ALSO BY JOHN JEROME

The Sports Illustrated *Book of Skiing*
The Death of the Automobile
Truck
On Mountains

The
Sweet Spot

in Time

by
John Jerome

With a New Introduction

A Touchstone Book
Published by Simon & Schuster Inc.
New York • London • Toronto • Sydney • Tokyo

Touchstone
Simon & Schuster Building
Rockefeller Center
1230 Avenue of the Americas
New York, New York 10020

Copyright © 1980 by John Jerome
First Touchstone Edition, 1989
Published by arrangement with Summit Books
TOUCHSTONE and colophon are registered trademarks
of Simon & Schuster Inc.
Manufactured in the United States of America

10 9 8 7 6 5 4 3 2 1 Pbk.

Library of Congress Cataloging in Publication data
Jerome, John.
Sweet spot in time/by John Jerome.—1st Touchstone ed.
p.   cm.—(A Touchstone book)
Includes index.
1. Sports—Physiological aspects.   I. Title.
RC1235.J48   1989
612'.044—dc19   89-4216
                                                                                               CIP

ISBN 0-671-68297-0 Pbk.

An excerpt taken from this book originally appeared in *Playboy* magazine, and other portions have appeared in *The Runner*, *Quest/80*, and
Esquire magazines, in slightly different form.

Acknowledgments

This book has drawn heavily on the intelligence and talents of more people than I can possibly acknowledge. But I owe a particularly large debt to each of the following. Some are mentioned in the text; some are never mentioned at all despite their very real help. (Some contributed whole ideas which I simply incorporated entire.) My permanent gratitude, then, to Robbie Barnett, Peter Cavanagh, David Costill, Dave Cowens, Art Dickinson, Janet Guthrie, Kathy Hewett, Nick Howe, John Ivy, Billy Kidd, Denise McCluggage, Dr. Rob Roy McGregor, Billy Salter, Dr. Richard Schuster, Phyllis Seidel, Frank Shorter, Chris Steinmetz, and Humpy Wheeler. I'm particularly grateful to Bill Fink of the Human Performance Lab at Ball State University, for his direct assistance with the manuscript.

Anyone who says
there is no free lunch
doesn't know Billy and Kathy,
Chris, and Sarah.
This book is for them.

Contents

Introduction

Tonight I watched the sports segment of the local evening news. It had been a busy day in sports—dramatic new developments with teams and individual athletes, wrenching personal changes and heroic deeds in that strange and wonderful world. I was struck by how big a world it is. Sports has become an established industry, of course, but it's more than that, it is an entire universe of concerns, involving great numbers of people. It has a remarkably powerful hold on our imaginations and our lives.

The Sweet Spot in Time is a study of one segment of that world, the area David Halberstam has called the "biophysical dynamics" of sport. It is the story of what we've learned so far about hard use of the human body.

The Sweet Spot in Time was first published in 1980, and the study of these matters, loosely called sports science, has grown exponentially since that time. Much careful scientific work has been done (and more than a little snake oil has been sprinkled over the subject). What is most surprising, however, is how little things have really changed in the sports themselves. Equipment has improved, training and preparation have been refined—and huge sums of money have been invested—but the only wholesale change in any aspect of athletics has been the names and faces. (And there have been exceptions there, too.) Many of the athletes used as examples in the earlier edition of this book have passed from the scene, or are now elder statesmen in their fields of endeavor. Those athletes were only exemplars of their time, however; in most cases, someone else has come along who does the same things, and probably does them a little better. This is not to take away from the uniqueness of the original examples as athletes or as human beings. There will never be another Walter Payton or an O. J. Simpson—but now there's a Herschel Walker and an Eric Dickerson, and the records continue to fall.

Only the faces have changed. We have learned a huge amount in sports science since 1980, but much of what it amounts to is embellishment—of such positive aspects as training details at the upper edges of endurance performance, of such negative ones as more sophisticated shades of drug use. The most important thing we've learned in those years is that this physiological aspect is much more important than we ever realized in the past. And the more attention we pay to it, the more we can improve performance. World records have improved as much as they have in recent years almost entirely as a result of focusing on this physiological aspect of sport.

The gossip and personalities and human dramas and all those wonderful other human aspects of sport provide a terrific additional device for understanding the world of athletics. But they, too, are filigree around the edges of the basic question: what *can* you do with the human body? Whether you are an athlete or a spectator, the physiological point of view will permanently enrich sports for you. *The Sweet Spot in Time* is an introduction to those riches.

—John Jerome
June 1989

CHAPTER 1
Sweet Spots

As a kid I spent a lot of time throwing rocks. The best place to do it was under a bridge, where there were always plenty of rocks and bottles—targets as well as missiles. You set up the bottles on one mudbank, then crossed over to the other side and you were in your own private shooting gallery. It was the only childhood activity I knew that ever involved anything like a warm-up. You would start out just lobbing the rocks, gradually working up the pace ("velocity," as the ballplayers now say) until you were zinging them in pretty hard, beginning to get the range. Finally, everything warm and working well, your arm loose, feeling strong, you'd find yourself really powering each throw, rearing back in unaffected natural windup, bringing them home. There is peculiar appeal in such rhythmic, repetitive activity, and this was one you could really bear down on. I think that was important.

I never indulged in baseball fantasies—bottom of the ninth with two men out, that kind of thing. I knew perfectly well what I was doing: I was throwing rocks, that was all. It was enough. I can still summon up in memory the way the rocks sizzled into the mudbank —and, now and then, sizzled into an old whiskey bottle with a satisfying *pop!* (Environmental damage hadn't been recognized yet; whiskey bottles were expendable because only they brought no cash refund.) I never did get to play much baseball, but I always had a strong throwing arm. Mostly I recall the haunting power I felt on that occasional throw when I knew as the stone left my hand that it was going to hit its target.

* * *

Biomechanics is the study of the mechanics of animate structures. It tells us that every human movement, from raising a cup of tea to the lips to pole-vaulting eighteen feet, is a product of levers moving through arcs. The joint is the fulcrum; the limb, or segment of limb, is the lever. Complicated movements require the arcs to be linked in series, but the arc is the inevitable basic unit, since at least one end of every segment is attached somewhere. This reductionist notion leads me to propose a Sweet Spot Theory of Performance. It is a way of perceiving good athletes (and various other performers) that can add a certain richness to the enjoyment of sports (and various other activities) for spectators as well as for participants.

If you've played any stick-and-ball game you are familiar with the wonderful sensation of hitting the sweet spot. You swing the implement—bat, racket, golf club, whatever—as usual, but you meet the ball a little more accurately than usual, make contact more squarely. The ball simply takes off: a remarkably smooth, easy, yet forceful result. In one sense the sweet spot is almost audible. When you hit it there is a characteristic sound—a sharp *click* (golf), *crack* (baseball), *whock* (tennis). A clearer signal comes not from the sound or the sight of the ball's flight, however, but from the startling information you get through the implement itself. It doesn't vibrate. No shock is transmitted to the hands. It is as if new force is created within the implement, exploding the ball into flight, driving it away harder than you actually swung at it.

Hitting the sweet spot is such a compelling sensation that a large part of our insistence on playing these stick-and-ball games may come from the desire to reexperience that.*click* of a perfectly hit shot. The feeling is almost mystical. There is nothing unreal about the actual spot, however. A biomechanist named Peter Cavanagh explained the lab procedures for determining it. "The sweet spot is not a figment of the imagination," he told me. "It is a mechanical reality in the implement, the center of percussion. Set up a baseball bat with oscillating machinery and you can determine the exact spot where, if you hit a ball there, minimum jarring will be transferred back to the hand. That spot will also likely give you the best shot. Of course, when you put a human being on the end of the implement, the problem gets much more complicated." At any rate, golf club manufacturers who advertise that they've increased the size of the sweet spot in their irons may or may not be fudging, but at least they're working with real-world physics.

We throw the word "perfect" around much too freely in sports, but for the moment let's assume that the 450-foot home run, for example, is a perfect stroke. It very likely comes off the sweet spot of the bat, but it also has a great deal of force behind it, which by some statistical miracle is lined up so that it is applied in a straight line through the dead center (another sweet spot) of the round baseball as well as through the center line of the round bat. Furthermore, this towering blast, as the sportswriters like to say, comes off a bat that is swung in a near perfect trajectory: a sweet line, so to speak. The bat moves through so true and even a trajectory that the ball is caught not only at the optimum spot along the length and width of the bat, but also at the perfect point in the arc of the swing to give it maximum force and distance. In effect, bat and ball meet at a sweet spot in time—a point in time in the arc. Or, perhaps, at an intersection of time and space. Thus we say the athlete hit the ball with perfect timing. There is even more exquisite timing to come.

The Sweet Spot Theory of (Sports) Performance goes like this: All athletic movement—all human movement—is generated by muscles pulling across joints to make limbs move. Grossly oversimplifying the baseball swing, for example, the batter cocks his shoulders and arms back away from the pitch, then begins the swing by rotating his hips, his lower body, and his shoulders toward the pitcher. After the shoulders get into motion, the upper arms start through, as in crack-the-whip; to the speed generated by rotation of the shoulder is added the speed of the upper arms as they are swung into action. After the upper arms are firmly launched, they pull the forearms into motion; after the forearms reach maximum velocity (actually, after the pitch has been met—or missed), the wrists "break," rolling over and bringing the hands through—the last and shortest pair of levers in the chain of action.

Each segment of this motion is an arc working off an arc; each is carefully timed to start as the previous arc reaches the best possible point. The superior athlete, according to my theory, anyway, is the one who in effect reaches the sweet spot of the arc for each segment of his or her skeleton as he or she goes through the athletic motion. The shoulders swing to the optimum point in the arc and at that instant the upper arms are launched into their arcs; at the optimum point of the arc traveled by the upper arms, the forearm motion is launched, and so on. Every good athletic motion has a crack-the-whip aspect to it, a chain of accelerating arcs, each taking the motion at the maximum from the arc before and using that speed to multiply its own acceleration. (Or, if less force is required, taking the motion at the best point in the arc for purposes of accuracy, and so on.) The sweet spots in the skeleton move around, of course, according to the purpose of the athletic motion, the implements used, and hundreds of other variables. There are whole chains of sweet spots within the human frame, if we can only learn to use them. Reggie Jackson has learned how to use them. Lynn Swann has learned how to use them.

There's more to this theory. Every human joint—the fulcrum point of each of those arcs—has several components of motion available to it. Some joints, such as the shoulder, work easily through several planes of motion; some, like the knee, are structured to move only through a single plane—to and fro, or up and down, or back and forth, but in no additional directions. Because of structural anomalies within and beyond the joint itself, however—loose ligaments, misalignments, and other angularities—no joint moves purely within a single plane. For the sweet lines, the true trajectories which will allow each segment of the skeleton to swing precisely through the sweet spots, angular displacement must somehow be removed. All else being equal, the better athlete should be the one who either has been blessed with superior alignment in the joints, or somehow can overcome the misalignments and can control the trajectories and keep them true.

The good athlete must be able to damp out the assorted wobbles and wasted motions and other excursions that would otherwise screw up the true trajectories. The motor-learning experts say, however, that ballistic motions cannot be guided once they are launched, which would preclude that kind of control. If so, then the good athlete must launch these trajectories with a great deal more accuracy than can you or I. Of course the motor-learning people don't get to work with Reggie Jackson very often. I suspect that the good athlete does both: through practice he or she learns to initiate motions with considerably more accuracy than the lesser athlete, and also learns to damp out extraneous motion as the act progresses. In fact I think the really superior athlete can do a great deal more in this regard.

(There are artificial aids for controlling excess motion, of course. Knee braces, in their various sizes and shapes, are an attempt to restrict that overburdened joint to motion in a single plane—particularly after injury. For that matter, so is athletic tape, as it is commonly used to tape ankles. "Orthotics," the running craze's newest status symbol, are another example—shoe inserts designed to help damp out extraneous motion all the way from the sole of the foot on up through the hip.)

We have specific organs with which we keep track of ourselves, called *proprioceptors* ("self-sensing"). These are internal measuring devices deep within the flesh that keep reading body position, change, rate of change, tension, loading. The job that these organs must do in telling the athlete when to fire off each consecutive body segment on its trajectory is truly remarkable. There is so much to go wrong. Witness high jumpers, who sometimes seem to set more records for inconsistency than for heights cleared. A world-class sprinter will run 10.1 for the 100 meters one week, 10.2 or 10.0 the next, but a world-class high jumper will often jump 7'6" one week and then fail to clear 7'0" the next. The ranks of high jumpers are frequented by flashes-in-the-pan, previously unknown performers who suddenly post a world-class mark and then never again come close to that height.

High jumping is a fiendishly complex series of movements, and if any one of them goes awry, the proprioceptive sequencing can go blooey. Everything from the speed (and angle) of the run-up to the last kick to get the heels over the bar is infinitely variable. Get a hundredth of a second off at any point in the sequence, and the timing for all the rest can be destroyed. A great athlete may be able to rearrange this schedule of movement quickly enough to get the sequence back; the lesser athlete kicks off the crossbar—or balks at the pit—then retreats to the practice field, and often finds that the frantic rehearsal aimed at getting the timing back just makes matters worse.

When an athlete is hitting the internal sweet spots—when the timing is right and the motion is smooth—the skill levels are higher, the athletic motions quicker, more forceful, more accurate. Injuries will be lessened; the athlete is performing "within" himself or herself, under control, within the limits to motion beyond which human tissue is overstressed. And there is one more advantage to this smooth-running vision of athletics: endurance. As the exercise physiologists point out, unskilled performance is like running on a bent wheel. One scientist has even proposed a skill index based on oxygen consumption per minute per unit of body weight: to do something badly takes more muscle and thus more energy.

Not too long ago there were two women skiers on the U.S. team whose results were so consistently equal that they were considered virtual competition twins. Yet one was so slim and delicate, so hyper-feminine, that she seemed unsuited to the rigors of international competition, while the other was exceptionally strong, a little pit bull of a ski racer. A friend of mine named Nick Howe, writing about the ski team, asked coach Hermann Goellner how this could be—that despite their widely disparate levels of strength they could post such similar results.

Goellner pointed out that the slim one was technically one of the best skiers in the world, and the strong one definitely was not. The slim one had never needed muscles: she stood on her skis so well, skied with such grace and control, that she never had to develop the musculature to ski powerfully—and had not done so. The strong one, on the other hand, tended to ski in series of linked recoveries. She had had to develop the strength to snatch herself back from disaster time after time. She skied by forcing her skis to do what she wanted them to do; she forced her way down a racecourse—and she had developed the physique to go with all that forcing. She had also suffered through several knee operations and other injuries. The slim one stayed injury-free.

The more highly skilled athlete simply performs in a higher gear; there is less of the grinding inefficiency of multiplying mechanical advantage to accomplish the task. It is the athlete's job to learn to do the hard thing easily. The result is usually very graceful. "Grace," says ski teacher Denise McCluggage, "is a warmer word for efficiency."

Most athletes perform with considerable grace; some don't and still get the job done, of course. There is always the occasional eccentric athlete who gets away with motions that bear no connection with grace, who has invented a totally unorthodox way of accomplishing the task. Compare the silken golf swings of Gene Littler or Sam Snead with the lurching blasts of Lee Trevino and Arnold Palmer. Littler and Snead are used to illustrate textbooks, while both Trevino and Palmer risk falling down on every drive. Golf may place horrendous demands on the nerves, but it doesn't really press the individual to the limits of physical endurance—which makes an unorthodox style less of a handicap. As endurance requirements go up, efficiency (or grace) becomes more important; anatomy being what it is, the movements of one performer will come closer to resembling those of all the rest. Although there are considerable differences in the running styles of Frank Shorter and Bill Rodgers, the differences are much subtler than the differences between the golf swings of a Trevino and a Littler. Fatigue hones away roughness. (Roughness burns energy.) In any case, unorthodoxy will never be taught; smoothness will be. Coaches refer to any unorthodoxy of athletic style as "herky-jerky."

*   *   *

I keep thinking about that high jumper on the practice field, trying to get the timing back. He'll say he's "lost his rhythm." Rhythm *is* timing, certainly—a means of signaling to each body segment the proper moment to initiate movement. Rhythm in athletic motion means that each segment of the body comes in right on the beat.

(Initiation can be the hardest part of an athletic movement. That's where all those bat wiggles and free-throw eccentricities and tennis-serve mannerisms blossom forth. That's why the "yips"—the aging golfer's typical troubles with the putter—often involve difficulty with drawing the clubhead back, rather than with swinging it forward.)

I happened to hear violinist Isaac Stern discuss his art one night, and a jazz musician (whose name escapes me) the next. Both of these immensely talented individuals would sing wordless snatches—"dum dum ti dum," and so on—to illustrate points about their very different styles of music. I am not a musician, and could barely catch the significant differences they were demonstrating so effortlessly. I could discern, but I'm sure I did not fully comprehend, these differences—in emphasis and tone, but mostly just in timing. Each man would illustrate one way to play a phrase, then an alternative, varying the timing of the notes subtly without violating the form, changing in major ways the emotional content of the music without changing a note. I suddenly realized that for musicians—and for athletes—there must be a great deal more *room*, in effect, in the flow of time than there is for the rest of us.

I tap my foot to music and think I'm on the beat; any real musician can demonstrate convincingly that I'm not, that I'm farther off than, for example, the bad TV singer trying to lip-synch to prerecording. It is as if the exact instant of the true beat is surrounded by several microseconds of available time. If I get somewhere in the vicinity, within those few fractions one way or the other, it sounds okay to me. It doesn't sound okay to a musician (and isn't likely to hold an audience spellbound). Within that span of microseconds lies room I never dreamed existed, room wherein the good performer can place the note, the beat—or the movement—with delicate, deliberate control. In those microseconds there is room for performing art.

Athlete, dancer, musician, all may fulfill the basic requirements of their task by getting precisely on the beat. In that sense the beat is like a point in geometry: dimensionless, not even a millisecond long. It is met exactly. To perform that way is only a kind of defensive approach to the task, however. (See Harold Solomon, jokingly referred to as a human backboard, indefatigably putting the tennis ball right back into the middle of the court every time—*every* time—until his opponent crumples in frustration.) Technical brilliance can spring from that kind of precision: just playing the notes. A machine can be made to replicate the beat perfectly, but the rhythm it produces will always be identifiable, instantly, as machine-produced. It is "cold." To warm it up, put a hand on it. Introduce human error.

Or human control. Imaginative performers control their material, and do so by using those microseconds that surround the instant of the beat. It is another order of precision entirely. For instance, delay: the dancer delays a step and introduces dramatic tension into the performance; the tennis player delays a return and pulls the opponent out of position; the basketball player hangs momentarily before letting go of the jump shot and is fouled, receiving a bonus free throw. Hurrying the motion, moving it minutely ahead of the natural rhythms of the form, can have similar effect. Feints and fakes are chiefly composed of just this toying with time. The musician moves notes micrometrically forward or backward in time, and in doing so makes the music witty, or sentimental, or sad. Or square (a plodding, unvarying microsecond too slow). The athlete similarly varies the timing of movements and "plays" the opponent as well as the game.

Put a human being on the end of the implement and the sweet spot in time also gets moved about.

But those tactical uses of time are well known, and beyond the Sweet Spot Theory. More interesting to me is what control of the time sequence *within* the movement does for skill. Fiddling around with the timing of moves can go deeper than delaying a return in tennis. The tennis player can also delay or speed up different segments, different arcs or portions of arcs within the sequence of motion, with brilliant results as far as the stroke is concerned. This does not happen because the athlete focuses attention on the segments and arcs of the motion. (It is almost impossible to do that. We grasp movements with the cortex, not with the muscles. That's why your handwriting is roughly the same whether you write with pen on paper, using small finger muscles, or stand at a blackboard writing with your whole arm.) It happens because the performer focuses attention on the time frame—inside the time frame—of the move.

A former ballplayer I know named Don Hewett used to advise his children, "You have to have the confidence *to take the time*" (to make the catch, to get to the return, to control the implement). Focusing on time slows it down. Next time you're having trouble with any quick-reaction sport—squash, racquetball, even table tennis or badminton—try telling yourself you have more time than you think you have. You'll find another several inches of incoming trajectory to work with, during which you can focus on and prepare to make your return. That few inches is enough: it is a few inches in time, if you have confidence enough to take it. All you've really done is make the sweet spot in time a little more accessible.

Most infield errors occur because the fielder starts his play before he catches the ball. A lot of dropped forward passes fall to the turf because the receiver starts avoiding tacklers before he finishes catching the football. This is the tiredest cliché in sports, of course—"Look the ball into your hands," even "Keep your eye on the ball"—but it illuminates a little more territory when it is understood in terms of available time. The good performer simply takes all the time there is

—for the particular move. There is a sweet spot in time for catching a ball just as there is for hitting one. The same capacities are at work, the same judgmental control of linked arcs—right down to the closing of the fingers—is involved. The sweet spot in time is merely the true finish of the move. Ah, but that is one hell of a "merely." (Follow-through is usually misapprehended. As it turns out, it is just a memory device to keep us from screwing up the motion that leads up to what we're following through. If you *intend* a smooth follow-through, that intention somehow takes you through the sweet spot of the move.)

Finishing the move is a startlingly important aspect of performing, although I have been unable to find a clear explanation of why it is so critical. In skiing, for example, if you don't finish one turn—carrying it out to its logical conclusion, metaphorically putting a stamp of completion on it—you will be in terrible shape to launch the next turn. The quickest indication of an unskilled dancer, gymnast, diver, figure skater, is the hurried move, which, surprisingly, doesn't come from starting the move too soon but from neglecting to finish the move that preceded it, cutting it off short of the sweet spot in time. It is a paradox: taking time to finish one move somehow gives you more time to get the next one started right. (Finishing the move probably restores the neuromuscular machinery to equilibrium, and thus gives you a new starting place.) Just as a wide receiver must, as they say, "put the ball away" before he starts to run with it, so must any performer put away the movement at hand before starting the next. There will be time. Finishing the move *makes* time. (Mikhail Baryshnikov has time. So does Julius Erving.)

Confidence, as in the advice from Don Hewett, may not seem to be the ultimate tool for getting control of the time sequence of performance, but it certainly helps. Concentration, that utter mystery, helps more. (Concentration slows time, as all of us obsessives know perfectly well.) Confidence allows you not to rush; concentration lets you have the time to choose when to rush. People who have played golf with Jack Nicklaus come away muttering about his absolutely frightening powers of concentration. They used to say the same about Ben Hogan. The same thing must be true of all outstanding performers, in sports and elsewhere. (Golf's slow pace may just supply a setting that makes gimlet-eyed concentration more evident.) Unfortunately, concentration is that peculiar power which by its own definition slips away when you try to hold onto it. I suspect that good performers have a better way.

*　　*　　*

I am haunted by the moment when the rock I threw went precisely where I wanted it to go. That moment hardly developed purely out of concentration, although it wasn't sheer accident, either. I think I probably stumbled onto several of the sweet spots in the same throw, and the result was simply a coming together, a moment when what my mind intended was matched by what my body accomplished. A momentary healing of the mind-body split, to overdignify it. It haunts me still because it was magic—pipsqueak magic, if you will, but magic nonetheless. It moved me; out of all those mindless boyhood hours of rock-throwing it is the moment I remember. It was a moment when the amount of time between letting fly the rock and seeing it arrive at the bottle seemed to stretch out forever. Time stopped. My mind's eye can still almost trace the flight.

The sublime moment in dance is the male dancer's prodigious leap. Ballet writer Herbert Saal, reviewing a performance of Baryshnikov, stated: "The most exquisitely chilling weapon in the arsenal of this complete dancer was his *ballon*, his ability to ascend in the air and stay there, defying gravity." Other dancers have had some of this capacity—Nijinsky more than most, perhaps more even than Baryshnikov. No one has explained it. It is electrifying to watch; we know we are witnessing a nonordinary event. When we see it we are moved. It is magic. Time stops.

It is my thesis—the Sweet Spot Theory—that this is true magic, the only magic there is. I am suggesting that there is a line between the banality of my rock-throwing experience—included here as a deliberately ridiculous example of Everykid's uncomprehending brush with performing magic—and the sublimity of Baryshnikov's great leaps. Along that line can be located much of the rest of what we refer to as magic in sports—from tennis players playing "in the zone" (Billie Jean King's last Wimbledon singles title) to Reggie Jackson's three consecutive World Series home runs to Bob Beamon's "mutation performance" long jump in the 1968 Olympics, a foot longer than anyone else ever jumped, before or since. On those occasions something magic did happen. A group of world-class marathoners was recently surveyed about their best performances; most of them spoke of some particularly fulfilling moment when "mind and body" seemed to "come together." Several of them used the word: magic. It was magic when that happened.

In *The Psychic Side of Sports*,* Michael Murphy and Rhea White have collected hundreds of stories of "mystical" experiences of athletes. The examples range from unusual bursts of speed or strength to whole games, even whole careers, which seem to exceed ordinary physical parameters. Not all of these examples can be reduced to fortuitous arrangements of limb segments and well-timed arcs of motion, but a surprising number of them have to do with strange dislocations—suspensions, really—of ordinary time.

Some of the most mystifying of these nonordinary experiences occur in the martial arts and other Eastern disciplines—movements too quick to see, uncanny reactions, moments when someone seems to disappear and rematerialize somewhere else.† Many of these Eastern disciplines make considerable use of meditation. As I understand meditation, one of its aims is to teach the individual to banish the distractions of past and future, to focus the mind on the reality of *now*, on the fleeting instant.

To stay securely anchored in the present is simply to concentrate without straining to do so: to *attend*. To stay in the present tense—to react, to respond only to the exigencies of the moment—is to take control of the time frame of performance. To follow with full attention what happens, as it happens, is to bring up to consciousness the possibility of the sweet spot in time—to spread out all those microseconds surrounding it, to expand time if not to stop it. The sweet spot in time is never anywhere but in the present tense.

I suspect that the reason a ballistic motion such as throwing or swinging an implement can't be adjusted once it has been started is because we abdicate control. We choose a ballistic motion because it is a means of gaining additional force, yes, but also because it is a way

---

* Addison-Wesley Co., Reading, Mass., 1978.

† In *The Ultimate Athlete* (Viking, New York, 1975) George Leonard describes a film of Morihei Uyeshiba, the founder of aikido, in which Uyeshiba is apparently trapped by two attackers, but between one frame of the film and the next—while the attackers move sequentially—Uyeshiba suddenly appears two feet away and facing in the opposite direction. That's what I thought happened with Renaldo Nehemiah in the 1979 World Cup II track meet in Montreal. Nehemiah hit the next-to-last hurdle (in the 110-meter event) heavily, and was obviously beaten. Yet he won the race. I watched the slo-mo instant replay through three or four repetitions, and I still can't see how he got from where he was at the next-to-last hurdle to where he was at the tape. But then we all know there's nothing "mystical" about track.

of starting a motion and letting it finish itself, of putting the motion on automatic. We feel it is necessary to do so in order that we might think ahead, preparing for the next necessity. But to think ahead is to ignore the present, and therefore to rush time ahead, to accelerate its passing. It is only when we stop thinking ahead that we can slow time sufficiently to open the possibility of adjusting a ballistic motion. Don Hewett is correct: we abdicate control because we don't have the confidence to keep our minds within the time frame of the motion.

Golfer Bobby Jones once said he didn't think it was possible to swing a golf club too *slowly*. Jack Nicklaus is reputed to have the slowest backswing on the tour, and during the early part of his downswing, some observers swear that his hands actually slow further. I'm not sure how or why this could be true, but what I am proposing is that that level of performer—the individual who now and then can find enough room in the flow of time to adapt the rhythm of the performance to his or her personal will—just might be able also to find enough time to vary the motor input into the ballistic motion. To make corrections as time runs by, to keep chasing the elusive sweet spots—in time, in space, in all the multidimensional complexities of sport (or art) to the last closing of the door of possibility. I'm sure the motor-learning people won't buy this explanation either, but then they aren't having much luck explaining these levels of skill any other way.

For several years now I've been trying to get a handle on the link that connects what seem to me to be *sensual* sports—skiing, surfing, cycling, and other sports and recreations that we practice noncompetitively, for the sheer pleasure of the act. (Many of them can be made competitive, of course, and many purely competitive sports offer the same kind of sensual pleasures.) Slicing across the face of a wave, leaning a bike into a high-speed turn, getting a solid edge-set in good snow—so that that, too, is an act you can bear down on— are experiences so similarly pleasurable and so distinctive a sheer physical joy that they must be related, but in ways I'd never been able to grasp.

Now I think that sweet spots provide the link. I think we play at these sports in large part just for the pleasure of getting the timing right, of feeling the physical forces fall into the sphere of our control. What's more, we get a different version of the same pleasure from watching others play at them. It can be ineffably moving to watch a performer control time, placing his or her movements—steps, motions, strokes, blows, notes—where he or she wants them in time, where the sweep of action will best be continued. Where the discipline and the performer's imagination combine to create something vivid in an otherwise rigid frame. And that placement, that sensual touch, that finger of magic on the precise point in time that is such a sweet spot, is so satisfying that it must be why we play.

CHAPTER 2
Edges

In the sports pages of most major dailies there is now a regular column that lists "transactions." In among the tabulated statistics for everything from last night's NBA games to local high school lacrosse contests, there is a compilation of the day's trades, court actions, fines, judgments, hirings and firings. Such a listing documents the industrialization of sports.

This industrialization is most clearly measurable in the sheer numbers of which sports is so fond—in this case not batting averages or yards gained, but the larger numbers that show growth: participants, spectators, teams, profits, costs, TV broadcast hours, ratings. All are on the increase. It is the effect of television on sports, of course—or, more bluntly, the effect of cash. (And tax incentives.)

The industrialization of sports is such a massive phenomenon that it has distracted us, unfortunately, from a subtler but ultimately more rewarding revolution in sports. It is a revolution in performance. If there is a single unifying thread that pulls together all the different sports and the interest of all the millions who follow sports, it is, simply, performance. The great moment in sports, the moment that is a kind of sweet spot in time in the experience of us all—participant as well as spectator—occurs when the human mechanism is called upon to perform at the exquisite limits of its capabilities. And the revolution sweeping sports right now is nothing less than a total revision upward of those limits.

Individual athletes and coaches are perfectly aware of the industrialization of sports. They see the evidence of the numbers. But working as they are within the specific applications of their particular disciplines, they may not see the other transformation that is taking place in sports. They see only bits and pieces, tiny tips and particles of information that just apply within the framework of attention to minute detail that leads to top athletic performance. Interested observers may be able to recognize the change more clearly than can the professionals. They can see it by researching no more deeply than the daily sports pages and TV coverage, so long as they look across sports, on what might be called a pandisciplinary basis, at athletic performance.

There's a temptation to call this upward revision of the limits of performance a technological revolution, the product of the application of science to sport, as in such futuristic developments as computer-based biomechanical analysis of athletic motions, or the isokinetic exercise machines. Much of the change is, in fact, based on such application of hard science to the athletic task, and greater changes are to come from that source. But there are also distinctly nonscientific aspects to the change, which are having their own effect. Basketball players and high jumpers now study ballet and the martial arts, learning more effective ways of moving their bodies. Coaches, traditionally the most pragmatic and nonmystical of citizens, point their charges toward yoga. Superstars cultivate nonrational mental disciplines, including deliberate trance states, to improve their performances.

The daily sports pages have begun to cover this different kind of sports "news"—both the technological and the other kind—although the unifying thread is not always readily apparent. I'm sure most sports page readers are familiar with such seemingly random items as the Soviet use of hypnotism to prepare athletes for competition; the decision of the U.S. Olympic Committee—finally—to invest heavily in sports medicine and research; the use of computers to determine the best way to make a slap shot, a free throw, a block on a defensive lineman; the use of steroids to add body mass in strength-dominant athletic events (and the efforts to trace the use of steroids and other drugs); the continuing speculation about mysterious, hyperscientific

Communist-bloc training methods. This documentation of the continued assault on the limits of performance has become a staple feature of the sports pages. It makes a welcome relief from play-by-play accounts, line scores, statistics.

It is also an indication of something more. Perhaps a better example of this change in sports emerged from a startling thirty-second postgame interview a few seasons back, when basketball star Dave Cowens returned to the Boston Celtics lineup after an extraordinary midseason leave of absence. In his first game upon returning, he played with his usual intensity, did a fine job of getting rebounds and feeding the break, but missed a lot of shots at the basket. After the game the interviewer asked Cowens if his shooting touch had been affected by his layoff. Well, Cowens replied, he'd trained hard during his time off, but training just couldn't match the intensity of the game itself. So by not playing for several weeks he'd lost a little lung capacity. That meant that in all the mileage he'd covered up and down the court, he'd built up some degree of oxygen debt. The lack of oxygen to brain and body did affect his total coordination, and, therefore, his shooting touch—just enough so the shots weren't dropping. Close, but no cigar. A couple of games to play back into shape—to stretch his rib-cage muscles and rebuild lung capacity, Cowens said—and he should be hitting again. A couple of games later he was.

Several things about the interview were startling to me. The first was that he'd managed to impart so much intriguing information about the athletic process in those thirty seconds. The second was that he had so clear, if complex, an understanding of the workings of his body that he could make the leap, in a linear, physiology textbook way, from oxygen capacity to missed baskets. And the third was not only that he bothered to tell us all this, but that it was obviously perfectly logical and intelligible to a modern sports audience, and of more than passing interest. The brief interview was a long way from the traditional jock response. (Hi, Mom, we played hard, I did my best.) Clearly, Cowens got interested in the question.

Dave Cowens is a remarkable individual in a lot of other ways, too, and it's not to be expected that you will hear that kind of analysis every time a microphone is stuck in the face of a modern athlete. But we can expect to hear more and more, and we can expect that complex content to become more and more intelligible. It is as if athletes, coaches, managers, trainers are finally getting a chance to let us in on what sport is really all about.

(We can also expect to hear a lot more airy nonsense, as athletes, with their infinite capacity for being fascinated by their own physical processes, spin out nutball theories to explain themselves. It may be difficult to separate the nutball from the merely complex, at least for a while.)

It isn't that there has been a conspiracy to silence athletes; it is more that as the athletes understand themselves more clearly, the audience is beginning to acquire a finer appreciation of their work. It is as if the general public level of athletic IQ is rising. Whether this greater understanding is cause or effect of the revolution in performance is moot. More, better informed athletes coming into sport will inevitably raise the level of performances; more and better informed coaching and training will have the same effect, whether or not the athletes even bother to understand the significance of the new training methods they are asked to follow.

And whether the performance revolution is cause or effect is also moot: it is under way. In the 1976 Montreal Olympics, world records were broken in twenty-two of twenty-six swimming events. By the time those games were over, there was only one world record left in swimming that was more than two months old. The argument was then made that the records in other sports tended to be much longer lived, indicating that the evolution of swimming performance is behind that of other disciplines. Yet in 1978 one man, Henry Rono, broke three major track records in one season, and the next year Sebastian Coe broke three more—of the most aggressively attacked records in all of sports (the 800 meter, the 1500 meter, the mile). The same effect is being felt in all of the record-keeping sports. The limits of human performance are rising at a startling rate.

*　　*　　*

I am an average sports fan, I think, and a little less than average athlete—not even a George Plimpton, pursuing Walter Mittyish fantasies. I am only one of those numbers that are rising so rapidly in the industrialization of sports; I think I'm a party to the rise in mass athletic IQ. Recently I've found that what I was learning about sports seemed to be accelerating. The more I've learned, the more enjoyment I've gotten out of sports, as an observer but also more recently, increasingly, as a kind of born-again participant. I really do love sports, and can find almost any of them endlessly absorbing. What I've started to see *in* sports—from looking at performance rather than at scores, outcomes, standings—has enriched the experience of sports for me immensely. It's been a steady growth.

As a child, like everyone else, I wanted nothing more out of life than to go out and *play*—every waking moment. At some early grade-school level that play began to mature, from running about and screaming a lot—from all appearances the principal activity on primary school playgrounds—into games. In search of a little more content for our play, we organized it. The games began to evolve into sports. I think this is the way most of us discover sports. In elementary school all of us are athletes.

"Physical education"—mostly hygiene lectures and organized push-up sessions—was as unsatisfactory to me as was any other kind of schooling. I was on a junior high swim team, played high school football and basketball with only moderate success. In my first semester of college I was a swimmer again, but soon abandoned that. I was a diver, a trampolinist—exhibitionist rather than competitor, if you will—for a few post-high school years. In most senses that was the end of my athletic career. I did race sports cars very briefly (an athletic task, I swear it), and later earned my living from writing about skiing, for which I had to ski a great deal. I loved that, for a while; I skied just about as well or as badly as I performed at any other sport.

Despite this limited and deservedly modest athletic biography, I would maintain that I've always *thought* like an athlete. I've always been spellbound by what the human body—my own or anyone else's —could do. The bodily experience of sport has always been intensely pleasurable to me, no matter how bad I was at it. But still it lacked content for me: it was pleasurable, but a thin and inconsequential kind of pursuit.

What turned me in my tracks was a simple backache, at about age forty. Attempting to relieve that, I began systematic exercise, which didn't help. For all my putative athleticism, I didn't know *how* to exercise, even with the advice of all the popular self-help books on the subject. Something was wrong; I began to research the problem a bit, to learn something about physiology. I learned how utterly baffled conventional medicine is by high-use injuries in a healthy body—what one poetic doctor has called the "diseases of excellence." (In fact I learned how confused, even hurt, the medical profession is by the very notion of good health.) I began to run, a few years before the running craze exploded upon us, in hopes that that might help my back. It did, sort of, but it brought new aches and pains to engage my attention. I researched some more, never on anything more than a dilettantish level, simply browsing my way narcissistically through the literature in search of relief of minor pains.

But that opened up whole new worlds. Instead of relief of pain, what I got was the aforementioned enrichment of the experience of sports—enrichment as both observer and participant. That was the process by which I plugged into this rising athletic IQ. I was amazed to discover, among other things, that most of what I "knew" about the processes of athletics was simply untrue. I was trying to understand sports from a background of information and theory that had been almost entirely supplanted in the past twenty years. And none of the usual sources of information about and explanation of sports had bothered to acknowledge the profundity of this change—or, in the rare case when they tried, they had usually managed to get it wrong. What I had stumbled onto was how incredibly large and complex a field of knowledge had gathered around the requirements of athletics in recent years, and what endless fascination lay waiting for the practitioners who are now attempting to put that knowledge to use in sports. What this meant for my own personal pleasure was a forcible shift in attention from the endless, sometimes nasty superficialities of the games, events, contests—meaningless franchise shifts, artificially created loyalties, bogus rivalries, and other such thin gruel —to what I insist is the real meaning of sports: finding out what the human organism can do. Performance: the endless riches thereof.

What I'm referring to as a mass rise in athletic IQ is more likely a common body of knowledge emerging into direct, conscious accessibility for the first time. We've always known a great deal about these matters, whether or not we've been able to express what we know. We recognize great athletic talent instantly, often without knowing why, without being able to put into words what it is about that talent that is so vivid. It is easy to be lulled to sleep by the seemingly undistinguished performance in, for example, the second quarter of any given regular season NBA game. But flash onto the television screen five seconds of a lower level of basketball—even good-quality college basketball—and the comparative lack of efficiency and fluidity of play is instantly glaring.

(We owe a wry debt of gratitude to what *Sports Illustrated* has so aptly named "Trashsports," those artificial TV games that move good athletes out of their narrow ranges of specialization or, more embarrassing, put celebrity nonathletes into athletic events. It doesn't take much of the floundering that results to demonstrate how high a level of performance we have come to expect when we watch good athletes practice their own true sports. Watch the super slo-mo film of a movie star attempting to sprint, and you will see great flabby shock waves travel up and down the leg muscles at each foot plant, unstable ankle and knee joints wobble under the stress—no matter how shapely and attractive those legs. Only then do you begin to realize how much stronger and more efficient are the legs of any normally fit athlete.)

I am continually surprised at how clearly we pick up tiny signals, even over the tube: the first hint of clumsiness in a hitherto graceful athlete, indicating that fatigue is beginning to set in. The emotional shift in a game—usually caught in a single glaring look between two players on the losing side—that means the other team has gained the psychological advantage. The lift in stride and carriage that tells you an athlete is getting hot, ready to mount a charge—and the charmed abandon with which he or she then proceeds to play the game, whichever game it is. I'm equally surprised at how seldom traditional sports coverage bothers to note these things.

I think our background, our sports heritage, is much deeper than any of us recognize. I have never studied baseball, and for a long period paid it no attention whatsoever. Babe Ruth was before my time, and I've seen him only on jerky old newsreel film. But I recently realized that I "knew" his swing. I could picture that hulking, water-filled balloon of a man taking that great, fat swing, as smooth a motion—from the pigeon-toes on up—as we've ever been privileged to see in sports. It is engraved forever on the back of my eyelids, and without even knowing that I knew that swing, I have unconsciously been comparing those of every other batter in baseball with that vivid memory. I think most of us do, if not with Ruth and baseball then with the other magnificent athletic practitioners. Excellence simply registers, whether we know it or not, in a kind of kinetic imprinting.

I think that that imprinting is the kind of sports experience that we are now beginning to understand much more fully. (I think that something in us knows when we see the sweet spots being hit.)

On the evening of the first Ali-Spinks fight, Leon Spinks remained at ringside through a preliminary bout, cheering for his younger brother through a very close fight. One of the more knowledgeable commentators—that is, one who came from boxing, rather than from broadcasting—opined that it was a mistake for Spinks to be there, that he was expending a couple of rounds' worth of energy on the effort to pull his brother through the fight. It was an interesting observation, even if it didn't prove, in that instance, to be terribly prescient.

During the remainder of the evening I kept noticing how much muscular energy I was expending, in the form of building tension during each round, as I strained with every punch and slumped with relief at the end of the round. After the fight I couldn't get to sleep. The very dramatic fight had dumped a load of adrenaline into my system; my heart rate was still elevated an hour or more later; and, sure enough, when I let my thoughts drift back over the boxing itself, I found myself tensing muscles all over again, tying myself into empathetic knots as I lay in bed.

Now it wasn't that there was anything special about my reaction to the fight. But my understanding of the physical results of watching that high drama, while by no means a penetrating analysis of exercise physiology or reaction to stress, was something new to me. The broadcaster's tip-off, and my absorption of it, were of a piece in this rising athletic awareness, I'm certain. Adrenaline, heart rate, muscle tension—and rib-cage volume and oxygen capacity—are part of a kind of new grammar of our understanding of the body, a new set of ways of relating the elements of physicality, now becoming generally understood and widely accepted. Understanding my own physiology that way—having access to this athletic grammar—enriches my experience of the Ali-Spinks fight, just as the Ali-Spinks fight enriches my understanding of my own physiology, my grasp of the grammar of athletics.

The relationship is seductively symbiotic. The tremendous explosion of participation sports, the growing mass interest in fitness, aerobics, and the management of athletic injuries, feeds this rising level of physiological understanding, of course. But the "new" sports news does the same. Injuries to major sports figures, for example, have traditionally been reported. But in recent years the coverage has expanded to become a sports page staple, to include the details of injuries, their probable causes, treatment procedures, rehabilitation strategies. Good sports physicians become superstars in their own right. Medical terms appear more and more frequently in the sports section of the newspaper.

It's a hoary truism that with very few exceptions—Babe Ruth, Jean-Claude Killy, Edwin Moses, Eric Heiden—the level of competition at the very top is dead even. The winners have little advantage in strength, technique, or training; the difference comes in psychology. The winners are better able to get "up," to achieve the state of psychic balance that allows them consistently to perform at their best. ("Up" is often precisely the wrong direction—it's a holdover in the language from before the Age of Drugs.) They are better able, in motor-racing parlance, to get their power down on the road. I was holding forth recently on the fact that Valery Borzov, the Russian sprinter, had written his doctoral dissertation on the first ten meters of the hundred-meter dash—intending this as an example of the development of new understandings that characterizes the performance revolution. A friend instantly countered, "Oh, yeah, if Borzov knows so much, then how come _____ runs faster?"—referring to a sprinter who shall be nameless, who is reputed to be illiterate, perhaps even retarded, but who wins sprinting medals.

My friend raises an interesting point. Here is a world-class sprinter who, one must assume, can find and put to use graduate-school-level complexities and refinements in the start of the dash. And here is another world-class sprinter who needs help from the coach to get his track shoes onto the right feet, but who must only be pointed in the proper direction and then in effect fired toward the finish line. For all Sprinter A's fine-grained knowledge, Sprinter B wins just as consistently.

There's long been a tradition in sports that in the pressure of competition, nobody is quite able to put to use all the conventional knowledge, the stuff we've known for generations anyway—never mind all this fancy computerized biomechanical whatzis that's being produced by the reams and tons now. It is the same point of view that insists that a football team spend all its time practicing "fundamentals," that talks a lot about "execution." Important sports contests are still lost, regularly, by the failure to "execute" those "fundamentals," of course. If Sprinter A spends all his time analyzing starts while Sprinter B is practicing them, then B is likely to be the consistent winner.

That means only that Sprinter A has to practice also; it doesn't mean that he's wrong, or wasting time, to delve into the minutiae of his starting technique. The execution-of-fundamentals school of athletics unfortunately tends to distrust intelligence. It also denies hope to the less fortunately endowed athlete, who must compensate with brains and energy for what nature left out in innate speed, reaction time, coordination. It also takes a great deal of the fun out of sports: three-yards-and-a-cloud-of-dust may win football games, but it is usually fun for nobody but the coach.

And, of course, in the end it doesn't work. All else being equal—*all* else—the smart athlete will always find a way to beat the dumb one. One source tells me that Dave Cowens has overcome foot problems that should have precluded his ever stepping onto a basketball court. He's done it by careful management of those problems, and in the process he's obviously acquired a sizable pool of knowledge about the way his body works. That's what gives him the analytical ability so quickly to link his shooting touch to the elasticity of his rib cage.

My source who spoke of Cowens' foot problems had gotten into a conversation with him that started with feet, drifted on to diet and nutrition—about which Cowens knows a great deal, and has strong opinions—and then uncovered the fact that Cowens has a basement full of the exotic new exercise machinery, which he uses to work on specific weaknesses, to prevent muscle imbalance from developing, to stay superbly conditioned. Musing on this, my friend, who has the expertise to know what he's talking about, said, "You know, he's the first professional athlete I've run into who recognizes and acknowledges the real problem, which is simply management of the body. Most pros don't bother. That gives Cowens an edge."

*　　*　　*

Edges are interesting. Every athlete wants every contest to be fair, to be even—which means he or she doesn't want the opponent to have an edge either. But every athlete will take any edge he or she can get. Borzov is willing to split all those hairs in researching the sprinter's start because if he finds a hundredth of a second advantage in those first ten meters, he will take it, consider it an edge, and win races with it. So long as it is not specifically in violation of the rules, no question of sportsmanship will ever enter his head over the question of his private, personal hundredth of a second. He'll take that edge even if he only thinks he has it—and he'll very likely win with that, too, since the confidence imparted by belief in an edge can be enough to make the difference in races that are decided by hundredths of a second. Science has just begun to isolate the placebo effect; athletes couldn't care less, since they seem to be able to win with placebos as effectively as they can with real edges. See the "bee power" craze—bee pollen, with no identifiable nutritional advantage over other sources of the same nutrients, ingested by dozens of world-class track and field athletes as a kind of supervitamin.

That's only one kind of edge, however. Biology has long been fascinated with edges: the perimeter of a woodlot, the shoreline, any boundary area where one kind of habitat joins another. That's where the biological action is, where species intermingle—partially to feed off one another, to be sure, but also just out of a kind of natural curiosity. It is there at the edges where everything is going on, where one species will try to overtake or crowd out another, where environmental neighbors come to congregate—and compete. Timberline, creek bank, power-line cut, roadside, even such a subtle line of demarcation as a change in soil composition—all are edges. All stimulate action, embroilment, vitality.

The same is true for the edges in sport. A clever athlete plays the boundaries, the sidelines, finding in them an added tactical element. He plays the physical limits of the playing surface just as consciously as he plays his opponent. Using the lines—in tennis, football, even chess or marbles—is often precisely what a given sport is all about. These edges—of boundary, barrier, rule (both meanings), dimension —are the same for every athlete (with the possible exception of seven-foot basketball players). The advantage comes in how well the athlete can use them; thus it is possible to have an edge in the ability to play the edges. To approach the edges, and play off them. These are the edges of skill, of judgment, of control.

There is yet another kind of edge in athletics, which is the edge of the title of this chapter. It is a different sort of limit: the edge of what it is possible for the athlete to do. The edge of strength, speed, endurance. World records are the curious institution by which we define these edges, these outer limits. The goal, in the record-keeping sports such as track and field, is to go over the edge of what is possible: to venture into unexplored territory, out there beyond the current realm of human experience, where no one has gone before. Imagine the thrill of that.

One way of ensuring that the athlete can approach those edges most consistently and most fruitfully is by the proper management of the body. ("Body" isn't quite right. "Physical self," perhaps—since it is specifically in attempting to close the old Aristotelian mind-body dichotomy that some of the most interesting attempts to overcome these limits are being made.) That management is a task that for generations received only the most superficial lip-service: clean living, plenty of rest, no self-abuse, train until it hurts. But it is a task that has now exploded, as a result of the same kind of exhaustive attention to detail that Borzov has given to the sprinter's start. The task is a fascinating balancing act: we now know so many ways of developing the necessary physical capabilities that the athlete begins to feel overwhelmed by choice.

Yet the limits of human performance cannot be grossly overpowered. This, too, is a balancing act. Any athlete who is ready to break a record—properly prepared in every sense for the effort—is also on the edge of breakdown, trained so fine that he or she can slump into the sour despair of overtrained staleness at the first whisper of a muscle pull or a head cold. It is another management problem of intricate complexity. We know fairly well how to prepare to come close to the limits of performance. But to prepare to go beyond them—or to prepare either to remain at that stage of readiness, or to achieve that stage of readiness at a specific time, for a specific event —requires a level of management that often eludes us.

It takes only a glimpse of what an athlete like Dave Cowens goes through to ensure his own stable, consistent, season-long performance, at or near his own limits, to vastly enrich our own involvement with sports, whether as spectators or participants. What's more, understanding what is possible in the management of the body to reach the limits can vastly enrich our own day-to-day capacity to manage our bodies, to prepare ourselves to experience a raising of the limitations to what is possible in our own lives.

I don't think we come close to our own limits. I don't think we've come close to the ultimate limits of human performance in any field.

In fact, I think that notion is a contradiction in terms: human performance implies a lack of limitation. The limit is only to the amount of energy, effort, enterprise that we find worthwhile to expend on exceeding those edges. (That may be the meaningful limit: not what can be done by human beings, but the point at which further extension of human capability comes at too high a price.) Nevertheless, the limits to human performance that we now perceive do not represent physical realities so much as they signify failure of the imagination. Those limits don't really exist; they are ghost images, lying there waiting for us to surpass and dissolve them.

Book I:
Systems

CHAPTER 3

Red Meat

The aspect of sports that first rivets our attention is movement: the joyous flow of the human body lifted into fluid motion. Movement is the athlete's principal medium. Movement requires muscle. Muscle, for some reason, gets a bad rap.

The larger culture has a tradition of sneering at muscle—all brawn and no brain, the meathead image of sports. Muscle is a metaphor for the failure of intelligence, the last resort of fools. It is inescapable that the basic stuff—red meat, human skeletal muscle—is the essential currency of sports, no matter what skills and intelligences are thereby ignored. The elements of athletics are effort and motion. Effort and motion, no matter how gross or fine, are produced by muscle.

We are also bone, blood, sinew, nerve, organ; analyze us finely enough and in the end we are nothing more than electrochemical soup. But muscle is what makes us quick and lively. Bone may hold man upright, but it is muscle that puts him there (and maintains his balance once he gets there). Without bone we couldn't stand, but we could still move; we could—and would—invent boneless sports that we could play, slithering over the ground in some unimaginable fashion. With bone but no muscle we would be reduced to clacking in the wind.

Movement gross and fine: using muscle to maximum effect, one man has raised 6,270 pounds in a single lift. (Well, he budged it, anyway—Paul Anderson, in a "back-lift," raising the weight off a trestle.) By such incomprehensible records do we reinforce muscle's brutish image. But you can't blink an eyelid without muscle, indeed, can't focus the unblinking eye. Life can't be maintained, unaided, without muscle. Forget about the hospital full of machines to take over your ailing functions, the technology of "heroic" measures; just slip into this well-tailored suit of red meat, your own personal life-support system, and it will get to work for you, pumping, churning, by its strength and elasticity keeping you alive.

It is not just that muscle makes us move; movement makes muscle, too, as anyone who has ever spent time in a cast knows well enough. Deny to muscle tissue the capacity to move, to exert effort, and it simply disappears. *Poof!* Skin and bones. Break an arm and by the time the cast comes off, your arm has shrunk to pitifulness. Rehabilitation will be rapid once you can move the arm, get the muscle working again. But not until you can move can you make new muscle. It is as clear a symbiotic relationship as you'll ever see.

("New muscle" may not be quite accurate. It has long been believed that we have all the muscle fibers that we'll ever have—in number—by about the fourth month after conception. Whether we take those muscle fibers and make ourselves into Caspar Milquetoasts or Arnold Schwarzeneggers depends on how much work we choose to do. According to standard theory, if we choose effort and motion we don't add muscle fibers, we simply add size to the muscle fibers that lie there waiting for activity to give them strength. Recent research is finding growing evidence that there may be some generation of new muscle fibers, by a process of division of existing fibers. But it isn't clear that this is the body's major process for developing new muscular bulk and strength, and it certainly isn't the way atrophied muscle is restored.)

Muscle tissue is a physiological one-way street. A muscle can exert a pull, and that's all. It is connected at either end, to bone, and all it can do is try to pull those two ends closer together. It works by contraction only. (Or, in some cases, by attempting to contract or resisting extension, in which case it does its work not by succeeding at contraction, but simply by not failing.) An individual muscle fiber is either contracted or it isn't; it doesn't contract partway, or contract with part of its length but not with the remainder. It is on or off, like a light switch. We get variations in the amount of effort or motion that we produce by varying the number of muscle fibers we contract, not by varying how much we contract them. How we vary those numbers is part of the mystery surrounding muscle tissue. That, perhaps, is the most wonderful thing about this flesh that gives us the gift of movement: we don't know quite how it does it. We know a great deal about it, but there is something essential about its function that eludes our scientists.

*   *   *

There are three types of muscle tissue in mammals: smooth muscle (involuntary), heart muscle (striated involuntary), and skeletal muscle (striated voluntary). While the first two categories are also of crucial significance to health and athletic fitness, it is only the last form—the muscle that is amenable to conscious control—that we are talking about when we speak of muscle in athletics. I don't have comparative figures for the Milquetoasts and Schwarzeneggers, but skeletal muscle, on average, makes up about 40 percent of body weight in adult males, 23 percent in females. There are about 600 significant muscles in the body; each has from 200 to half a million cells, or fibers. A skeletal muscle fiber is a single elongated cell that can vary in thickness from 10 to 100 microns. (A micron is one-thousandth of a millimeter.) Some individual muscle cells may run the entire length of the muscle. A single fiber in the sartorius—the longest muscle in the body, running across the front of the thigh from the hip to the knee—may be 30 centimeters in length.

Thanks to the electron microscope, we can zoom in on muscle tissue, going deeper and deeper in search of explanations for its clever capabilities. Each whole muscle—biceps, sartorius, etc.—is ensheathed in fascia, a sac of fibrous connective tissue; within that sheath there are bundles of muscle tissue, and each bundle has its own encompassing sheath. One bundle is made up of a great number of separate muscle fibers, usually several thousand. Each of these individual fibers—each of them a multinucleated cell—has, in turn, its own protective covering. All of the connective tissues come together at the ends of the muscle to form the tendons, which anchor the muscle at either end. The tendons are of dense, extraordinarily strong material. There is a tendon of origin, where the muscle starts, usually at the less mobile skeletal end, and a tendon of insertion, where the muscle ends, toward the end of the bone with more capability of movement. The tendons are attached firmly to the outermost covering of the bone. Tendons and their attachment sites are generally stronger than muscles. In injury the muscle should tear—a muscle "pull," a "hamstring," even a "charleyhorse"—before the tendon gives way. It doesn't always happen that way, of course.

None of this superstructure gives us clues to the capacity for movement. For that we must go deeper yet, to the very striations, the stripes themselves, those bands of light and dark flesh that are signboards indicating that this muscle tissue is available to voluntary control. Within the cell membrane of the muscle fiber there is *sarcoplasm*, the specialized protoplasm of the muscle itself—a viscous reddish fluid full of bits of biochemistry, the minutiae of science. Floating in this syrup are globules of fat, glycogen, phosphate compounds, small molecules, ions.

Also within this fluid are hundreds upon hundreds of strands of protein, laid down in orderly parallel fashion. These strands contain the capacity for contraction. There are two kinds: thick filaments of a substance known as *myosin*, and thin ones of *actin*. The ends of the myosin and actin filaments overlap; where they do, a darker band is formed across the muscle fiber. Between bands, where there is only one material or the other, the muscle tissue appears lighter in color. Voila! Striations. When the muscle fiber contracts, shortening in length, the thick and thin filaments slide past each other in telescopic fashion, in a kind of microminiaturized interdigitation, pulling the striations closer, so that the distance between the stripes is shortened.

Ah, but *how?* What causes these filaments to pull themselves along each other's length, telescoping the muscle cell? To find out we must screw the focus tighter yet, and we begin to enter the realm of speculation, of theory. Microscopy becomes insufficient, as the processes at work stop being mechanical and become electrochemical.

The signal for contraction comes from a motor nerve, transmitted to end plates on the muscle fiber. It is assumed that the signal depolarizes the cell membrane, allowing it to be permeated by various chemicals. That would explain how the signal is transmitted simultaneously throughout the fiber, making the entire fiber contract as a unit, rather than in waves. With the signal to contract, calcium is released from storage vesicles that surround the protein filaments—part of what one writer calls the "plumbing and fueling system" of the muscle fiber. The calcium triggers an enzymatic reaction in which a new protein compound, *actomyosin*, is temporarily formed.

The actin filament has binding sites spaced at regular intervals along its length. The myosin filament has little protrusions—the heads of molecules—extending outward along its length, reaching toward the binding sites. In contraction the heads of the myosin molecules link with the binding sites on the actin filaments. These molecular crossbridges linking the fibers are made of the actomyosin created enzymatically by the initiating jolt of calcium.

If there is no change in the length of the muscle, as when you are holding steady tension, the two filaments bind, release, and rebind at the same sites, continuing to do so as long as there is energy supplied to the muscle. There is contracting tension but no actual movement of the filaments alongside each other.

More commonly the muscle shortens when it is used. In that case the filaments bind and release as before, but when the bind is broken the head of the myosin molecule swivels toward a new site in the direction of contraction, and rebinds there, in effect pulling the myosin filament along over the actin strand. Contraction: the muscle works. It is a ratcheting process, working like a bumper jack does to raise a car. Relaxation occurs when another signal causes the calcium to be withdrawn.

The foregoing is mostly theory. There is still some question about whether the filaments actually do slide over each other to shorten the muscle, although no other explanation, mechanical or otherwise, seems to make sense. Much of the chemistry has been worked out to scientists' satisfaction, however. For example, neither actin nor myosin can contract, but actomyosin does so under proper conditions, even in the test tube.

The governance of the making and breaking of the linkages, the mechanisms for relaxing the muscle, the variations in strength, are still mysterious. For example, muscle fiber can be stretched out beyond its resting length; when this is done, the ensuing contraction will be more powerful than for an unstretched muscle. (This is a useful principle in athletics.) The opposite would seem more likely: as the amount of overlap between thick and thin filaments is decreased, fewer binding sites would seem to be available and fewer crossbridges could be formed. The assumption—which still lacks proof—is that the crossbridges are stronger near the ends of the

filaments. It has been demonstrated that there is a limit to this enhancement of contraction strength through stretching. It is possible
to stretch a muscle fiber so that there is no longer any overlap between filaments, so the myosin and actin sites can't reach each other
in order to bind. But that degree of stretch is likely only in a laboratory situation, with dissected muscle, without the support of all those
connective tissues. It won't happen to you or me on the tennis court;
a lot of other tissue would have to rupture first.

*   *   *

"What's a cramp?" I asked Dave Costill. We were returning to the
Human Performance Laboratory at Ball State University, of which
he is director, after lunch. Bill Fink, Costill's principal assistant, was
with us. Costill and Fink looked at each other and began to chuckle.
"Nobody knows," Costill finally said, smiling at my puzzlement.
"How are you going to study one? You'd have to take a sample of
tissue while the muscle was cramped, and then find a way to keep it
that way while you studied it. Nobody has figured out a way to do that
yet."
The same problem forecloses research on a lot of other muscle
phenomena. To prove that new muscle fibers are created by training,
you'd have to catch a specific fiber in the act of splitting. Or find a
way to count every fiber in a given muscle before training—without
harming it—and then count them all again after training. (The evidence that this may, in fact, take place comes from dissecting animal
muscle and teasing each fiber out of the group, in search of a fiber
that starts as a single cell at one end and finishes as more than one
cell at the other end. In effect, finding a cell with split ends. Some of
these have, in fact, been found. Bill Fink also points out that there is
another theory that credits satellite cells for fiber neogenesis. I don't
think the weight lifters have heard about that one yet.)
The problem reminds me of the time when "frogging" swept my
junior high school. You would sneak up on a friend and rap him
sharply across the belly of the biceps with a hard knuckle. If you
caught the muscle just right against the bone, a hard lump of temporary swelling—a "frog"—would pop up and ripple across the
surface for a few seconds before subsiding. We thought this
phenomenon was hilariously funny, and became so fascinated with it
that we would sit around frogging ourselves in the biceps, competing

to see who could raise the largest lump. School authorities outlawed the process, but not before all our upper arms turned black from the abuse.

This kind of 13-year-old self-punishment in the interests of science startles me now to recall it. But considering that we also experimented at great length with spinning around on tottering feet until we threw up, with trying to go so high in playground swings that we looped over the top bar, with clamping off our own carotid arteries until we began to pass out, perhaps it shouldn't be so surprising.

*   *   *

I am a fairly rapid typist—fast enough so that I am usually eight or ten characters past a mistake before my brain registers that I have mis-hit a key. Sixty words per minute, perhaps—roughly three hundred characters a minute, or five a second. (A really good typist goes almost twice that fast.) For each of my fingers to be able to jerk down onto the proper key, there must first be a little squirt of calcium juice in the finger muscle which will allow crossbridges to form between protein filaments. That's a notion that threatens to drag me to a halt—like the distraught centipede in the doggerel verse, trying to determine which leg to move first. My typing is absolutely snail-like compared to what a violinist or a pianist does with his or her hands. In either case we are making small motions involving tiny forces.

Consider instead the following four seconds. The pitcher fires a 95-mph fastball over the plate; the batter cracks a sharp grounder to third; the third baseman scoops, plants his feet, gets the throw away; the second baseman takes the throw, whirls, and relays it to first, dragging his toe across the bag as he does; the sprinting baserunner from first has reached full speed by the time the third baseman touches the ball, but he's still thrown out by four feet; the batter has likewise accelerated from the instant bat met ball, but to no avail; the first baseman stretches, extends, does a complete split, takes the throw at the earliest possible moment. Double play.

Consider *those* calcium squirts. Six men (not counting the short-stop and the catcher, who backed up their teammates at second and first bases), performing at the edge of athletic possibility: a routine double play, exactly as the manager has every right to expect. Much more than mere effort and motion are involved here, clearly—discriminations, estimates, linked series of rehearsed moves performed at speeds that preclude conscious control. The calcium squirts, the sliding of muscle filaments over each other that actually cause all this action, these are only the end products. The process starts with the sensory organs, receiving information that ignites that six-man, ten-second burst of hyperactivity. A great deal of that sensory information comes, curiously enough, through the muscles themselves and their ancillary tissues.

One early decision required of the central nervous system is just how much muscle will be required to accomplish the task. The term "muscle" is used here as a slang term for force, or effort—but that is literally the determining factor: how many muscle fibers will be required. The amount of force generated is precisely determined by the number of muscle fibers involved. There are a quarter of a billion muscle fibers in the skeletal muscles of an individual, but only about four hundred thousand motor nerves, so each motor nerve has to fire numerous muscle fibers. One motor nerve plus all the muscle fibers it serves is a *motor unit*, in which all the fibers contract and relax on the same signal. In muscles required to operate with great precision and delicacy, such as those of the eye, there will be as few as four or five muscle fibers under the control of one motor nerve. In muscles used for heavy work, as in the thigh, a single motor nerve may control a thousand or more muscle fibers. Something—a visual estimate, a preconceived idea, a mere reflex—must give the system some notice of how many motor units to fire to accomplish the task at hand.

Peculiarly enough, the more automatic the response—the farther its origin is removed from conscious control—the more accurate the muscular reaction is likely to be. It is when our dithering minds get involved that our muscular reactions tend to become inappropriate. I like to think that says more about the slick efficiency of our reflexive systems than it does about the interference caused by our conscious "intelligence." But in the brains-vs.-brawn arguments, it is inescapable that our bodies are often smarter than our minds, if we could only learn to trust them.

The muscles have their own network of sense organs, but what those organs sense is of another order of sophistication than the conventional five senses. The argument can be made that the muscle-generated information is only some variation on the sense of touch—there are, for example, pain receptors in the fascia of the muscle fibers, the arterial blood vessels, and the connective tissues.

Much of the data received from the musculoskeletal system is indeed touch, or "feel," but there is also something else being sensed there. There's a name for it: *proprioception*. (It is heavily involved in my sweet spot theory.) It is the sense that tells us where our body parts are in relation to their environment and to each other. Coaches sometimes refer to it as "muscle sense." It gives us the capacity, not always fully realized, of smoothly coordinated movement. And in another close relationship, this time with the organs of balance in the inner ear and with sight, the proprioceptive organs aid us in keeping bodily equilibrium.

There are three types of proprioceptive organs. *Muscle spindles* are bundles of muscle fiber that have the peculiar capacity, when stretched, to send signals to the central nervous system, rather than receiving signals from it. They are thus adapted to the particular job of measuring the degree of stretch in a muscle, which helps the body decide how many motor units to devote to a task. Muscle spindles let the central nervous system know the length of the muscle when it is loaded, and the rate of change in the length when it is overloaded. Muscle spindles even send messages through the central nervous system and back to the muscle itself, telling the muscle to contract in order to reestablish a sense of its own state. In effect the spindles are making the muscle contract just to feel itself, so it can determine where it is and what state it is in.

Drop a book into your outstretched hand. The hand and forearm dip downward before the load is accommodated, the muscles momentarily overloaded. Muscle spindles fire rapidly, notifying the central nervous system how many more motor units must come into operation to stop the dip and hold the book steady. The additional motor units fire; the arm yanks back upward and steadies with its new load. It might be possible to lock the arm muscles so rigidly before the fact that the accommodating dip could be dispensed with, but to do so would be a much less efficient, more energy-consuming method of dealing with the problem. As nature abhors a vacuum, so does the body abhor rigidity. It is the unconscious choice of flexibility, of suppleness, of accommodating reaction over unyielding firmness, that brings such fluid grace to human movement.

There are also proprioceptors, located in the ligaments and the capsules of the joints, called *joint receptors*. Some joint receptors signal movement in the joint, some signal the position of the joint without movement. Joint receptors signal to more conscious levels of the brain than do the muscle spindles. For complex and unusual tasks of coordination—such as touching the tip of the nose with the forefinger when the eyes are closed—it is the joint receptors that provide most of the information to make the controlled movement possible, rather like the radio homing beams that guide airliners from airport to airport in bad weather.

Finally, there are the *Golgi tendon organs*, located near the junction of muscle and tendon. These too are activated by stretch—at very high loadings—but they signal the muscle to relax rather than to contract. They are the opposite side of the cybernetics of movement, inhibiting muscles to prevent injury. In arm wrestling, when the loser's arm is suddenly slammed down against the tabletop after an extended strain, it is the Golgi organs that have caused the muscles to let go, in order that the arm may live to wrestle again another day.

The proprioceptors are what guide Dr. J on his whirling, driving, space-walk slam dunks. They are a kind of muscular early warning system, a network of controls deep within the flesh that keep reading position, change, rate of change, stress. This is the network that gives that second baseman enough sense of location—of himself, the base, the basepaths, the approaching runner—to drag one toe subtly across the bag even while dealing with the arrival and departure of the hard-flung relay throw. These same controls let the high jumper know when to drive his lift leg up, when to drop his head back over the bar. They let the pole vaulter reach that upside-down position sixteen feet off the runway with enough sense of where he is that he can still in effect do a push-up off the end of the vaulting pole. At the sight of David Thompson twirling in yet another lay-up from the wrong side of the basket, four feet off the floor with defenders hanging from him like pilot fish, the TV commentators speak of "body control." It is not so much control of the body as it is the ability to read the proprioceptive information he's receiving: the sum total of all the firings of all the receptors within the musculoskeletal system, telling the athlete what his body is doing, what the linkages are up to, what the relationships of the body parts are and where they are headed.

It is common practice to refer to this or that star performer as a "great athlete" for capabilities that lie outside the narrow specializations of his particular game. (Capabilities that may consist of little more than a particularly fluid style of running or a distinctive throwing motion.) It's a categorization that we'll examine in more detail later, but one theory has it that the superior athlete is the individual who just happens to be endowed with more, and more sensitive, proprioceptors.

*　　*　　*

The notion of proprioceptors is so powerful that I'm reluctant to let it go. I find myself searching for psychological equivalents to these organs by which we keep ourselves oriented. Farfetched, perhaps— yet I certainly have patterns of thought, ways of dealing with the world, that occur so regularly and dependably that they might as well be located in my physiology as in my alleged intellect. In my psychological joints and tendons.

When confronted with a difficult new task, for example, my instant reaction is that I can't do it. This just has to be the psychic version of the dip of the hand when catching a dropped book. Psychological muscle spindles: the mind goes *with* the new load, at first. It is necessary to spend a certain amount of time merely wondering at the new task, shuddering at its size and complexity. One is unconsciously assessing it, measuring how much mental energy—rather than how many motor units—will have to be fired off to deal with it. Only then is it possible to start solving the problem instead of standing around fearing it. Fleeing it.

The psychological equivalent of the joint receptor might be the psychic compass that tells you where, as they said in the 1960s, your head is at: the reality-testing function. It works so smoothly that you don't know it is there until it fails you, of course. Mine fails most frequently when I travel too much, when I wake in a hotel room and have to cogitate hard—stirring into activity my psychic joint receptors—in order to remember what town I'm in. (After extended foreign travel I've also had to work fairly hard to remember *who* I am, but I don't know the psychological proprioceptor responsible for that one.)

There is also the psychological equivalent of the Golgi tendon organ, I'm sure—some kind of mental measuring device that tells you when you're trying to push things too far, resisting pressures that you'd be better off to let go. I'm positive there is a perfectly common psychological version of that function, but I just can't seem to come up with an example of it right now. Besides, it's five o'clock: the hell with it. It's time to cover the typewriter and go buy myself a drink.

*　　*　　*

There is another form of cybernetics in the musculoskeletal system that assists in the smooth coordination of complex movements. No matter how completely a muscle may be relaxed, there remains a residual level of tension in it: *tonus*, muscle tone. This inherent resiliency of relaxed, resting muscle is assumed to be the product of random firings of motor nerves. If either the motor or sensory nerves to the muscle are cut, or suffer any of several degenerative nerve diseases, such as polio, the tonus is destroyed and the muscle begins to atrophy.

(You can toy with your own level of muscle tone, and experience the necessity of tonus to proprioceptive information. Lie perfectly still, preferably on your back, and relax your limbs progressively, starting at the extremities and working toward the body core. If you achieve a thorough enough level of relaxation—without falling asleep—your level of tonus will seem to subside so that your proprioceptors begin to turn off, and you'll lose track of where your limbs are. It's a disconcerting experience at first; if you stumble into the state unwittingly, you'll likely move your limbs immediately to reestablish your sense of position. But if you sink into the state deliberately it can bring a wonderfully oceanic sensation of freedom from the body. I suspect that some mystics' "out-of-body" experiences have this physiological basis.)

Tonus maintains the muscle in a state of preparedness, ready for action. It has been compared to the idling of a car engine. Set the idle too slow (as in flabby, unfit tonelessness of muscle), and the engine will stall if you floor the gas too suddenly. Set it too high (the near-spastic condition of overworked, overfatigued muscle) and you're wasting gas, generating too much noise, wearing out your car too fast. The idle must be just right for smooth performance. Good muscle tone is an elastic buffer against the shock of sudden action. It also supplies a sustained capacity for low-level muscular work that is performed outside of conscious control—holding actions, such as the maintenance of posture, where a slight tension in the muscles is all that is required to do the job. Such work is performed much more efficiently with muscle tonus than with conscious control; the more of your muscular requirements that you can fulfill with muscle tone, the less fatigued you'll be.

When the doctor raps your kneecap to test your reflexes, he's checking out another feedback mechanism that helps maintain muscle tonus, the *stretch reflex*. He taps the patellar tendon; the tap stretches the appropriate proprioceptors, which send contraction signals to the quadriceps; your foot kicks upward "of its own volition." The stretch reflex means that if you subject a muscle to a pulling force, it contracts reflexively. It's a more significant reflex for athletics than it might seem at first glance. The pitcher's windup, for example, is a complex motion that puts the arm and back muscles in a substantial stretch at the start of the actual throw, so that the stretch reflex adds force to the willful control of those muscles. Almost any sports motion that requires force has some kind of windup preceding it to enhance its power—the golf swing, the football kick, the sprinter's crouch, the tennis serve. A deliberate elongation of the muscle precedes the contraction, pulling more motor units into play. It's also an energy saver. If you can use a reflex to start a motion, you reduce the effort expended. You do so every time you walk, stretching the hip flexors to initiate each step.

In throwing we depend on the stretch reflex so heavily that when it is bypassed the resulting motion feels impossibly awkward. In the standard American overhand throwing motion (which incidentally is not totally natural—European kids, brought up playing soccer, have trouble learning it), we step forward with the leg opposite the throwing arm, cocking the muscles, in effect, with the stretch reflex. When an athlete is caught in a situation that requires that the throw be made without that anticipatory step, off the wrong foot, we generally say he or she is throwing off-balance. Lack of balance is not what makes the throw difficult. Throwing off-balance is easy, so long as you have the correct leg in front. It's throwing without the stretch reflex to help power the throw that is difficult, when the force on the throw must come from the arm muscles alone.

The stretch reflex also serves to protect joints from overextension, and plays a substantial role in maintaining equilibrium. It is the basic reflex in controlling posture. The pull of gravity works to stretch the "antigravity" muscles, and they automatically—reflexively—resist that pull, holding the body upright with minimum effort. We get an assist from postural sway: the tendency of a freestanding individual to swing the center of gravity of the body through a random pattern of swaying. The frequency of this sway is about five or six cycles per minute; it's perfectly unconscious, of course. Much as the muscle spindles make the muscles feel themselves periodically, so does this postural sway cause the muscles to cycle through periods of activity and inactivity, reducing fatigue. The swaying helps promote blood flow, assisting venous return.* The fatigue you feel from standing upright for long periods comes less from muscle fatigue than from poor blood circulation. You can reduce the fatigue by deliberately increasing the amount and frequency of sway. (Even the subtlest exercise can be beneficial. Doctors consider the rocking chair to represent a significant exercise for the aged and infirm, stimulating both musculoskeletal and respiratory systems into gentle action.)

One more interesting sidelight to posture: the theory is that the stretch reflex sends impulses to the central nervous system, which relays the signals to the motor units and thus to the muscles. One important relay center is very likely the hypothalamus, and it has been theorized that generally upbeat feelings—alertness, elation, attention—increase the signals relayed back to the muscles. Feelings at the other end of the spectrum—drowsiness, inattention, depression—may decrease the signals. That would explain why an individual's mood can so often be read from the posture. That's why "attitude" refers to postural as well as emotional stance. I like to think it is further confirmation of the indivisibility of body and mind.

*   *   *

The muscles that maintain posture are predominantly of the "slow-twitch" variety. The muscles that you use for quicker motions, for shorter periods of time, are "fast-twitch" muscles. These are the two basic types of muscle fiber in mammals. Slow-twitch muscle tissue is often referred to as red fiber, fast-twitch fiber as white. Light meat vs. dark: it is an oversimplification that the sports world finds irresistible.

* The stretch reflex even helps control heart rate. The body relies to a great extent on muscular activity in the extremities to pump venous blood back to the heart. As you begin to exercise, working the muscles more strenuously, a greater volume of blood is automatically pumped back to the heart. That volume of blood stretches the heart chambers slightly, in turn firing the reflex that speeds up the heart rate, providing more freshly oxygenated blood back to supply the exercising muscles.

Slow-twitch or red muscle fiber has a richer supply of that basic muscle soup called sarcoplasm, which is responsible for the darker coloring. It is better oxygenated, more capable of extracting and using oxygen from the blood. Red fiber is slower to respond to a stimulus, but when it does respond it does so tonically—in sustained contraction, rather than in alternating phasic waves of contraction and relaxation. Slow-twitch muscle fibers are preferentially recruited by the central nervous system for long-term endurance type activities.

Fast-twitch or white muscle fiber is quicker to respond, quicker to fatigue, capable of greater strength of contraction but only over shorter periods of time than slow-twitch muscle. Fast-twitch muscle fiber is preferentially recruited for high-intensity work of short duration, such as sprinting.

Wild ducks, which make long-distance migratory flights, are predominantly dark meat; domestic chickens, which seldom cover longer distances than the sprint to the next bug, have more white meat. The comparison is too pat, leading to oversimplifications, but it is a handy memory device. In man, our muscles are composed of both types of fiber, the predominance depending on use. In the calf of the human leg, for example, there are two major muscles, the soleus and the gastrocnemius, both inserting into the Achilles tendon at the heel. The soleus, inside the gastrocnemius, closer to the leg bones, is predominantly of slow-twitch fiber; it is used mostly for long-term work such as standing upright. The gastrocnemius, covering the soleus, lying just under the skin, is used for running and jumping. It typically will have more fast-twitch fiber, or at least more of a mixture than the soleus.

A muscle biopsy (a small tissue sample) from your thigh can tell a lab technician whether your legs are better suited for sprinting or distance running. In recent years it has been regarded as the gospel, particularly in track and field, that that's the way to determine your athletic future. Once you've gotten the word about your own personal muscle-fiber heritage, you then devise your training and your plans for competition accordingly. The ratio of slow- to fast-twitch fibers is genetically determined—or so the studies, particularly those done with identical twins, have shown. All the training in the world, it has been assumed, can't change the ratio. According to the physiologists, the only way a muscle fiber could be changed from red to white, or vice versa, would be to change the type of motor nerve that supplies it with signals.

A lot of would-be athletes have taken comfort from this immutability. If you have sprinter's muscles, there's no point in expending the effort to try to make yourself a distance runner; no sense in fighting your own genes. Then scientists came up with a curious new finding. Individuals with scoliosis (curvature of the spine) tend to have different types of fiber in the muscle on either side of the curve. The differentiation serves no known functional purpose. It is not yet known how or why the differentiation develops, but it seems clear that the hereditary determination of ratios of red to white muscle fiber is open to question. It is possible that the muscles on each side of the spine of the scoliosis victims are already, genetically, of different types before the curvature develops, rather than the other way around, but it doesn't seem likely. In any case, no explanation is yet available. For now, the physiologists say only that there's a strong genetic factor. The betting seems to be that several other determining factors for muscle fiber type will eventually be found.

The simplicity of this endurance-vs.-sprint picture has recently been further clouded by the discovery of a third fiber type. In between the slow-twitch, fatigue-resistant fibers and the fast-twitch, fatigable fibers (known now as fast-twitch Type B), we must insert a *fast*-twitch, fatigue-*resistant* fiber, known as fast-twitch Type A. All three types are mixed throughout our muscles, although of course ratios vary. The third type does not seem to dominate any particular muscle groups.

As if that weren't confusing enough, now some adventurous physiologists predict as many as eight different muscle fiber types will eventually be found, as categories are drawn finer and finer. In fact there is some evidence that researchers may finally be able to come up with motor units strung along a continuous spectrum of contraction speeds—the speed of contraction related to the size of the nerve fibers leading to the motor units, rather than to the type of tissue within the muscle fibers.

The original neat dualism of slow- vs. fast-twitch muscle structure fit without a hitch into our traditional concepts of athletic achievement and work physiology; these new categories just confuse the issue. Athletic training is so far still conducted largely along the old sprint vs. endurance lines. What new sophistications in training may result from a more detailed understanding of muscle tissue is impossible to say, but the research races ahead, and training techniques will surely follow this scientific lead. Meanwhile, science seems to be telling us to beware athletic predeterminism. As soon as you settle on simplistic categorizations, someone will come along and tear up your categories, if not with scientific research then with sheer performance and dogged human stubbornness. That's what makes trying to understand athletics so bewilderingly entertaining.

* * *

When muscle is contracted or stretched its temperature rises. In dynamic exercise, up to 80 percent of the energy that is chemically available to the muscle is converted into heat. As the muscle heats up it becomes, within limits, stronger and more efficient. The strength of the contraction increases, also within limits, with repeated stimulation of the muscle fiber, in part because of the beneficial effect of increased tissue temperature. Warm muscle fibers simply slide over each other more easily than cold ones. Warming up increases strength; it's a positive gain. Warm-up also helps avoid a loss, of course: stone-cold muscle subjected to heavy work loads can give way, tearing muscle tissue—the "pulled" muscle that is the despair of every athletic trainer.

All else being equal, a muscle's strength of contraction will be greatest if the muscle is stretched out to about 120 percent of its relaxed, resting length. Although the fulcrums and lever actions of muscular attachment may mean that the body generates more force with a given limb when the muscles that power it are at less than this optimum length, still, the stretching principle applies. Furthermore, if the muscle is prestretched before contraction, it stores a certain amount of elastic or potential energy, which works as a kind of rippling overlay of extra energy in the contraction that follows. If there is too much time lag between prestretch and contraction, the stored energy will dissipate, but a conscious routine of prestretching just before muscular effort can add measurably to the available force.

The batter stalks to the on-deck circle, swinging a weighted bat before proceeding to the batter's box. He takes hefty swings in both directions several times before knocking the bat weight loose and tossing it aside. He then will usually hold the bat at each end, at arm's length, and extend it back above his head, using it as a stretching tool for his upper torso and shoulders. He may intentionally rotate his upper body a few times without the bat, swing his trunk down to stretch his hamstrings, go through various other wriggles and twitches, in a routinized series of motions that will continue all the way to the batter's box.

He may be going through all these motions only because they feel good, they leave him feeling "loose," "ready." In fact he is pulling muscle group after muscle group toward that optimum stretched length of 1.2:1, pulling individual muscle fibers to the length at which the actin and myosin binding sites can exert maximum pull on each other. He's prestretching muscles to cock them for extra energy, just as he will also draw the bat back in windup to load up the stretch reflex, to put additional energy into his swing when he actually takes a cut at a pitch. He is, in effect, waking up the motor nerves, preparing them for the rapid-fire activity that will be required of them to snap the bat through the strike zone with maximum force. There's no concern about fatigue: these are motor nerves that can comfortably fire seventy times a second, and they're only stimulated to readiness by the practice swings. He is also raising the temperature of the muscle tissue by all that random flexing, thinning the viscosity of the very sarcoplasm, "getting his juices flowing"—literally. He quite specifically gains strength and quickness by these few seconds of preparation. With the added strength and quickness he can then put greater force into his swing without having to overswing, attempting to overpower the ball. The force can come with a nice, loose, easy swing, as one sees in the better golfers.

It seems likely that most athletes only sense all this physiology, that they can in fact feel when their musculoskeletal structure is ready for action and when it is not. That's okay. It certainly isn't necessary for the athlete to think about binding sites and stretch reflexes in order to prepare for action. But if athletes do understand the significance of those physiological mechanisms, it seems likely that they will "feel" more carefully, read proprioceptive information more attentively, prepare more thoroughly. It is an approach to athletics that is gaining adherents. To the extent that athletes have traditionally prepared themselves in this manner, they've usually done so out of fear of injury, to avoid problems that could curtail careers. I suspect that if the results to be had were presented as percentage gains in strength and quickness rather than as protection against loss, the whole warm-up procedure would be enriched considerably—particularly so for younger athletes, who tend to depend on their natural resiliency to take the place of a careful warm-up.

One other bit of physiological minutiae. I made mention previously of "getting the juices flowing." This is so literally true that it deserves expansion, although in this particular case the gain doesn't apply specifically to muscle. Back in the 1950s a Swedish physiologist observed that when rabbits were removed from the relative freedom of their cages and held with their knee joints immobilized, the thickness of the joint cartilage was reduced by about 10 percent *within 30 minutes.* When the rabbits were allowed freedom of movement again, the joint cartilage thickness shot up by 13 percent within a mere 10 minutes. The 10 percent reduction reoccurred after another half hour of immobilization.

The changes in cartilage thickness are the result of changes in the amount of fluid in the tissues, of course—mostly synovial fluid, the lubricant that ordinarily bathes the joint. Since the joints are so much more susceptible to serious, potentially permanent injury than muscle and bone, anything the athlete can do to ensure their smooth functioning has got to be worthwhile. With a 10 percent increase in the amount of lubricant available from 10 minutes of gentle motion, the warm-up becomes even more valuable to the athlete. That perennial battle cry of the singles' bars, "use it or lose it," would seem to apply to outdoor sports as well—and it never had a more graphic illustration.

*   *   *

I once worked on a documentary film that required interviews in several different locations. After each interview, when the room was cleared, the sound man would go back in with his recording equipment and run his tapes for a minute or two in the empty room. I asked what he was doing. "Gettin' room tone," he said.

The sound man was recording the sound of the empty room: the subliminal buzzing, echoes of passing traffic, the hum of the mechanical systems of the building. It is different for every configuration of walls and drapes and furniture; it can't be precisely matched by artificial means. Later, if we needed to dub in additional material, we could record it in a sound studio (deliberately constructed for minimum room tone). Then, to keep the added material from sounding strangely out of place, the sound man would mix in some of the original room tone. When this isn't done, there's a jarring variation in the sound tracks when the new material comes in.

Muscle tone is the room tone of the body: the buzz and hum of your own electromechanical systems, the echoes of reaction to passing sounds. Damp out that tone too severely and the quiescent muscles go eerily dead. Let the background noise get excessive, however, and the result is tension, aches and pains, a jittering inability to relax. Overreaction. I suspect that's an epidemic disease of modern society that has led to our massive dependence on tranquilizing substances. And I suspect that it is just that buzzing jitteriness that has led to the fitness craze, to our turning attention, finally, back to our bodies.

CHAPTER 4
Brutes

All else being equal, the stronger athlete will always prevail over the weaker one. That's a truism that the less muscularly endowed among us have resisted for years, but it is inescapable. A lot of the propaganda that we weaklings have perpetrated on the subject—that too much muscle makes the athlete slow, or less agile, or liable to injury—simply isn't true. Muscle, it turns out, is good stuff to have going for you. Acceptance of that fact—grudgingly given in the beginning, now sweeping throughout sport—is bringing radical change.

One result has been a substantial increase in the amount of training effort that the athlete gives over to strength building. And that means weight: weight training, pumping iron. Nowadays, however, it may be pumping hydraulic fluid, or cleverly designed cams, rather than pure iron: along with this revolution in training has come a curious abandonment of the traditional barbell, the very symbol of weight training, for something better. Technology has come to strength building. So has science, of course—that's where the technology comes from—but in the interpretation and application of that science all is confusion. One hilarious result has been sport's own pipsqueak version of industrial warfare among equipment makers. A less humorous development has been considerable counterproductive effort expended by athletes and, through misinterpretation of the new research in strength building, dissemination of programs that can do more harm than good.

The rush to weight training in almost all sports has been truly remarkable. We expect it in brute-strength disciplines such as football and wrestling, but much of the initial impetus toward weight training came from the seemingly languid and gentle sport of swimming. Baseball players are often accused of being poorly trained, and have never particularly fit the image of hulking musclemen. (Unlike our other major sports of football and basketball, baseball offers equal employment opportunity to the smaller athlete.) But check the fore-arms on almost any modern-day baseball player as he steps up to the plate. In recent years a great number of baseball players have been spending their off-seasons in programs of weight training, often to the dismay of old-line devotees of traditional training methods. The field-event athletes in track and field have always worked with weights—particularly the throwers—but now even the distance run-ners, men and women, are experimenting with weight machines.

There may be sports in which speed is not advantageous, but I can't think of any. Simply put, within limits, muscle = strength, and strength = speed. That is, bulging muscles are in fact stronger than slim ones—never mind that wiry little devil you used to know who seemed stronger than anyone else. The strength of a muscle depends directly on its effective cross section. Muscle tissue is theoretically capable, under lab conditions, of exerting a maximum contractive force of about 140 pounds per square inch of cross section. A 16-inch biceps has 3 square inches more cross section than a 15-inch biceps, and should thus, theoretically, have 420 pounds more contractive force. Of course, it doesn't turn out quite that linear in real life, in practical application, but the principle is inarguable.

Speed depends to a large extent on strength, so strength-building exercises increase speed, within limits, as well as the power of mus-cular contraction. Similarly, if weight-training exercises are per-formed throughout the full range of motion of the affected limb, flexibility may actually be increased, rather than diminished. So much for the notion of "muscleboundedness." Physiologists came up with that idea when it used to be believed that speed of contraction could be limited by the size of the muscle. It was assumed that an enlarging muscle would eventually develop so much internal viscosity that it would more than use up the increased strength the new bulk provided. To the disappointment of us Milquetoasts, later research has failed to demonstrate that any such phenomenon occurs.

Measuring strength—as a basis for beginning a strength-building program or for just about anything else—is a bit of a problem, the first of many that have clouded research in weight training. Strength is usually defined as the force that a muscle or muscle group can generate against a resistance. To measure strength you must find the maximum force available for a single effort.

(*Force* is the application of the energy of physical strength to a task; *work* is the application of force through distance; *power* is the performance of work over time. Lift a pound from rest and you've generated one pound of force; raise it a foot and you've done a foot-pound of work; do that work in one second and you've generated one foot-pound per second of power. One horsepower is 550 foot-pounds per second. A very strong athlete might generate six horsepower in a single movement of less than one second's duration, but for tasks that last as long as five minutes, two horsepower is about the maximum possible, and over periods longer than five minutes, half a horsepower would be extremely high production of power.)

What could be simpler than to measure the maximum force an individual can produce—as in the maximum weight that can be lifted? Well, in the first place, the maximum amount of weight that an individual can lift depends to an unfortunate degree on that person's skill at lifting weights. Balance, timing, coordination, all come into play. The same is true to a lesser extent even in the use of the various spring-loaded dynamometers and other test instruments devised for measuring strength.

Furthermore, a given individual may vary plus or minus 10 percent in the amount of force he or she can generate from day to day—for utterly indecipherable reasons that seem to range all the way from the subject's mood to the ambient humidity. In the generation of muscular force, motivation may well be much more important than anything else—as when the frail mother lifts the burning car off an injured child. (Instances of that kind of muscular overachievement are too well-documented to be merely legend.)

Because of the all-or-none principle of muscular contraction, the force generated will depend on the number of muscle fibers contracted, which in turn depends on the number of motor units brought into play. In untrained muscle, during any given contraction only a few motor units will operate; as fatigue sets in, the exhausted motor units turn off and others take up the slack. Strength training is aimed at preparing the muscle to be capable of firing as many muscle fibers as possible, as well as at bringing all fibers up to maximum contractile capacity. The heroic mother can perform that amazing feat because jolts of adrenaline and other ordinarily unavailable stress mechanisms enable her momentarily to activate all the motor units at one time. Athletes may not be able to achieve that level of activation, but that's the direction in which they want to work.

Increase in the muscle's cross section, and therefore its strength, is brought about by systematically overloading the muscle, by working it against that overload. Immobilize a limb, as in a cast, and the muscle that moves the limb will lose about 1 percent of its strength per day of immobilization. But if the limb is free to move and is worked regularly at loads above those normally encountered, its muscles increase in cross section, and therefore in strength, by a process known as *hypertrophy*. Hypertrophy is the goal of all weight training. In the modern version of the discipline there can be systematic control of the amount of overload, the number of repetitions, the speed of the work, the point of loading—in short, of all the possible variables. There are research-based rationales for toying with these variables, but there may be too many of them for the athlete to keep up with. There, too, confusion begins to set in.

It should be clear that the subject here is strength building, not body building or weight lifting, which are allied but very different endeavors. The body builders—Arnold Schwarzenegger & Co.—use weight training as a means of sculpturing their bodies, with highly selective (and generally well-informed) use of the principles of hypertrophy, as a kind of massive, effortful beauty treatment. They seek not only bulky muscles but greater "definition"—visual distinction between muscle groups. They aren't much interested in strength, as strength, at all.

Weight lifters, by contrast, are athletes. Their training is aimed at increasing their capacities and skills at a very specific and demanding sport. Their aim is to lift weights: to lift as much weight as possible, in a set style and in proper form. They care little about what appearance their bodies present. They train for speed and quickness as well as for sheer strength, since one principle of the sport says that the faster the lifter can move the bar on which the weights are mounted, the more weight one will be able to lift. The world records in weight lifting are being revised upward as quickly as in any other sport today.

Strength training, on the other hand, is simply a conditioning and training routine aimed at laying a better base under the athletic capacities the individual can bring to bear on a sport.

*   *   *

The self-sculpting of the body builder is an overachiever's version of an attitude toward the body that informs more and more of modern athletics: if you don't like it, change it. After a season of observing and reporting on the U.S. Ski Team, Nick Howe told me that those young athletes regard their bodies much as racing drivers might regard their cars. The body is merely another piece of equipment on which one must do maintenance work from time to time—but you can also modify it as needed, when new requirements outstrip the capacities of the old machine. At the end of the season, Nick says, some ski racers almost routinely put themselves into the hospital for the physical equivalent of a ring and valve job—usually in the form of having the year's damage to the knees repaired.

One particularly sanguine young ski racer is Abbi Fischer, who may eventually make more headlines in medical journals than in ski racing. In one recent off-season (which for ski racers now constitutes about three weeks in late spring), Abbi had Dr. Richard Steadman, the team physician, "do" both knees. For rehabilitation, she began running quarter-mile intervals in series. She ran them at about a minute and thirty seconds per lap, which wasn't too bad, considering that she was still in casts and on crutches when she did it. She was concerned about losing cardiovascular conditioning while she waited for her knees to heal. This regimen allowed her to "max out" at a heart rate of about 220 beats per minute, which did provide considerable training effect.

The last time Nick talked to Abbi she said she was considering having her kneecaps *removed*. She has a congenital instability, she said, and she figured she might as well get rid of the source of trouble. How much of this was Abbi pulling Nick's leg, or Nick pulling mine,

I'm not sure. But even to make jokes about such a matter bespeaks an acceptance of the mutability of the body that's hard for me to comprehend.

*   *   *

The enlargement of muscle that the strength builder is seeking is an increase in the cross section of the individual muscle fibers, which results from an increase in the number of protein filaments—actin and myosin—within the cell. In untrained muscle there is great variation in cross-sectional area from fiber to fiber within the same muscle group, and strength training is aimed at bringing the smaller fibers up to match the size of the largest ones within a given muscle.

To train a muscle you contract it. There are at least four different kinds of muscular contraction, each of which has had its period of popularity among physical culturists, in a curious kind of rotating popularity. *Isotonic* contraction (*iso-*, "constant," *tonic*, "tension") is the commonest form. It is what happens when you lift a weight by bending your elbow, for instance. The name isn't quite accurate: the weight that is lifted does remain constant, but the tension generated in the muscle varies as the limb changes angles and gains or loses in mechanical advantage. This kind of contraction is also called *concentric* (the muscle always shortens as it does its work) or *dynamic* (the limb always moves).

Eccentric contraction is isotonic contraction upside down: the muscle is lengthened while it is under tension, the muscular effort resisting the lengthening. When you use muscle to lower a weight— even as in walking downhill—you are performing eccentric contractions.* There is evidence that eccentric contraction builds strength faster than isotonic contraction. This means that weight *lowering* may be more efficacious than weight lifting—and sure enough, it is not unheard of for a serious weight lifter to have assistants lift weights up to height, lodging them there on stands, so the athlete can come along and simply lower them.

---

* You're also getting sore muscles. Muscle soreness—the kind that hurts the next day— comes from microscopic injuries in the muscle fibers, from overwork, and from the resulting edema. In eccentric contraction, as the muscle is stretched out to its full length, the job of maintaining tension falls on muscle fibers near the ends of the muscle, where there is less cross section and therefore less strength. Each muscle fiber must work harder to maintain the tension. You'll tear more muscle tissue in eccentric contraction than in concentric contraction. If you're not used to it you'll get sore from hiking a hill, but the soreness actually comes more from the climb up than from the walk back down.

"Isometrics" was a great fad about thirty years ago. In an *isometric* contraction (*iso*-, "constant," *metric*, "length") you strain against an immovable resistance, so the muscle is worked without its length being changed. Actually, Charles Atlas, the mail-order body builder who put the phrase "98-pound weakling" into the language, was selling isometrics long before science defined the principle. He called it "Dynamic Tension"—pitting one muscle against another in one's own frame. Serious exercise physiologists paid him little attention, mostly because he never bothered with scientific verification. "Isometrics," on the other hand, had a sufficiently scientific-sounding name to sweep all before it, and in the 1950s the paperback book racks blossomed with isometric exercise schemes. Isometrics caught on in part because the exercises brought sizable strength gains from very brief exercise periods—ten contractions of six seconds each, and so on. A whole new body in fifteen minutes a day, said the popularizations. (Twenty-five years later an even bolder popularizer would promise us Total Fitness in but thirty minutes of exertion per *week*—corroborating P. T. Barnum, if contributing little to public health.)

When properly applied, isometric contraction is a perfectly valid technique for building strength. But for various reasons—the limitation of the strength gain to a single fixed joint angle at which the contraction is performed, the lack of flexibility training in conjunction with those fifteen-minute-per-day routines—isometrics have turned out to have some serious drawbacks, too. What originally seemed a great exercise breakthrough became a very specific tool to be used precisely and carefully. The most fruitful use is by therapists in rehabilitative applications.

There are problems with isotonic and eccentric work as well. The amount of resistance with which a muscle can train is limited to the amount that can be moved at the position of greatest mechanical *dis*advantage—the weakest point in the range of motion of the exercise, known to weight lifters as "the sticking point." A lifter can cheat past a sticking point by lifting the weight ballistically: by yanking or "throwing" the weight into motion so that once inertia is overcome, it helps move the weight past the weak point in the motion. (That's why the speed of the lift is so important.) Because of inertia a weight gives full resistance only at the beginning and the end of the lift, and those are the only points at which the muscle is getting maximum work. Ballistic lifting allows heavier weights to be used, but limits their strength-building effect. Inertia has a certain distorting effect in any conventional weight-lifting program.

What the strength builders want is a way of achieving the maximum manageable overload, at any speed of movement, throughout the full range of motion of the muscle's contraction. To compensate for changing mechanical advantage and to damp out the ballistic effect, they seek exercise that matches resistance precisely to force: "accommodating resistance exercise." That's a more accurate description for what has become popularly known as *isokinetic* exercise (*iso-*, "constant," *kinetic*, "motion"). Such contractions are the fourth type of muscular action, in which the muscle can exert its maximal force at a given constant speed over the full range of motion. It is the type of contraction that theoretically has more strength-building potential than any other type. It is a type of contraction not easily achieved. Enter the exercise machines.

Not all the new exercise machines provide resistance that is precisely isokinetic, but many of them approach the isokinetic concept or some variation of it, and the world of athletics has come to refer to them all by that term. They are clearly the hottest items in sports training equipment right now, a whole stable full of exotic and extremely sophisticated machinery for which the manufacturers make very strong claims. Many of the devices are now into their third and fourth generation of design evolution. The race is on among manufacturers to bring down the size, price, and complexity of the equipment to make it practicable for private consumer use. (Most current customers are institutional athletic departments, professional sports teams, and health spas—and the occasional wealthy movie or rock star.) Competition among manufacturers is fierce, and lawsuits, charges of industrial espionage, and other bad-tempered behavior are becoming epidemic. But the efficacy of the machines, when used in programs properly designed to achieve specific results, has not been seriously challenged.

The four major manufacturers are Universal Gym, Nautilus, Mini-Gym, and Lumex. All four lines of equipment involve rather elaborate structural cages, tables, levers; the attempt has been made with most of the devices to provide resistive exercise in positions and with motions that reproduce those of common sports.

Universal Gym equipment provides isotonic exercise, with "dynamic variable resistance" (Universal's terminology) as an added extra. The Universal Gym consists of a central weight rack with up to sixteen exercise stations arrayed around it, connected to the weight rack with cables and pulleys. "Dynamic variable resistance" involves a lifting mechanism designed to require maximum muscular effort throughout the range of motion of the given exercise. The athlete controls the speed of the exercise.

Nautilus has taken its name from the nautilus-shaped cams that its machines use. These change the effective moment arms and thus vary the force required to lift weights on pulleys. (In both Nautilus and Universal equipment the weights slide in racks that allow vertical motion only, reducing the amount and direction of motion that the lifter must control. It's much safer that way.) The Nautilus lineup consists of several different self-contained machines, one for each of various muscle groups. Each provides accommodating resistance, leaving the speed of the exercise up to the athlete. The exercises thereon are isotonic. Aggressive promotion has made the name "Nautilus" almost generic, a synonym for exercise machine.

Mini-Gym uses a centrifugal braking mechanism in place of weights. This device is a speed governor which automatically adjusts to provide just as much resistance as the athlete is supplying in force. The basic control unit adapts to several rack and table arrangements. The Mini-Gym units are specifically isokinetic in function, controlling speed of motion by accommodating resistance. One researcher has reported that the Mini-Gym can be accelerated slightly, but the unit is designed to keep speed changes to a minimum.

Lumex manufactures a series of purely isokinetic systems designed for both training and rehabilitation, such as the Orthotron and the Cybex. These are extremely sophisticated electromechanical devices that provide accommodating resistance by governing speed. Speeds are preset, before exercise. When the athlete or patient moves a lever arm at a speed less than that preset, there is little or no resistance; when the lever is accelerated to the preset speed, it responds with resistance precisely equal to the force applied. The basic resistive unit can be positioned to exercise most limbs and joints.

Nautilus and Lumex systems isolate specific muscles or muscle groups; Universal and Mini-Gym equipment are less specific, and perhaps a little more closely keyed to common athletic movements. All of the equipment is expensive—the Cybex II with strip chart recorder and all the fixings can run nearly $10,000—but well-heeled training facilities are finding useful ways of taking advantage of the specific benefits of each. For rapid rehabilitation of injury, these so-called isokinetic machines have proved their value. (And the $10,000 figure is for a clinical rather than an athletic training setup; equipment for sports programs alone can be much cheaper.) For training aimed at reducing injuries by increasing the strength of vulnerable areas, they are similarly effective if properly used.

For sheer strength building—increasing the athlete's overall strength and power, or the strength and power of specific athletic motions—the machines have produced wildly varying results. Some remarkable strength gains have been reported; some equally remarkable failures have been registered, using essentially the same techniques and programs. It is when one of the manufacturers attempts to prove that his machines build strength more efficiently than do those of his competitors that the claims begin to get a little wild. Each holds up a wonderfully clear picture of immense training rewards for exercise done Just the Right Way. And whose fault is it if you don't follow the instructions, eh?

*   *   *

Our modern capacity for hype makes us forget that the isometrics kick of the 1950s and, to a certain extent, the exercise machine—at least in some of its more highly touted forms—are part of an unbroken line of physical foolishness that goes back to such saviors as Émile Coué ("Every day in every way I am getting better and better") and chewing each mouthful twenty times.

Isometrics has been the source of considerable fun. Legend has it that the technique was discovered when a researcher restrained a live frog with one leg free to kick, the other held fast. The expectation was that the free leg would grow larger with the exercise, developing new muscle, and the fixed leg would wither in atrophy. The opposite happened, of course: the leg with which the frog struggled against immobility developed great bulging muscles, while the free leg, kicking against no resistance, merely maintained its original size. Voila! Isometrics. Suddenly busy executives were taking thirty-second isometric breaks right at their desk, pushing and straining one muscle against another, getting all red-faced and bulgy-eyed from the effort.

There's one isometric exercise that predated the isometric fad by decades. It involved the rear bumper of an automobile, in a common folk remedy for a short-term affliction peculiar to adolescent (male) lotharios. The ailment was painful genital congestion, brought on by prolonged periods of unconsummated courtship. Relief was alleged to come from the act of straining to lift the rear of an automobile. The remedy never worked, but it was nevertheless handed down from aching high school swain to swain over the generations.

*   *   *

Muscle responds to overload. If a muscle is worked only against accustomed loads, no increase in strength occurs. Because overload does cause the muscle to gain strength, the amount of resistance against which it works must constantly be increased if strength gains are to continue. This is "progressive resistance," a concept with which physiologists have been perfectly comfortable since the turn of the century. In the 1940s Dr. Thomas DeLorme—in some senses the father of modern strength training—codified it further, establishing certain key principles. Weight training, he said, was best done in *reps* (repetitions of a given exercise) and *sets* (groups of reps performed without resting); the last set should be at the maximum weight the athlete can lift through the appointed number of reps. Strength is built into muscle by high loadings with few reps, DeLorme said; endurance is best increased by low loads and many repetitions. A perfect formula of reps and sets should be possible for most efficient training.

Since DeLorme, weight training has gone through years of tangled search for that perfect formula. Just about every possible variation has been tried, and most of them end up producing both "best" and "worst" results. Specificity again: everyone is different. The number of reps and sets turns out not to be as important as the amount of load. In training for sheer strength the important criterion is how close the final set comes to the maximum that the athlete can lift. In training for endurance the formula is less easily determined.

In either case, the goal is to work to exhaustion as many muscle fibers as possible. As muscle fibers within the body of the muscle become exhausted, they stop contracting, and fresh, hitherto uncontracted fibers begin taking up the slack. What you're trying to do is exhaust *all* the muscle fibers. But weight training has been shown to increase the cross section of fast-twitch fibers, and endurance training to increase the size of slow-twitch fibers. The trainers reasoned that there is little point in wasting time and energy developing fibers you aren't going to use, and so they began trying to come up with programs aimed at developing the specific fiber types.

Enter the exercise machine manufacturers, with fists full of theories. *Speed* of exercise, they proposed, is the key. Vary the speed at which you do the strength-building exercise, and you should vary the color (type) of muscle fiber you are developing. Perform your weight training at high speed and develop white fibers, improving your speed and explosive power. Train at slow speeds over many repetitions and increase red fiber dominance, improving your endurance. At least that's the claim of the isokinetic machine makers, whose equipment, not unexpectedly, makes possible accurate control of the speed of exercise.

Not so, say the makers of the variable resistance isotonic equipment. Strength is strength; endurance is endurance; anything you can do to increase either will represent a positive gain. Specificity is indeed a powerful factor, but what that means is that you must do plenty of training in your specific sport. That builds strength, endurance, *and* skill. Then if you want the extra edge, you build raw strength the best way you can—which is through maximum-load repetitions, irrespective of speed, with Nautilus, Universal, or even barbell.

The controversy goes on, but recent research shows that the point is probably moot. Every muscle is a mix of slow- and fast-twitch motor units. As you begin to exercise a limb, the slow-twitch motor units are fired first and most easily. As more force is required, more motor units are fired and more fibers are engaged, but the fast-twitch motor units don't come into play until after the slow-twitch units are engaged. In fact, there is a "ramp" effect as more force is required. First the slow-twitch, then the Type A fast-twitch (the ones with relatively good endurance capacity), and finally the Type B fast-twitch units are brought into play. It is the amount of force required that governs the type of muscle fibers brought into play. The speed of the exercise has nothing to do with it.

Neither side of the controversy argues against the principle of specificity in athletic preparation. Both sides claim that their own method is the most efficient means of bringing more strength to bear on the specific activities required by any given sport. Both sides imply that their competitors' methods risk missing the specificity boat in the way coaches fear most: by preparing the athlete in the wrong way for the wrong movement. The coach's nightmare is the good athlete who gets into a weight program and, out of insufficient or faulty guidance, builds strength that not only can't be used but actually interferes with performance. Not muscleboundedness, exactly, but it does sometimes seem possible for athletes to overdevelop themselves for their athletic specialty.

Pro golfer Johnny Miller may be an example, although his story does not involve weight training. After a blazing couple of seasons a few years back, Miller took some time off the golf tour to work on his ranch, doing heavy construction labor, operating chain saws and the like. According to the press he developed so much new strength in neglected muscles and unused parts of his body that he "lost" his golf swing. At this writing he is still struggling to get back his winning touch. Since the Miller affair, any established athlete who so much as touches a weight machine and then has a poor season (or suffers an unusual injury) is automatically accused of this kind of "overdevelopment." It might be called training de-specificity.

The controversy among the weight-machine makers seems to involve a lot of bad science. This whole area of muscle development and strength building is so complex, with so many variables and so much purely human inconsistency at work, that carefully designed experiment after experiment comes up with inexplicable results. Experiments that seem to produce perfectly bulletproof findings turn out to be unduplicatable even when repeated by the original researchers. Tests designed to check conflicting concepts end up producing impossibly similar results. Human cussedness keeps making the strict order of science look foolish.

Because of the elusiveness of consistent results, and because a huge volume of research has been done in related areas, the manufacturers of the exercise machines have been able to pick research papers that help sell their own designs and that predict dismal results from using the machines of their competitors. The journals in the field have shown a distressing tendency to publish research papers more distinguished by the newsworthiness of their findings than by the soundness of their methodology.

The manufacturers reprint the research papers that bolster their claims and tuck them into their sales brochures, of course. Results that conflict or disagree are dismissed as faulty, based on poor research design. (Such conflicting papers then find their way into the sales kits of the competition.) One manufacturer's sales literature, already heavy with reprints of allegedly scholarly papers, claims that "scientists" have approached the manufacturer for research funds, promising "scientific" results from experiments as yet undone that will support the claims made for the machines of the manufacturer and will shoot down the claims of the competition. Claims of bad science are a time-honored dodge when the ground gets shaky, in any field, but there are certainly enough contradictory research findings available here to throw doubt in every direction.

Needless to say the resulting confusion, plus the background level of industrial bickering, has soured a lot of reputable trainers on the use of exercise machines. Add to that the consternation and ill will that result when an athlete occasionally somehow mistrains with the machines and loses, rather than gains, in athletic capability. Play all this against the innate conservatism of coaches, managers, and trainers, and the future of the exercise machines would look anything but bright.

Yet the lure of the exercise machines is simply irresistible. The equation seems too clear. We know how to develop muscles. We now have the means to find out which muscles, operating in which sequences, enable the athlete to perform his particular athletic task. We can even analyze the muscular components of world-beating athletic performances and compare them to those of merely workaday athletic performances, finding out the specific differences in timing, angle, force, speed, placement. The scientist is now *almost* able to tell the athlete and trainer that by speeding up this facet or slowing that one, by strengthening here or retiming there, the athlete can expect to begin producing world records. Or games won, or opponents defeated. (Some scientists claim they can already do this.) With the aid of the exercise machines, the athlete can *almost* expect to identify and isolate the particular muscle groups, and strengthen or speed up or retime precisely as prescribed.

The ideas, the knowledge, and the equipment are all there to do just that. We don't quite yet know how to make them all work together, certainly not all the time. So far the equation remains too complex. But we're learning. And here and there, when just the right combination of athlete, concept, guidance, and equipment come together, the results are coming to pass. When they do, we get what seem like athletic miracles. The edges are exceeded; the limits recede.

CHAPTER 5
Chemics

Cut to the quick. The quick and the dead. The term is archaic in that usage, but "quick" used to mean "alive"; later it came to mean "fiery," "intense," before we devalued it into a description of mere speed. Still, I think, athletics are the quick part of our lives. Sports are the verbs of our existence, depending on action, motion, on quickness in both the archaic and modern senses of the word.

The motion that makes sport possible is generated out of energy; how energy makes motion remains mysterious. The textbooks tell us that energy is always the same stuff, whether it comes from your friendly neighborhood power generating station or from fruits and nuts. It comes in six more or less complicated forms—nuclear, electrical, light, heat, mechanical, and chemical energy. For athletics (as for life itself) we convert one form into another, chemical energy into mechanical energy. All energy starts as solar (nuclear) energy, but some of it is transformed by photosynthesis and stored in plants as chemical energy. We eat the plants, or eat animals that have eaten the plants. We convert the chemical energy in food into mechanical energy in the muscles, allowing movement. Allowing life. So why doesn't the athlete, in search of more, longer-lasting energy, just eat more food? Ah, groans the coach, if only it were that simple.

The components of chemical energy from food break down in the metabolic process, in the presence of oxygen, into carbon dioxide,

78

water, and . . . energy. But what that energy really is, in any concrete sense that my imagination can grasp, still eludes me: this mysterious *push*, this force that enables all these glorious properties of movement and life. The chemists can explain it further.

The energy that is liberated from conversion of nutrients is not used directly by the muscles to do work. Instead, that energy powers yet another chemical conversion which manufactures the compound *adenosine triphosphate*, or *ATP*. And ATP is the real stuff, the super-soup, the best carrier of energy within the cell: it is the wonderful substance that extracts energy from the nutrients and makes it available at the biological furnace within the muscle, at the site where it can be used to do mechanical work.

It is the three phosphate radicals at the end of the ATP molecule —the *tri*phosphate part—that hold the capacity to generate energy for us. The phosphates are bound to the adenosine by a high-energy bond. ATP is stored in the muscles; a nerve impulse triggers the breaking of that high-energy bond, and in the dissolution of the bond, energy is finally released, ready for use by the muscle cells. "We make our living," as Dr. Lewis Thomas so poetically puts it in *Lives of a Cell*, "by catching electrons at the moment of their excitement by solar photons, swiping the energy released at the instant of each jump, and storing it up in intricate loops for ourselves." The energy can be used for other things besides the purely mechanical work of contracting muscle, of course, but the muscle cells are specialized for producing mechanical work from chemical energy.

It is possible to take a strictly mechanical view of the process, looking back to the protein filaments, the actin and myosin strands, within the muscle cell. The crossbridges that form between those strands, enabling them to contract, are where ATP is stored in the muscles. The signal for contraction causes calcium to be released into the muscle cell. The calcium activates the actin binding sites, making them receptive, and "charges" the crossbridges, preparing them, too, for action. The crossbridge and the binding site are electrochemically attracted to each other, and link in a physical-chemical coupling of actin and myosin. This forms actomyosin, the enzyme that releases the phosphate from its high-energy bond, and releases energy in the process. It is this released energy, finally, that causes the crossbridges to swing forward in the direction of contraction, making the actin filament slide over the myosin. The muscle contracts; the limb moves.

To maintain contraction, the crossbridges must rapidly make and break the physical contact; to break the link between the binding site and the crossbridge, the crossbridge must be recharged. For this a new ATP molecule is required, which means another phosphate radical must be supplied. Stored in the muscle is another substance that has a terminal phosphate group, also attached with a high-energy bond: *phosphocreatine*, or *PC*. When PC is broken down, phosphate and energy are released. The energy drives the free phosphate to recombine and resynthesize ATP. Thus the PC reaction is the source of the new molecules of ATP needed to reload the crossbridges so the contraction can be maintained or extended. The ATP-PC relationship is known in biochemistry as a coupled reaction: each drives the other, filling the other's energy requirements.

I have a little trouble getting my head around this. In an earlier chapter I spoke of the inconceivable series of calcium squirts required in all the muscles of all the athletes involved in a routine double play in baseball. I marveled at the complexity of those reactions. Yet the calcium squirts are only the signals that initiate the activity. What really drives the muscle, what drives *us*, is this swapping of phosphate radicals deep down there in the electrochemistry of the cells. "Swiping the energy released at the instant of each jump" indeed: at the jumping free of the phosphate radical. That's hard to envision.

(It is withdrawal of the calcium, incidentally, that signals the muscle cells to relax. But if the resynthesizing of ATP is interrupted, or no new source of ATP is available to reload the crossbridges to allow them to break the links, then the muscle locks up rigidly. The supply of ATP is totally interrupted only in death; we call the resulting muscular rigidity *rigor mortis*. Death in effect seals the crossbridges in place, in a purely mechanical linkup.)

I make a fist, gripping a pencil as tightly as I can. The muscles of the hand and forearm go tight, the ordinarily soft, rubbery feel of the limb straining toward hardness. Something—not quite pain, a little more than just effort—swarms through my arm. It is a suffusing feeling of, well, *feeling*, that's all. Molecules dancing, my imagination tells me: the whirling exchange of phosphate radicals, the kicking free of tiny dabs of chemistry, the buzz of energy resulting from that casting free. I can almost feel the hum.

I spoke earlier of a mysterious *push* that is energy. Some sensory vision of that push is beginning to emerge for me now. The image I keep getting is from my childhood: combing my hair with a hard rubber comb, then holding the comb near my face, feeling the wafting current of static electricity play across the surface of my skin. Electric wind. Energy. To put that energy down deep into the belly of the muscle, to make it available to power the needs of flesh and blood, that's the marvel in the biochemistry of muscle.

* * *

In these terms, it is amusing to contemplate the robot. There are all these Hollywood sci-fi dreams of building the perfect electromechanical person, with capabilities surpassing those of mere human weaklings. Yet every one of our muscle cells is at least metaphorically a small electric motor, and limited though the horsepower may be on a cell-by-cell basis, the aggregate is overwhelming. Duplicating the variety of muscular capacities alone would be inconceivably complex, never mind the control system that could make sense out of the subtleties of choice behind all those calcium squirts.

* * *

The coupled reaction of ATP and PC is the simplest and most readily available system of energy conversion for the muscles, but it is not the only one. Since this system needs no oxygen and no energy sources other than those already stored in the muscle, it is the system that is called upon first, for brief, explosive physical tasks—running up a flight of stairs, lifting a heavy weight, jumping over an obstacle. It is sufficient for only very short periods of activity—a few seconds at best—and then another source of ATP is needed by the muscle tissue. If the physical task lasts a little longer—up to about two minutes—energy is produced by what physiologists call the *anaerobic pathway*, or *lactic acid system*, which also requires no oxygen. After a couple of minutes of hard physical effort, the respiratory system is stimulated sufficiently to start producing energy through the *aerobic pathway*, or *oxygen system*.

Thanks to the jogging boom and the good work of Dr. Kenneth H.

Cooper, who first wrote about "aerobics" and founded the Aerobics Center in Dallas, anaerobic (no oxygen required) and aerobic (oxygen-using) exercise are reasonably familiar concepts now. But anaerobic exercise involves a little more than running out of breath (running up an "oxygen debt," another familiar term), and aerobic exercise does not just mean jogging at a pace that allows you to chat as you run. The systems of energy production to which these two terms refer are affected by everything from diet to altitude, and in turn affect everything from muscular soreness to how an athlete should best spend the recovery time in between closely spaced competitions.

For energy conversion via the ATP-PC pathway the chemical fuel is the PC part—phosphocreatine. For the anaerobic pathway the fuel is carbohydrates, specifically sugar; nothing else will do. For the aerobic pathway, the fuel can be carbohydrates, fats, even proteins. The ATP-PC and anaerobic pathways produce relatively few molecules of ATP per molecule of PC or glucose consumed, and under load they quickly either run out of fuel or become so loaded with waste products that the muscle can no longer contract. The aerobic pathway, on the other hand, produces a great many ATP molecules per molecule of fuel, a supply of ATP that in fact is virtually unlimited so long as fuel and oxygen hold out. The waste products of the aerobic system are easily disposable carbon dioxide and water. But the aerobic system is slow to kick in, and has an upper limit to the *rate* of energy production, which effectively means a limit to the rate of exercise. When that rate is exceeded, the exercise becomes anaerobic again, and waste products begin to build up. This may have a familiar ring to it: anaerobic energy production is clearly suited to the type of activity that recruits white, fast-twitch muscle fiber, and aerobic exercise to red, slow-twitch fiber.

In the anaerobic system, glucose (sugar), which has been stored in the muscles and in the liver in the form of glycogen, is broken down by a series of complex chemical reactions into ATP and pyruvic acid. Without the presence of oxygen, pyruvic acid is converted into the waste by-product *lactic acid*. If ATP is the super-soup in the exercise equation, lactic acid is the super-sludge, the major poison, the source of muscular fatigue. When the level of lactic acid in the muscle gets high enough, the muscle just can't contract anymore. The chemistry of energy delivery in the muscle drags to a halt. Considerable discomfort is felt. Anaerobic exercise is thus necessarily short-term: the body does simply run past its own capacity to continue.

* * *

One of the most painful maturational experiences for the young athlete can occur at the level of lactic acid buildup. We are reared on romantic fantasies of athletic achievement, triumphs of will over flesh. We are told, in our youth, to gut it out, to be tough; "quitter" is the final insult. When, in sustained athletic effort, we run into that level of lactic acid buildup, the discomfort is considerable, but the reason we finally have to stop the activity is because the muscles just won't work anymore. Nobody tells us that.

Because there is discomfort we almost automatically, guiltily, assume that it is inability to bear pain that stops us. (In fact that's precisely what some coaches "suggest.") The chemical truth is that lactic acid has momentarily removed the muscle's capacity to function, and pain is only a secondary effect. Athletic training is aimed to a great extent at increasing the capacity to tolerate higher levels of lactic acid, and to ignore the discomforts of fatigue, but these are capacities that do have to be trained. Young athletes are seldom prepared for the shock of this failure. They tend, secretly or otherwise, to put the failure to character deficiency rather than to chemical sabotage from the anaerobic pathway. The phenomenon is a stimulus to train harder, yes—when it is understood. When it isn't, it is another reason that brawn gets a bad name: it is associated with those painful instances when the unbrawny are made to feel inadequate in moral as well as muscular fiber.

Lactic acid is also responsible for the unfortunate and unnecessary linkage in the minds of many adults between exercise (indeed, any muscular effort) and pain. It may not actually reduce the level of pain to know that the source is lactic acid—but placebo effect or not, I find it easier to deal with. If you don't know what the pain is, you automatically assume that it means damage, that it will at very least leave you aching with soreness. The discomfort that comes with sustained anaerobic exercise seems much more manageable when you know it is merely sludge in the muscles, bound to be washed away once the circulatory system catches up.

* * *

In anaerobic exercise you run out of breath; in aerobic exercise you run out of fuel—eventually—but until you do, your system keeps up with the lactic acid and you can continue the exercise. Aerobic exercise produces energy by breaking down sugar (glycogen) just as anaerobic exercise does. So long as there is enough oxygen delivered to the muscle cells, however, the pyruvic acid is not converted into lactic acid, but broken down into carbon dioxide, water, and additional ATP.

It is the athlete's capacity to consume oxygen—called *maximal oxygen uptake*—that determines when an exercise switches from anaerobic to aerobic and back again. The state of rest is aerobic (although there is a low residual level of lactic acid in the blood at all times). When the body switches from rest to exercise there is an adjustment period during which oxygen uptake is gradually increased. At the beginning of exercise it takes a few minutes for the system to step up delivery of oxygen to the muscles. More energy is used during this period than the aerobic pathway can supply. The ATP-PC and anaerobic pathways take up the slack in energy production, but in doing so cause the body to build up an oxygen deficit. In short-term, high-intensity exercise the oxygen deficit lasts throughout the period of exercise; afterward the athlete has to have recovery time, repaying the deficit by hard breathing until he or she catches up.

When the exercise lasts longer, the athlete builds up an oxygen deficit in the first few minutes, and lactic acid does begin to accumulate. But if the pace is low enough, oxygen delivery catches up and a steady-state level is reached. Lactic acid stops accumulating, but the oxygen supply is not likely to be able to clear out the accumulation until after the exercise is finished. If the early pace is too high, then there will be too great a handicap: the athlete will either have to drop the pace considerably, to allow oxygen to catch up with lactic acid, or will be forced by fatigue to abandon the exercise.

The best performance in an endurance event will come from maintaining the highest possible steady pace, rather than varying the pace with tactical moves, such as fast early laps or a hard sprint at the close. The aim in the endurance event is to run out of energy and to "tie up" with the accumulation of lactic acid just as one crosses the finish line. The athlete who can maintain the fastest steady pace throughout the event and finish at that elegant moment at which he or she is empty of glycogen and full of lactic acid will be the athlete who has the highest maximal aerobic capacity, which means the highest maximal oxygen uptake. He or she will also likely be a winner.

It is an interesting symbolic point, a matching of peak (lactic acid) and valley (glycogen) that indicates that the athletic organism is, temporarily, used up. To be able to move that juncture about, to place it at the point in space that is the finish line or at the moment in time signified by the final buzzer, that is a rare and exciting talent. To do that is to hit another kind of sweet spot in time. It produces world records, as well as heart-stopping finishes.

Bill Fink, who kindly attempted to straighten out my often shaky science in these pages, says that I'm stretching the point too far here. "Only in long endurance events such as the marathon is the runner likely to run out of glycogen," Fink points out, "and then he does so without any appreciable accumulation of lactic acid—unless he 'dies' on a sprint, which is not likely if he's run out of glycogen. At races of shorter distances, such as the mile or 10,000 meters, the runner may be full of lactic acid, but he will not be empty of glycogen. The timing is critical, but the nature of the exhaustion is more often a case of *either* empty of glycogen *or* full of lactic acid."

Clearly, I've overstated the case. Few forms of exercise are powered by only a single energy system. The examples cited, from bolting up a flight of stairs to running a marathon, are intended to indicate only the ends of the spectrum—a spectrum more characterized by blend than by distinct extremes. Exercise that requires effort lasting less than about two minutes gets its energy almost entirely from the ATP-PC and anaerobic pathways; exercise that takes longer than about nine minutes of sustained effort is almost entirely aerobic. But most sustained exercise falls in between. Training principles for improving either anaerobic or aerobic performance are fairly well understood. But when both systems of energy production are needed, the training methods get remarkably complex, the parameters fuzzy, the athletic task more judgmental. The 1500-meter run, for which the world record is currently just over three and a half minutes, is estimated to require almost exactly equal inputs from the anaerobic and aerobic systems. Training for it drives athletes and coaches alike to despair.

That's why track and field experts have given such significance to the 1500-meter and mile runs. That's why the mile has endured as a regular event in major meets despite the worldwide switch to metric measurement in all the rest of track and field. It is such a classic contest, with so rich a history of great performances, that the organizers are reluctant to let it become an extinct form. But it gets those great performances because it is so maddeningly effective as a test. In these middle distances the athlete is required to perform the most delicate balancing act in running—of sheer speed versus the immutable chemical requirements of the body, of strength and endurance against the irreducible realities of time and distance. The runner who goes out too fast begins to tie up—to lose form, and thus speed, as lactic acid dips the muscles in agonizing sludge. The runner who holds back, hoping to build up less oxygen deficit, attempts to judge the precise point from which to launch the final kick to the finish. Each runner becomes a metaphor for the energy pathway that he or she draws upon for race strategy. Peak matches valley at the finish line. The scales balance.

*   *   *

One staple in the pulp-novel athletic fantasies of my youth was "second wind." It came at the critical moment when our hero, laboring painfully out of breath, about to lose the championship to the hated crosstown rivals, reached down into his inner resources and somehow found renewed strength—the will, and the wind, to continue, even to pick up the pace. Perhaps because of that pulp-novel popularization, for decades "second wind" was considered to be a myth.

Our hero was simply woefully out of shape. Shortly after the Tokyo Olympics, exercise physiologists put Abebe Bikila, the Ethiopian who had just won his second gold medal in the marathon, on a treadmill. For the first two or three minutes his heart rate and other physiological measurements rose steadily, just as they should have, just like those of anyone else. Then the measurements dropped off sharply and stabilized at remarkably low levels. There they remained for the next hour or so of treadmill running, or until the physiologists got tired of taking readings. Eureka, cried science: second wind is a real phenomenon. It exists.

Curious. Second wind would seem to occur regularly at the time when oxygen delivery catches up with energy consumption, switching the system over from anaerobic to aerobic exercise. Actually, it's a little more complicated than that. In early stages of exercise the carbon dioxide content of the blood is high and the acid-base balance is upset by accumulating lactic acid—conditions that cause you to hyperventilate. So there is respiratory distress: you can't seem to get your breath. As you continue, these factors equilibrate, your breath "comes back," and you may feel euphoric. Second wind. It is available to every jogger, every time he or she goes out for a run. Trouble is, he or she won't notice it. Training reduces the time before physiological equilibration takes place, and also reduces the degree of discomfort before it does. So it is only the untrained person who clearly experiences the dramatic switchover and the accompanying euphoria of second wind.

Maybe that's why it eluded confirmation for so long. The people interested in such a phenomenon—athletes, coaches, exercise buffs —were effectively immune to the experience because of their levels of training. The scientists who might have been "eligible," so to speak, because of their own poor conditioning, would have found it hurt too much to exercise through the switchover point, and would likely have abandoned the effort before second wind kicked in. Unless they were about to lose the championship to the hated crosstown rivals, of course. This is very unscientific speculation on my part.

It reminds me of how Fritjof Capra contrasted Eastern and Western science in *The Tao of Physics*. Deep thinkers of the East, he points out, tend not to trust any phenomenon unless they can know it as a result of direct subjective experience. That, to Easterners, is scientific; anything that can't be experienced is mere theory. For Westerners, scientists in particular, subjective experience is no confirmation of anything. We trust ourselves and the evidence of our senses last. It is only when instruments can provide numbers, when measurements can be taken to provide objective verification, that the existence of a phenomenon is "proved," and the proof obtained thereby is accepted whether the phenomenon can be experienced subjectively or not. Each view holds that the other is absurd, of course.

Forget about Bikila's marathon medals; we needed the numbers off the machine to "prove" that he could go on running those distances at those speeds. There are some runners who talk about third wind, fourth wind, and so on, but no one has come up with any numbers for anything like that. So they must be mystics, deluding themselves, right?

*   *   *

The exhausted athlete stops, panting; his system immediately begins to work to replenish his energy stores, to ready him for further exertion. It takes energy to put back the energy stores in the muscles. That energy is provided via the aerobic pathway. The labored breathing of the recovering athlete pumps oxygen through the system, which combines with glucose (and free fatty acids) to produce ATP, carbon dioxide, and water. Some of the ATP is restored directly to the muscles; some is immediately broken down further to restore PC supplies. (The ATP and PC stores are referred to, more simply, as *muscle phosphagen*.)

Restoration of the muscle phosphagen is amazingly quick, virtually complete within about three minutes of hard breathing—a period referred to as the *alactacid oxygen debt*. An untrained adult male can incur a maximum alactacid oxygen debt of about 2 to 2.5 liters of oxygen, but that capacity can be increased with training. All else being equal, in anaerobic events, the athlete who can run up an alactacid oxygen debt of 3 liters will defeat the athlete who can incur only a 2-liter debt. He can use more energy at a faster rate, and thus can do more work before total exhaustion.

After about three minutes of hard breathing, oxygen consumption slows to something closer to normal, but it is still elevated. You've "got your breath back"; with your muscle phosphagen restored, you're ready for another brief few seconds of muscular activity. But if you've been performing anaerobically, you still have an accumulation of lactic acid in your system that threatens muscular shutdown again as soon as those few seconds of energy are used up. To get rid of the lactic acid you have to continue to process extra oxygen for a while. That period of slower but still elevated oxygen uptake repays the *lactacid oxygen debt.* The lactacid oxygen debt is repaid thirty times more slowly than the alactacid debt.

Gentle aerobic exercise will remove the lactic acid in the system more quickly than will total rest. If you keep the blood moving at a slightly faster rate, you pump it through the liver and oxidize out the lactic acid more quickly. So after one bout of exhaustive exercise you'll recover more quickly and be ready for another bout sooner if you keep moving. Most athletes know this, instinctively if not bio-chemically. That's one reason for all the restless jogging you see in the infield of every track meet. It's not all warm-up. Since it helps restore blood glucose, which is necessary for brain functioning, one might even say it is also good for the head. At any rate, an athlete who has a brief recovery period between two anaerobic events would do well to keep moving.

If there is a single standard of measurement that tells us the level of fitness of an athlete, it is *maximal oxygen consumption*. So clear and convenient is this measurement that exercise physiologists some-times speak of it as "athletic capacity"—roughly akin to horsepower in an automobile. (Athletes, who nowadays are becoming more and more sophisticated about exercise science, are starting to use the same language.) Maximal oxygen consumption is the capacity of the body to process oxygen. It is usually expressed in milliliters of oxygen consumed per kilogram of body weight per minute of exercise, or *ml/kg/min*. It can definitely be increased by training. You can also increase it by losing body fat, and thus weight; in *ml/kg/min*, the effect is the same whether the *ml* figure increases or the *kg* decreases.

A few years ago some exercise scientists began proposing another measurement of athletic capacity, which they called the *anaerobic threshold*—the point at which energy production begins to switch back from the aerobic to the anaerobic pathway. If an athlete with a low capacity for processing oxygen competes against an athlete with a high capacity, the low-capacity athlete will have to "go anaerobic" earlier than the competitor. That means he or she will start produc-ing lactic acid earlier, risk tying up earlier, run out of athletic capacity sooner. By measuring the level of lactic acid in an athlete's blood during or at the end of a bout of exercise, these scientists theorized, you might be able to compute backward to determine how much of the energy used was produced by the aerobic pathway, and how much by the anaerobic pathway.* Some researchers have assumed that just as with maximal oxygen consumption, an athlete's anaerobic threshold could be raised by training. Some others don't think so (see Chapter 12), but the question has stirred considerable interesting research.

Measuring maximal oxygen consumption requires that an elaborate air-bag setup be mounted on the athlete, complete with noseclips and other paraphernalia, throughout the exercise, as all gases inhaled and exhaled must be assayed. Measuring lactic acid levels takes only a quick blood sample—a drop of blood from the earlobe will do.

The vaunted East German sports program (regularly used by our own media to intimidate congressmen and athletic budget committees) recognized the comparative efficiency of measuring lactic acid levels a few years back and began using that method to train swimmers. They developed a computerized system for analyzing blood and began taking samples before and after hard workout sessions, particularly at intervals of one, three, five, seven, and ten minutes after exercise stopped. The athlete would then be put through another slightly different workout session, and the sampling procedure repeated.

The East German theory was that the limitation to athletic performance, particularly in high-pressure programs such as their own, was more likely to be from overtraining than from undertraining. Too much work, rather than too little. When lactic acid levels accumulate and are not washed away by sufficient rest and gentle aerobic exercise, the athlete becomes susceptible to injury or illness. More important, workouts can't be conducted at levels of sufficient overload to achieve any additional training effect. The trick is to keep workouts at the maximum possible level of aerobic expenditure without allowing lactic acid levels to rise. Hence the constant monitoring.

According to reports of the East German approach, if the computer is given enough data on an athlete it should be able to determine not only the maximum possible aerobic workout, but also the maximum pace that the athlete can carry through to the end in a

* There are some real problems here, Bill Fink points out. Some lactic acid is burned by the system even during the exercise that produces it. To determine how much energy comes from which pathway by measuring lactic acid levels would require that *all* the lactic acid show up in the blood, which doesn't happen. "This is not to say," Fink says, however, "that there is no value in knowing relative degrees of anaerobiosis during a work task or over the course of a training session."

competitive event. After the athlete trains for a sufficient time at one pace, the tolerance for lactic acid should increase. Theoretically, the anaerobic threshold should therefore be raised. The continuously updated blood samples should reflect this change, and the computer can calculate new, more strenuous workout programs to go with the higher threshold.

Observers maintain that the East German "breakthrough," if any, is not in basic science, not in the physiology of training, but in development of the computer programs which can plan workloads with such precision. For the East German women, who dominated world swimming for a period of years before and after the 1976 Montreal Olympics, the method seemed to work, at least for a while. For the East German men, interestingly enough, it did not. American men, who train anaerobically much of the time, hold the bulk of the world records, regularly defeating the East Germans and everyone else in swimming.

A more significant aspect of the East German programs is the provision of that level of constant scientific backup to practicing athletes. Efforts to inject these particular training methods into American athletics have so far been frustrated by both technology and politics. Few question the validity of this kind of measurement, but the limited attempts to duplicate them in this country have had mixed results. One large problem is the availability of that level of technological and medical backup throughout the long periods of training that a world-class athlete must put in. Or as Frank Shorter put it when someone asked him if he could win the 1980 Olympic marathon: "If I can find the right doctor." Meaning, if he can find the backup from sports medicine to help him prepare as thoroughly as he feels his competitors are now doing.

It is for that purpose that the U.S. Olympic Committee has finally begun to invest a few of its many millions in sports medicine facilities for American athletes. Do not expect instant technological or scientific successes, however. The men's swimming results alone argue against the basic premise—that overtraining is the primary culprit in limiting athletic performance. And so long as such arguments go on, there is little likelihood that U.S. national teams in any sport will go completely for the high-technology approach. In sports, we tend to choose democratic chaos over the monolithic technological steamroller. Except in football, of course.

*   *   *

It is everyman's essential nightmare: you are running desperately, fearfully, away from something, but it is as if you are running in deep sand, your limbs coated with some mysterious sluggishness that makes you unable to move quickly. Or in another version, a recurrent childish nightmare of my own, you find yourself in a fist fight, but the blows have no force because you can't move your arms fast enough. It is like fighting underwater.

It is a dream of glycogen depletion: the brain's signals to the limbs can't be carried out because there is no energy left in the muscles to make the limbs move. It is not a lactic acid dream; there is not that leaden discomfort. It is just that there isn't any energy available, no electric buzz in the muscles to get things working again.

And in the end it comes down to that: energy is all. Energy is what sports is all about. One can delve deeper and deeper into the muscle cell, seeking the mechanism that makes motion happen, because motion is sports and muscle makes motion. But the muscle requires energy to make motion, requires that swiping of phosphate radicals, the electrochemical attraction, the microminiature magnets of actin and myosin crossbridges pulling threads of protein molecules along, sliding over one another to turn on the machine, to make the limb move. All of us can do that, but the athlete can do it better than you and I because all the channels are freed up and clear, the connections better made. The athlete has kept the pathways open. I haven't. Maybe that's why the blows I launch in my dreams never land.

(Ah, but there's a postscript. I started running, and found myself much less pursued in my dreams. Furthermore when I run—in dreams—I run faster rather than slower; I run with wings, bounding down the road, second and third and fourth winds coming regularly along to help me sail. Unfortunately the sluggish limbs and the feeling of running in sand have transferred to my waking life, my daytime running.)

CHAPTER 6

Pumps

"Blood," said Goethe, "is an entirely wonderful sap." It is also the essential medium of exchange between the body's major pumping systems, the heart and the lungs. How effectively that exchange can be maintained, how well those pumping systems work, governs to a large extent how effective an athlete can be.

It is not the sap itself but the heart that pumps the sap that holds our imagination: always the heart, the tough old gristle of implacable, tireless, unyielding heart muscle. (Its strength as a muscle can't be measured; it has no tendons on which to tie transducers or other instruments for determining contractile force.) It is synonymous with the center, the core, the very source. Yet if the athlete goes by incoming information only, by the sensory reports received from the body—effort, discomfort, pain—the lungs quickly come to seem more important than the heart ever was. You *feel* insufficiency in the lungs; it hits you there first. You are reduced to imagining the struggle the heart goes through. Angina sufferers aside, of course.

You might even say that the breath—as in the breath of life—is at the heart of the matter. Corny or not, such metaphors are instructive. Take the body as universe and the ancient elements of earth, air, fire, and water become apt. One pump pumps air, the other "water"—or, in this case, that entirely wonderful sap. The fire comes from the central nervous system, of course (Chapters 7 and 8). And for earth, it is not too farfetched (as metaphors go) to consider the muscle tissue itself, the ground for the circuitry that begins with the brain. These are only writerly conceits, but I find their examples useful.

Energy drives the body, oxygen is required to produce energy, and it is the heart that sends oxygen to the tissues where energy is produced and used. Simple enough, on the face of it. The lungs pump air to the blood supply, where the essential gas that is oxygen can be extracted and fed to the body. Simplicity again.

But the heart is not one pump, it is two. The right heart gets carbon-dioxide-loaded blood—venous blood—from the body and pumps it to the lungs. The left heart gets oxygenated blood from the lungs and pumps it to the body tissues. Two circuits, two systems. And as oxygen absorbs all our attention, we overlook the outgoing carbon dioxide, which is not mere waste but is also an important medium of control, helping govern, among other things, how hard the pumps work to meet the demands of the body.

None of this is ever simple, and no circuit, system, or mechanism can be extracted from all the rest to be examined in pure simplicity. There is even a feedback system, for example, which cuts down production of urine when blood viscosity gets too high. During exercise, working muscles require more body fluid. (That's the "pumping up" the body builders do to expand their muscles for display purposes.) The fluid is extracted from the blood supply, which means the blood tends to thicken. Shutting down urine production helps preserve fluidity.

And so on. As energy needs go up, both pumps—heart and lungs —must work harder to supply more of the raw materials necessary for the process to continue. Both pumps need energy themselves, which has to come from the same sources, the same nutritional and oxygenation processes, that supply the rest of the body. Exercise physiology is a Möbius strip.

The lungs are passive, unmuscled air bags hanging within the rib cage. They don't breathe, exactly; they *are* breathed by that marvelous muscle that is the diaphragm. (The diaphragm does have some help: hard breathing can require the coordination of some ninety muscles.) The diaphragm is the sheet of muscle that divides the trunk in two parts, heart and lungs above, all the rest of the internal organs below. It is dome-shaped; contract it and the dome depresses, increasing the volume of the upper trunk, sucking air down into the lungs. A "stitch" in your "side" may in fact be a cramp in the diaphragm muscle. When you laugh or cry its movements become spasmodic.

*   *   *

Actors and singers learn subtle control of the diaphragm to help them project their voices, to ensure plentiful supplies of air to the voice box for extended passages, to play variations in timbre and volume. One school of psychological theory holds that the rest of us learn to control the diaphragm too well: it is the second major set of muscles we bring under conscious control (after the sphincters that permit toilet training), and much adult tension and unease come from controlling it too tightly, from never giving that tortured muscle a chance to stretch and relax. The diaphragm is a metaphor for Western consciousness, with the ego (head, heart, lungs) above, the id (the *pudenda*, Latin for those organs of which we should be ashamed—sex and elimination) below. Yogis and practitioners of various other psychophysiological disciplines seek to control the diaphragm—the breath—first. It is the one bodily system that operates perfectly well on automatic controls but that is also amenable to conscious control; the yogis consider it the entering wedge between the autonomic and voluntary nervous systems. Athletes, preparing for the beginning of action, take deep breaths, not to get their bodily processes going faster, but to get their "nerves"—their emotions—under control. Deep breathing does help one gain access to the emotions. We use the diaphragm to cry; we also use it to keep *from* crying.

*   *   *

For ordinary uses—until exercise increases your need for air—you can exhale sufficiently just by relaxing. As you inhale, the elasticity of the chest wall stores enough energy to pump out the used air; relax, and out it goes. As air requirements go up, you use additional muscles. The *intercostal* (between-the-rib) muscles are laid down as short fibers crisscrossing like the cords of a bias-ply tire, with the inner fibers organized in one direction, the outer fibers crossing them at right angles. Contract the external intercostals and the ribs are pulled apart slightly, the rib-cage volume increased. The lungs suck more air. Contract the internal intercostals and the ribs are pulled back together, forcing exhalation. For even more forceful breathing, you use the abdominals and various muscles of the back and neck to increase airflow in as well as out. Incidentally, the comedy skit in which the old duffer can't blow out the candles on his blazing birthday cake is based on one of aging's more explicit realities. Force of exhalation diminishes so predictably that it provides an index to the physiological toll of aging.

The volume of air inspired or expired per breath is known as the *tidal volume*. The maximum amount of air that can be expired after maximal inspiration is called the *vital capacity*. There's a certain volume of air left in the larynx, trachea, and other respiratory passages on every inhalation, air that can't get to the lungs to give up its oxygen; that volume is referred to as *anatomical dead space*. There is a certain volume of air left in the lungs at complete exhalation, known as the *residual volume*, which reduces the amount of new air that can be drawn in on the next breath. In fact there are at least eight different measurements of lung volume and respiratory capacity, useful for physiologists if for no one else; all of them are affected by exercise, and most can be improved—for "increased ventilatory efficiency"—by training.

The act of breathing itself requires oxygen, to produce the energy to work the ventilatory muscles. At rest only 1 or 2 percent of the body's oxygen consumption is used to supply the respiratory muscles. As the rate of exercise increases, the muscles have to overcome air resistance in the respiratory passages, the elasticity of the rib cage, and other restrictions, which increases the energy demand, and thus the oxygen consumption, markedly. Under extreme conditions the oxygen cost of ventilation can shoot up to 8 to 10 percent of the total oxygen consumption.

That's why it is worthwhile to train for increased ventilatory efficiency. If you can make the ventilatory muscles work more efficiently, you decrease their oxygen consumption and make more oxygen available to the skeletal muscles. Scientists disagree about the limits to total oxygen consumption. One theory has it that the limit is simply the heart's capacity to pump. (The heart uses oxygen also —a great deal of it.) The other theory is that above a certain rate of exercise any additional oxygen that the system can acquire must be used to power the ventilatory muscles. But in either case increased ventilatory efficiency pays off in more oxygen made available to the working muscles.

* * *

The supercharger increases power in an internal combustion engine by cramming more gasoline (mixed with air) into the combustion chamber at each power stroke. The supercharger is basically an air pump hooked to the carburetor. An air pump needs power to operate. Early superchargers took their power from the engine's crankshaft. They eventually bumped up against a point of diminishing returns: power increases from supercharging were just about sufficient to make up the extra power needed to turn the supercharger. That's approximately the same situation that the body faces in the energy costs of increased ventilation.

Then engineers devised the turbocharger, which uses the flow of exhaust gases, which would otherwise just be wasted, to turn the air pump. No athletic equivalent of the turbocharger has yet been discovered, although some athletes have nominated amphetamines for that role.

* * *

One way that training increases ventilatory efficiency is by increasing *diffusion* capacity. The crucial part of respiration is not so much circulation of blood and pumping of air as it is the exchange of gases (oxygen for carbon dioxide) between those two media. The exchange of gases is by the process of diffusion. It takes place in the alveoli— the tiny air sacs, roughly 150 million per lung, each surrounded by its own network of capillaries like a macramé sling for a hanging flowerpot—and in the muscle tissue itself, also intricately interlaced with capillaries. The capillaries open and close on demand of the circulatory system, with perhaps ten times as many capillaries open in a working muscle as in the same muscle at rest. The alveoli respond similarly, opening for the increased demands of exercise, closing when lesser activity reduces the need. (When the alveoli open, so does their network of capillaries.) The surface area of all the alveoli of a pair of adult male lungs is estimated to be about the same as a tennis court; that same male will have about 60,000 *miles* of capillaries.

The gases are diffused directly through the permeable alveolar and capillary walls. The rate of diffusion depends on several things, including the length of the pathway of the gases, the available surface area, the number of red blood cells, and, most importantly, the pressure gradients between the gases. These gradients, in turn, depend on the partial pressures of the gases, which at sea level are quite manageable but which vary considerably at high altitudes and under water—environments in which some of us, nonathletes as well as athletes, insist on performing heavy exercise. Troubles can result, ranging from the altitude sickness of mountain climbers and skiers to the "bends" suffered by divers.

Oxygen is diffused chemically into the red blood cells, forming oxyhemoglobin—a process that increases the oxygen-carrying capacity of the blood by a factor of better than sixty. At the same time, much smaller amounts of oxygen are simply dissolved into the blood plasma. The amount of dissolved oxygen is inconsequential for meeting the body's requirements, even at rest. But this oxygen in solution does determine the partial pressure of oxygen in the system, which in turn controls both the rate of breathing and the rate of red blood cell production. (The system destroys and replaces several million red cells per second, so the latter function is not trivial.)

The partial pressure of oxygen also governs the level of saturation of the hemoglobin with oxygen. Each molecule of hemoglobin has a maximum capacity to combine with four molecules of oxygen, but only does so under ideal conditions. The more oxygen the hemoglobin carries, the more efficient the system; the higher the partial pressure of oxygen, the higher percentage of saturation of the hemoglobin with oxygen.

The oxygen that the hemoglobin picks up must eventually be given back to the body tissues, in a process called dissociation. The rate of dissociation of the oxygen from the hemoglobin varies to protect the system. Blood temperature, blood acid levels, and the amount of carbon dioxide in the blood also affect hemoglobin saturation. All three increase with exercise, and the increase causes oxygen to kick loose from its bond with the hemoglobin more easily, to speed up oxygenation of working muscles. Training increases this capacity.

Carbon dioxide, like oxygen, is carried in the blood in both chemical and physical solution. In chemical reactions it combines with water in the blood to make weak carbonic acid, and with proteins in the blood to form carboamino compounds. In physical solution the dissolved carbon dioxide in the blood helps to control various cardiorespiratory functions.

* * *

Here we go swapping free radicals again: hemoglobin in the blood making itself attractive, somehow, to lure the oxygen molecules into jumping on board for the ride. The harder we exercise—the more oxygen-hungry the muscles—the more attractive the hemoglobin is able to make itself.

There's another image that works better for me. The inner diameter of the capillaries is so small that the individual red blood cells must line up in single file to pass through, and can actually be squeezed out of shape as they pass. Still, the transfer of gases takes place, and in less than half a second; that's all the transit time the red cells spend in the capillaries. The squeezing of red blood cells actually enhances the transfer of gases: the oxygen is virtually *sprayed through* the capillary wall; then the cell sucks up plasma—and carbon dioxide—like a sponge. And vice versa, at the alveolar end.

When I first started running, attempting to get back into decent cardiovascular shape after fifteen years of sluggardness, I didn't know about any of this. But I kept having these mental images of forcing blood down into long-unused capillaries, the red cells stubbornly poking their way through. Very likely I'd seen and forgotten some television documentary about the process. I dismissed the image as childish, but it kept popping back into my head. More truth than poetry to that image, as it turns out.

A year or so later my wife, Chris, started running also. Her reaction, when she began developing some aerobic capacity, when all that buzz and thrum and tingling activity began happening out there in long-passive muscles, bordered on fright. She was not sure, for a while, that she *liked* having all that strange business being transacted in her body. It went away after a while. Now she says she thinks it was the freeing of clogged capillaries that caused the electrical singing sensations, and once they were freed up the noise died down.

(Bill Fink says this kind of "intuitive physiology" is very misleading and has little to do with what is really going on. More likely, Chris just got used to the sensation.)

*　　*　　*

The processes that improve gaseous exchange during exercise—the opening up of alveoli and capillaries, the increased saturation of hemoglobin, and all the rest—can multiply the amount of oxygen delivered to the muscles by a factor of three over resting rates. But the demands of the musculature during the same exercise may be thirteen times as high as at rest. To make up the difference, you have to move a lot more blood through the system.

There are two ways to increase cardiac output: You can increase the heart rate (more beats per minute) and you can increase the stroke volume (more blood pumped by each heartbeat). The latter increase is more healthful in the long run; more blood pumped per heartbeat means that the same amount of total blood flow can be maintained at a slower heart rate, which means that the heart doesn't have to work as hard.

The heart increases its stroke volume by making a sharper, more effective contraction of the ventricle which pumps arterial blood out into the tissues. At resting rates that ventricle may not be terribly efficient, often emptying only half its contents with each beat; at maximum output it discharges the total volume, doubling its efficiency. The change is brought about by stimulation from the central nervous system and by hormonal changes induced by exercise.

Those same stimuli speed up the heart rate, too. Training has a considerable effect on heart rates. In a healthy but untrained adult male, at rest, the heart usually settles to something on the order of 70 to 90 beats per minute. (Smokers' heart rates will usually be higher.) But train that same individual sufficiently and the resting rate can be brought as low as 45 to 50 beats per minute—and the strain on that overworked muscle is reduced accordingly.

(As I was working on this book an acquaintance in his late forties, a physical-fitness buff who was in superb shape, suffered a near-fatal glider crash. He was rushed to an emergency ward, unconscious. The attending physicians, finding a heart rate of roughly forty beats per minute in a middle-aged man in severe trauma, put him on the intensive care heart monitoring equipment, assuming he was near death. The doctor couldn't conceive that so low a heart rate could mean anything other than incipient heart failure. In fact the heart was stronger than normal, and played a major role in the victim's remarkably quick recovery.)

Because maximum heart rate is closely related to maximum oxygen uptake, heart rates, taken at the pulse, are among the handiest of training guides. All else being equal, the athlete who can sustain a given cardiac output at the slowest possible heart rate will have the most endurance. Among other advantages, the heart itself will use up less oxygen from the supply that could otherwise be going to the musculature.

When you begin loading up the cardiovascular system through exercise, the stroke volume and heart rate both adjust quickly for increased cardiac output. Stroke volume increases to its maximum at only moderate work loads—at about 40 percent of maximum oxygen uptake. Heart rate is slower to react, and is keyed more closely to specific oxygen demands. After thirty minutes or so of heavy exercise, the stroke volume decreases slightly and holds there. The heart rate continues to increase, however, and in cases where extreme work loads are continued uninterrupted for long periods, as in running a marathon, the heart can spend an hour or more pumping away at very high rates. The physical load to the system entailed by that kind of energy expenditure is, of course, immense.

The heart can't pump blood that it can't get its ventricles around. The total cardiac output is therefore ultimately dependent on the capacity of the body to get blood back to the heart: venous return. This is accomplished in various ways. There is no specific venous pump, no heartlike single mechanism that is responsible for venous return; the heart can't "suck" blood back up from the extremities. But a system for enhancing venous return is built in. Exercise involves contraction of the muscles, and those contractions themselves compress the veins, pushing blood back toward the heart as a milkmaid pushes milk out of the cow's teat. The veins contain valves within them that permit blood flow in one direction only—toward the heart. (Muscular effort that requires that you exert a force and hold it doesn't involve a contraction-relaxation cycle, and therefore hinders, rather than helps, venous return.)

The heavy breathing that accompanies exercise also adds pressure to the return system: the veins of the thorax and abdomen fill when you exhale and are pumped out, emptying toward the heart, by the pressure on those veins when you inhale. There's also a natural reflex constriction of the veins that occurs rhythmically during exercise, which pumps blood on toward the heart.

Sitting on the back of your neck watching TV or sleeping, you may be pumping only 20 percent of your blood to skeletal muscles. The great bulk of the blood flow goes to internal organs, to the heart itself, and to the brain. (Rumors that TV-watching automatically shuts off the total blood supply to the brain are as yet unproven.) When you begin to exercise, the body quickly compensates, redistributing the blood flow so that as much as 90 percent of it begins to go to working muscles.

As you start to exercise, the temperature rises in your working muscles, and your lactic acid and carbon dioxide levels rise while your blood oxygen levels drop. These changes, plus the same kind of hormonal and central nervous system changes that govern stroke volume and heart rate, kick off a reflexive redistribution of the blood supply. The arteries that supply the viscera and the skin contract sharply, reducing the supply of blood to those organs (except in conditions of extreme heat, in which case the skin continues to get a healthy supply of blood for cooling purposes.) At the same time the vessels that supply the skeletal muscles automatically dilate. The blood supply to the heart is increased—it, too, is a working muscle —but the brain's supply is kept close to resting levels. (This may help explain episodes of cloudy judgment under extreme work loads, such as often occur near the end of a marathon.) These reflexive adjustments are sufficient to increase the blood supply to the skeletal muscles by as much as 15 percent without any change in cardiac output at all. More importantly, the changes prepare the route, in effect, for the great rivers of blood required by oxygen-hungry muscles during heavy exercise.

* * *

Venous return, hindered by steady, constant muscular straining, is also seriously affected by the *Valsalva maneuver*—and so are several other important physiological responses. The Valsalva maneuver occurs when you close off your glottis and strain against it: you tighten your abdominal muscles and make an "expiratory effort," as if to exhale against the closed glottis, during any brief, heavy muscular exertion. It is the habitual response for most of us, a very natural way to lock up all the muscle and skeleton of the upper body to provide a firmer base for maximum effort. The respiratory muscles do, in fact, help provide a great deal of stability to the trunk.

It's a bad habit. If you've been breathing heavily beforehand, it can make you faint. It can raise your blood pressure to the danger point. It can even collapse the major vessels returning blood to the heart.

You can avoid all that trouble by remembering to exhale during a straining effort. That's one reason why weight lifters are trained to give that mighty grunt when they expend their maximum strength: to keep the glottis at least partially open, and prevent any of several disastrous kinds of internal blow-outs.

*   *   *

The control centers that govern respiration and circulation are located in the brainstem and near the heart. Stimulation of the respiratory control center changes the depth and rate of breathing. Stimulation of the circulatory control center changes the heart rate, stroke volume, distribution of blood to the various organs, and venous return mechanisms. But the centers are so closely linked that stimulation of either of them usually results in stimulation of the other. They are cybernetic mechanisms, sending feedback messages from one to the other. Ventilation affects blood flow, and vice versa.

Furthermore, the kinds of stimuli are also closely linked. Stimuli can come directly from the blood chemistry. Oxygen deficiency, carbon dioxide overload, or rising levels of lactic acid, for example, can all cause dilation of the arterioles of the heart, which in turn causes redistribution of the blood flow. Stimuli also come directly through the nervous system. Mental states themselves—fright, elation, grief —can cause the cardiorespiratory control centers to react, primarily from hormonal changes from the adrenal gland. Limb movement, pain, changes in blood pressure, even the stretch of the rib cage associated with taking a deep breath (another kind of stretch reflex) can cause the control centers to change blood flow and ventilation.

In fact these controls of respiration and circulation are so intertwined that they remain largely mysterious, despite generations of study. We know of several factors affecting blood pressure, for instance: the internal resistance of the arteries to blood flow, the elasticity of the arteries (which helps damp out the pulsations from the heartbeat by the time the blood gets to the capillaries), the viscosity of the blood (which increases as temperatures drop, an important consideration for winter sports), the blood volume (increased ty training). Yet we still search for the cause of hypertension.

Response of the respiratory control center is extremely individualistic. With subjects in an experimental chamber the oxygen content can be dropped to the point at which one person may lose consciousness before the rate of breathing is affected at all, and another's ventilatory rate may double under the same conditions. We know that ventilation increases with work load, but we don't know the details and specifics, particularly of what seem "improper" adjustments that the body sometimes makes to those work loads. For instance, working with small muscle groups, such as the arms, causes harder breathing at a lower oxygen uptake than does working with larger muscle groups, such as the legs. Heart attacks associated with shoveling snow are assumed to be related to this phenomenon. Negative work—lowering weights, running downhill—is off-scale in the other direction. There's a condition called *exercise hyperpnea* (abnormally rapid breathing during exercise) that just doesn't compute, as far as oxygen uptake and ventilation are concerned; no explanation has been found. The surprisingly small ventilatory response to the first few moments of extreme effort, such as occurs in the sprints, is similarly "inappropriate."

The scientists tell us that there are stretch receptors in the lungs and muscle spindles in the respiratory muscles which tell us when to stop inhaling and start exhaling. This seems a little more complicated than necessary. You stop inhaling when your lungs are full. Your lungs tell you to exhale; your head, your *need* tells you to inhale. You can feel these impulses immediately and clearly just by holding your breath. It is possible to concern oneself with chemoreceptors in the carotid and aortic bodies, or linked inspiratory and expiratory centers in the medulla oblongata, but you'll get the same amount of data anyway, when you need it, whether you have the Latin for it or not.

Despite the accessibility of these controls to conscious manipulation, it seldom helps much to take the breathing off automatic. If you attempt to step up the rate of exchange by breathing more heavily or more rapidly, you soon find that the oxygen demands of the ventilatory muscles themselves increase enough to wipe out the intended gain. You may not experience it quite that specifically: conscious breathing usually just seems to interfere, however subtly, with the rhythm of the work you're trying to do. You either abandon the attempt to control your breathing, or put up with gross inefficiency in the work you're trying to accomplish. More commonly, you'll work hard for a brief spell, then stop to breathe hard—consciously—to make up the deficit.

One particular folk belief says you should breathe just through the nose during heavy exercise, keeping the mouth shut. For purposes of filtering out particulate matter with the nostril hairs, there may be some small benefit from the practice. But you pay a heavy price: breathing just through the nose can require three times as much energy expenditure as breathing through both nose and mouth. There may also be some slight advantage to nose-breathing to pre-warm cold air, to reduce the shock of frigid air hitting the lungs. But experiments with cross-country ski racers have shown that mouth-breathing alone warms incoming air sufficiently to prevent damage to the lungs at almost any temperature at which exercise is feasible. The idea that cold air may frost-burn lungs is not borne out by cold-weather (and high-altitude) experience. If your system needs more air, you might as well suck it in any way—the easiest way—you can.

There is one situation in which you won't necessarily get the experiential data you need for proper breathing. Swimmers, attempting to stay underwater longer in breath-holding dives, sometimes hyperventilate before submerging. It's a good way to drown. The intent is to saturate the blood with oxygen to increase breath-holding endurance, but that's not what happens. You're really blowing off carbon dioxide, which can also turn off your respiratory centers so that you lose consciousness before your system tells you to come up for air. Losing consciousness underwater is not healthy.

There's a similar but less dangerous phenomenon that can occur at high altitudes, usually experienced by mountain climbers (and cardiac patients). It's called Cheyne-Stokes breathing: the respiratory centers become disoriented by the unusual partial pressures of oxygen and carbon dioxide at altitude, and for brief periods "forget" to make you breathe. You may neglect to breathe for thirty seconds or more, then suddenly find yourself gasping for breath. Skiers, during their first night at the higher altitude of a ski resort, often suffer from mild visitations of Cheyne-Stokes breathing in their sleep. It is one source of the disturbed sleep that is an early symptom of the onset of altitude sickness. (Whether the greater disturbance is to the sleep of the sufferer from Cheyne-Stokes symptoms or to that of a roommate —who must lie there all night listening to the alternating spooky silences and gasping hyperventilation—is moot.) Mountain climbers, bivouacking at higher altitudes in tiny, carbon-dioxide-collecting tents, suffer a more severe version of Cheyne-Stokes.

John Havlicek, the perpetual-motion machine who played basketball for the Boston Celtics for what seemed like generations, is noted for owning a pair of lungs so large that for a proper chest x-ray, two exposures—top and bottom—are necessary. It's a safe bet that his other pump, his heart, is also quite large; no other physiological explanation would serve for his tireless style of play. Many living athletes have heart volumes well beyond the statistical norm, and autopsies of deceased athletes have frequently turned up "enlarged hearts." Although this variation from the norm has pretty well been discounted as a source of concern, one still occasionally hears of the dangers of "athlete's heart" from the uninformed—usually from that peculiarly disgruntled element who are frightened of exercise.

With regular endurance-type training the heart muscle does indeed hypertrophy, just like the biceps. It grows larger, and it grows stronger, able to contract faster and with more force. It has a very high capacity for oxidative metabolism, but almost no anaerobic capacity. In fact anaerobic work for the heart muscle—as when the blood supply is interrupted—is another term for heart attack.

A larger heart has several things going for it, and only a single small disadvantage. When a heart contraction starts with a larger volume, more blood volume can be ejected per stroke with less shortening of the heart muscle fibers. A larger, "dilated" heart loses less energy from internal friction and tension within its own walls than does a smaller heart. A stretched muscle fiber can provide a greater contractile force than an unstretched one. When the contractions are firing off rapidly—as a smaller heart must do to maintain a given cardiac output—there's more energy loss than when the contractions are slower. (A kind of economy of scale applies to the energy losses in heart contractions.) These are all advantages accruing to the larger "athlete's" heart. The sole disadvantage is that to sustain a given intraventricular pressure, the greater the volume of the heart, the more tension is required of the heart muscle fibers. And as it happens, with a large, well-trained heart, the blood flow to working muscles may be slightly lower than with an untrained heart. But the trained working muscle extracts more oxygen from a given volume of blood flow to make up the difference. (And you can't train a heart without training some muscle to go with it.)

*   *   *

I smoked for more than twenty-five years; I just purely loved tobacco, in just about any form anyone wanted to sell it to me. I think I know as well as most how little rationality has to do with the question of smoking or not smoking, and the difficulty of quitting. I try to restrain myself from the tiresome role of nagging reformer. But as I researched this chapter, as I looked into these two interacting pumping systems which so immediately sustain our lives, I found myself descending into growing horror.

You see, when you draw that thick, tasty blue roil of smoke into your mouth, it contains fifteen known carcinogens and a few more cocarcinogens—the latter are substances which don't cause cancer themselves but which assist in the production of other carcinogens. You also get a mouthful of gases: four hundred times the level of carbon monoxide considered safe for industrial purposes, a hundred and sixty times the safe level of hydrogen cyanide. The tars in the smoke begin coating teeth, tongue, gums—enough tar in six years of smoking to make you drink a full pound of the sticky brown stuff. The nicotine begins poisoning the nerve endings responsible for your senses of taste and smell. The irritants in the smoke also stimulate secretion of mucus, which you swallow; that sends a portion of the chemical load and products of combustion into the gullet and stomach. (Some of this poisoned mucus goes into the lungs, too.) The coating in your mouth contributes to periodontal disease—but you can probably postpone the dental surgery for quite a while.

As you inhale the smoke, the resistance to airflow in your bronchi and bronchioles increases, instantly, by two or three times. Particulate matter in the smoke irritates the sensory receptors in the airways, causing the passages to narrow reflexively. The effect of a cigarette lasts from ten to thirty minutes. It is hard to detect subjectively, but it may well be that the reopening of the passages, however subtle, is the signal that reminds the addicted smoker to light up another butt. During heavy exercise the resistance to airflow can rise to four to five times normal, nonsmoking values.

So the "shortness of breath" blamed on smoking is a real phenomenon. What's more, it is measurably fatiguing: smoking wears you out. Even at rest, chronic smokers have to work twice as hard as nonsmokers just to get enough oxygen into the system to work the muscles to keep breathing. Heavy smokers may work four times as hard. That's how much the oxygen cost of breathing itself is raised by smoking. The smoker's working muscles therefore get less oxygen too, no matter what the level of activity, because less is left over from supplying the ventilatory muscles. (Not to mention the supply of oxygen to the racing heart. The nicotine in tobacco smoke alone would raise the heart rate markedly, even if that rate hadn't already been boosted upward to achieve the increase in cardiac output necessary to supply the ventilatory load from restricted airways.)

All this means decreased performance for athletes, of course, but also for anyone else who smokes: seriously decreased all-out performance, a lowered anaerobic threshold, early fatigue at less strenuous levels of activity. Fatigue even at near resting levels, if you smoke enough. Twenty-four hours of abstinence will restore a quarter of this lost ventilatory capacity, incidentally, so it behooves the athlete who smokes to lay off, even if only temporarily, before important competitions. The "spacy," amphetaminelike, hyper feeling that smokers usually experience during the first day or two after they quit is very likely the result of this restored ventilatory capacity, the grossly easier respiratory process and the resulting excess of energy that accrues.

The costs—oxygen and otherwise—don't stop there. That overload of carbon monoxide has a much greater affinity for blood hemoglobin than does oxygen; it binds up the hemoglobin molecules so they can't carry oxygen to the tissues. (That's the way carbon monoxide eventually kills, with sufficient exposure.) The effects of carbon monoxide are cumulative, and take much longer to wash out of the system than they do to get into it in the first place. Smoking alone can cause carbon monoxide to supplant as much as 8 percent of the oxygen that would otherwise be in the bloodstream—which means another 8 percent increase in ventilatory costs, more cardiac output to make up the difference, and all the rest. Carbon monoxide in the system inhibits the dissociation of oxygen into the tissues, also—as it is quicker to bind with the hemoglobin, so is it reluctant to let go. It raises the required pressure gradient between capillary and muscle cells for transmitting oxygen, which can mean that out at the extremities the oxygen supply is seriously diminished. (When I was a smoker, my hands and feet were usually cold, a condition I only really noticed by its sudden absence when I quit.)

All of which is as nothing to what happens to the respiratory cilia. The cilia are the microscopic hairlike growths on the mucous lining of the lungs. Millions upon millions of them. These actually wave, whiplike, lashing fifty thousand times an hour, driving particulate matter and other irritants back up out of the lungs so we can swallow or spit them out. When inhaled cigarette smoke hits the cilia, it paralyzes them. They wilt, stop their protective flagellation, subside into the mucous sea that surrounds them. "Mucus, tar, dirt, and bacteria then collect in the lungs in festering pools," as one writer describes the process, "encouraging tissue degeneration and hindering gas exchange." Or as another puts it, "They [cilia] turn from looking like a healthy little forest to looking, under the microscope, like a deeply napped Oriental rug that's been chewed in patches by a dog. This throws the alveolar interface wide open to invasion." Infections, erosion, edema, emphysema. Lung cancer.

Smoking raises the levels of fatty acids and cholesterol in the blood, and causes the platelets to have a tendency to stick to each other and to vessel walls. It may convert linoleic acid into a toxic lipid oxide. The nicotine in cigarette smoke constricts the blood vessels, raises blood pressure and blood sugar levels, affects such central nervous system activities as the control of secretion of epinephrine (adrenaline). Small amounts of nicotine stimulate the central nervous system, but larger amounts sedate it. Sedate you. Seventy milligrams of nicotine—in one dose, as in an injection—will kill you. There is from 100 to 400 milligrams in a carton of cigarettes.

Smokers have five times as many gastric ulcers, twice as many duodenal ones, as nonsmokers. If you're a smoker you're seventy times more likely to have lung cancer, four times more likely to have cancer of the mouth or pharynx, five times more likely to have cancer of the larynx, twice as likely to have cancer of the stomach, the esophagus, the bladder. Smokers have four times as many accidents as nonsmokers—perhaps just because their reaction times are slowed. Smoking doubles your chances of dying before age 65. It makes you run the same risk of death as if you were ten years older than your chronological (nonsmoking) age.

I repeat: I smoked for twenty-five years. I dearly wish I could claim that it was strength of character that allowed me to quit, that I over-came the demon only after enduring the horrible twitches and fidgets that accompany cold turkey withdrawal. I can't. I simply ran away from smoking. Or, perhaps, smoking quit me; I didn't have to quit it.

The only strength of character involved was that required to get through the first few weeks of regular exercise, during which time I smoked as usual. Once I could run for thirty minutes at a time—"trot" is a better adjective—I became addicted to that, rather than to smoking. Tobacco, as a significant element in my life, began to shrink like the bar of soap in the soap dish. It simply went away.

I'd tried to quit plenty of times before, by conventional methods, and failed—so I know the pain and psychological disruption that ordinarily accompany those efforts. I only include this tale here be-cause it was so shockingly painless a process, and I suspect that phys-iological changes took place during it that reflect, in ways I can't quite track down, the training phenomenon as it applies to lungs and heart. At any rate, I take no credit. The only thing about it that continues to tug at my curiosity—other than it was so easy—is that it took me so long to arrive at the point where it could happen. Beyond that, it was a gift.

CHAPTER 7
Electrics

"When a joint is bent or a muscle is stretched, the intensity of the mechanical event is conveyed in numerical terms. In other words, both action and experience are counted out rather than weighed. Like the instructions which transmit the hereditary details from one generation to the next, the information moving within the nervous system is conveyed in coded bits."—JONATHAN MILLER, *The Body in Question*

An event transpires in the real world: a starter's gun goes off, for instance. The event communicates itself to a brain; the brain in turn communicates an urgent message to a 150-pound package of meat (or of chemicals and electricity, if you prefer). The package—which happens to include the brain and all the necessary receptors and transmitters—communicates itself, physically, over one hundred meters in the next ten seconds. This is communication of the highest order: Mailgrams, Ma Bell, even the technological immensities of NASA can't compete.

The medium of this communication is, always, from start to finish, electricity. Pardon the fanciful metaphors, but they are inescapable. To move the body, the nerves stimulate the muscles, the muscles move the bones, yes. Yet when you penetrate to the core of the matter, to the cells where these messages are finally received and sent, all *is* metaphor, at least for my imperfect understanding of electricity: that magnetic breeze again, the same stuff that makes your pants legs cling to your socks when you stand up. As in the muscle cells, with their swapping of free phosphate radicals to liberate the energy to bind the actin and myosin fibrils to contract the muscle tissue. By contrast with the events of neural stimulation, the mechanisms of muscular contraction seem about as complicated as a cold chisel.

Strangely, I still catch myself assuming that there are athletic tasks that require only brute force—that muscle mass alone will do the job, that for these tasks there is no learning, no signaling, almost no neural component at all. That's much too easy. As antidote to that kind of oversimplification, it is helpful to hear from David L. Costill, director of one of our most respected human performance labs, at Ball State University. Costill runs marathons himself, at age 44, partly as a kind of hobby, partly to experience in his own body the physiological changes that his research turns up. I had asked him about "The Wall"—another metaphor, this for the last five or six miles of the marathon, when the body has run out of normally available supplies of energy.

"It isn't that you hit the wall suddenly," Costill says. "It's slower than that. What happens is that you have selectively depleted [of energy] a lot of muscle fibers, the ones you've been calling on to do most of the work. As you deplete your glycogen supply, you have fewer and fewer fibers available to develop tension. You have to call on nearly everything you have left. When you start doing that, you're hitting the wall. You have to concentrate harder, because by the process of concentration you are literally trying to get more muscle fibers to fire up.

"In the early stages of a marathon you run with ease. The actual motion of running doesn't take much willed effort from the cortex except to tell the system to continue, to go on as before. But later the drive for recruiting these fibers is considerably more complex. How do you turn these on? When you need these less frequently used fibers, you have to have a high cortical input. The motor centers of the brain have to generate a greater number of impulses to turn on the fibers that you don't ordinarily use.

"It's the same way you have to concentrate harder to lift a heavier weight. That's why a weight lifter concentrates so hard when he approaches a heavy bar. To him at that moment, nothing in the world exists but that bar. He's focusing all of his cortical output to every muscle he's going to fire. A lot of weight training is aimed at learning to do just that. One of the early phases of weight training is to train the nervous system, rather than the muscles. Because to lift heavy weights, you have to learn to recruit a lot of muscle fibers that you don't ordinarily use.

"In running marathon distances you learn that as you lose certain capabilities of the muscle, the only fibers that have any fuel left are fibers that require a stimulus of higher frequency—a stronger input —to fire. They have a higher threshold of recruitment. It's only when the other fibers leave you that the load is heavy enough to force the unused fibers to come into play. You concentrate to do that. The ideal way to run a marathon is just to dissociate for the first eighteen miles or so, enjoying the run. If you find you're having to concentrate hard at twelve miles, you're in trouble."

* * *

To move the body, the nerves stimulate the muscles, the muscles move the bones. At every juncture, at every step on that progression —external stimulus, sensory receptor, spinal cord, cortex, spinal cord, motor neuron, end plate, muscle fiber, movement—there is room for improvement. Theoretically. It may someday be possible to improve speed, accuracy, frequency, stamina, strength of response. Any point on the loop, from initiation (the starter's gun) to recovery (the cool-off lap, the next night's sleep) could be a point of entry for uncovering whole new worlds of human performance. In one sense we already know a great deal about what happens, electrochemically, in each of those steps, and each can seem finite, immutable. Yet every step is also clouded in mystery. Debate still rages about how we crook the little finger as we balance our cup of tea.

* * *

The *motor neuron*—the nerve cell that controls the contraction of the muscle fiber—is the essential communications unit of the nervous system. It has a cell body (with nucleus), *dendrites* on one end (shrublike branches of nerve endings which receive impulses and carry them into the cell body), and one or more *axons* on the other end—usually only one. The axon can be several threadlike feet long, and carries nerve impulses from the cell body to the muscle fiber. At the muscle end the axon branches, and each branch terminates in an *end plate* on a muscle fiber. One motor neuron may signal to several muscle fibers; one muscle fiber may have end plates from more than one motor neuron, although it is more common for a muscle fiber to receive signals only from a single nerve cell. One motor neuron and the muscle fibers it signals make up a *motor unit*.

The end plate is the motor neuron version of the synaptic cleft—the physical gap between nerve cells through which nerve impulses must be transmitted. There are semipermeable membranes on either side of the end-plate cleft. Within the nerve cells there is an electrochemical solution that is high in potassium but is electrically negative; outside the cells—within the cleft itself—the solution is high in sodium and chloride, and electrically positive. Ordinarily there should be diffusion of these chemicals across the gap to reduce the electrochemical gradient. But at rest, the polarity of the semipermeable membranes does not permit this diffusion. A strong electrical potential is maintained.

When a nerve impulse arrives at the end of the axon, a chemical agent, *acetylcholine*, is released from tiny vesicles on the axon side, into the end-plate gap. The acetylcholine binds to receptor sites on the muscle-cell side of the gap, depolarizing the cell and allowing sodium ions to flood into it. This causes a voltage spike within the cell which initiates the contractile mechanisms. Zap: the little finger crooks, the weight is lifted, the marathoner strides on.

There is a delay of perhaps one millisecond between the arrival of the nerve impulse at the end of the axon, "uphill" of the end plate, and the arrival of the impulse in the muscle fiber. This synaptic delay represents the time necessary for the acetylcholine to be released and make its way to the postsynaptic binding sites. The nerve impulse travels through the length of the axon at speeds of up to 100 meters per second. (Large, thick nerve fibers transmit impulses faster than thin ones.) The acetylcholine is broken down by another enzyme to interrupt the transmission of the impulse, and ion pumps located in and between the cells restore the resting potential of the cell membrane—repolarizing it, in effect—within one to ten milliseconds.

The "spike" of the nerve impulse—which, incidentally, can be read directly on a cathode-ray oscilloscope—is interesting. Like the muscle cell, the nerve cell operates on an all-or-none basis: if there is sufficient stimulus to breach the threshold, the nerve cell responds completely. That is, the height of the spike or the strength of the impulse is completely independent of the strength of the stimulus that kicks it off. Within a given bundle of nerve fibers, however, some fibers may fire and some may not. A weak stimulus may not fire all the nerve fibers or axons within the bundle—some may be out of physical range of the stimulus, some may have too high a threshold of excitation. If a strong stimulus causes a more powerful reaction, it is by recruiting more neurons and thus reaching more muscle fibers, rather than by generating a stronger reaction in a given fiber.

For about one millisecond after the impulse passes through, the nerve fiber is impervious to further stimuli. It can't transmit impulses at all. For another one-half to two milliseconds the nerve fiber can respond only to stimuli much stronger than usual. There follows a period when the nerve is hypersensitive and can respond to weaker than normal stimuli, and then there is a brief return to a partial refractory state. All of these variations in the threshold of excitability cease within eighty milliseconds. No fiber can transmit more than two thousand impulses per second; most fibers, under normal body conditions, can handle no more than about five hundred impulses per second.

"Quick reflexes," "good reaction times," are presumed to be among the standard equipment of any good athlete. Yet reaction time—the time between the initiation of the stimulus and the muscular response—depends on several kinds of irreducible physiology. The stimulus comes into the system through receptors which have their own latency periods. It must travel through incoming, *afferent*, nerves to the central nervous system, through an association neuron within the spinal cord which takes it to the outgoing or *efferent* nerves. There are synaptic junctions, with attendant delaying periods, at every step of that journey. The length of the neural pathways affects reaction time, as does any latency of reaction in the affected muscle fibers at the end. An individual whose nervous system is rested, perfectly tuned, undistracted by confusing and half-read signals or neurological "noise," may have a marginally better reaction time than someone less sharply tuned to the requirements of the athletic task. But a good portion of the time lag is simply built into the system. The superior athlete's advantage comes not from reduction of this physiological time, but from reacting more decisively to the incoming information in the first place, and from reacting more judiciously—with more effort, speed, accuracy, with more attention to the possibility of sweet spots.

*   *   *

The interior of the cell is negatively charged—heavy with potassium—and the surrounding matter is positive, loaded with sodium. This is true for the entire cell: there's a constant "resting potential" of about seventy millivolts across the semipermeable membranes of the cell, at the cell body and all along the length of the axon as well as at the motor end plate.

At a stimulus the membrane depolarizes *locally*, and there is a rapid exchange of positive and negative ions across the cell wall. This changes the resting potential from an electrical difference between the inside and outside of the nerve cell into a difference between one region of the cell and the next, and ions begin to flow from one to another internal part of the cell.

Down the length of the axon, the electric potential difference across one point of the membrane excites the next, which amplifies the signal and sends it on. Each point along the axon receives the signal from the point before, boosts the signal, and sends it on to the next. At the point of impulse, as it moves along the axon, the interior of the nerve fiber has become momentarily positive, the outside of the membrane negative. At the leading edge of the impulse the negative ions, now on the exterior, are attracted to the as-yet unstimulated positive exterior ions that await—a minielectromagnet on the outside of the cell wall, yanking the impulse forward. The same thing is happening inside the cell, in reverse—positive attracted to negative. "The nerve fiber is, in effect, a chain of relay stations," according to Sigmund Grollman, from whose *The Human Body* (Macmillan, New York, 1978) this description is adapted.

Yet Grollman also says, "The nerve impulse is not an electric current, it is a wave of physiochemical activity in the nerve which moves rapidly along the fiber . . . and is accompanied by a potential charge." So the stuff that goes zipping along the axon, telling the fingers to crook and legs to run, is not electricity, exactly, but something else. An "impulse," says the physiologist, raising images of whimsy in my head. The signal goes rippling down the length of the fiber, pulled along by dancing ions like one of those 400-mph electromagnetic passenger trains of the future that the Sunday supplements are always teasing us with. What is it, this signal? An *idea?* (Of movement, reaction, response.) Intent, perhaps? Or, simply, change?

* * *

Nerve cells consume oxygen and give off carbon dioxide just as other living tissue does, and during periods of neural activity, oxygen uptake and carbon dioxide liberation are increased about one-third over resting levels. Similarly, the firing of nerves produces heat, just as does the working of muscle. These increases take place during the restoration phase, after the spike of impulse has passed, rather than during the actual period of activation. At five hundred or a thousand impulses per second, however, whether the increase in metabolic activity occurs at or just after an impulse seems beside the point. Energy nevertheless is required. (So thinking *can* raise a sweat. I've always had trouble accepting the notion that mental effort could make you tired. Protestant ethic, I suppose—if the muscles don't ache afterward, it wasn't work.)

Yet nerve cells themselves don't get fatigued. So long as circulation to the nerve tissue is sufficient, a nerve cell can't really be fatigued to the point of failure. If you keep sticking someone's foot with a pin, the reflex will eventually fail and your victim will stop yanking the foot away. But the failure, the fatigue, is in the central nervous system, not in the nerve cells that go to the foot. After the reflex response has stopped working completely, you can still apply a stimulus directly to the nerves to the muscles that yank the foot away, and the response will work as swiftly and directly as before.

If the structural unit of the nervous system is the nerve cell, the functional unit is the reflex. The classic reflex is the familiar *knee jerk*, so much a part of the language that it has come to stand for any kind of unthinking response. A tap to the patellar tendon activates the exquisitely useful proprioceptive organ in the quadriceps tendon, making the leg hop, extending. But reflexes come in droves—reflexes that control blood pressure, respiration and heart rates, the secretions of the glands, the diameter of the pupil of the eye. Seldom is any reflex as simple as it might seem. The knee jerk seems to be merely an extension brought about by contraction of the quadriceps muscle. But for the quadriceps to be able to extend the lower leg, the flexor muscles at the back of the leg must relax—and that, too, requires a signal from the nervous system. (The same is true for any other extensor/reflexor reaction.) There are, in fact, inhibitory responses that take place in the neural junctions, too, just as there are excitatory ones. One theory has it that rather than depolarizing the cell membranes at the synaptic cleft, the inhibitory reactions cause an *increase* in the polarization of the cell walls, shutting off even the merest trickle of ions that might otherwise be maintaining a certain degree of tone in the muscle. Another theory says that inhibition may be achieved when impulses fire so rapidly that they keep the cell body in a prolonged refractory state. There is still considerable disagreement about just how inhibition takes place, neurologically.

If you clench your fist while someone taps your kneecap, your knee-jerk reflex will be considerably stronger than if you are entirely relaxed. The more activity that is going on in the nervous system, the more pronounced the reflex reactions will be: increased activity reduces resistance to the passage of signals in all the synapses. If you step on a tack, you will reflexively flex the leg of the offended foot, trying to withdraw from the pain. To do so you must shift your weight to the other leg, which means that you'll have to fire the extensor muscles on that side of the body to hold the weight. This kind of linked reflex reaction is built-in. A strong stimulus to one side of the body ordinarily causes a flexor response (the withdrawal from the tack) on that side, and an automatic, linked, extensor response simultaneously on the other side.

There's food for thought for the athlete in all of these linked, crossed, boosted reflexes. The more active the body is, the quicker, stronger, more effective its reflexes are. There is a snowballing effect in physical capability that accrues with activity, with the revving-up of the system, that goes beyond the accepted training effect on the muscular and cardiovascular systems. We probably can't specifically rely on such things as these crossed reflexes to accomplish athletic tasks, at least not in the sense of planning them out ahead of time. Rather, we learn to live with them unconsciously, making them a natural, unthinking part of our athletic armamentarium—as natural as our ability to avoid falling down when we step on a sharp object. But in the biomechanical analysis of athletic motions to come, it is certain that new ways of performing those tasks—ways that draw upon deep-seated, brainstem-generated responses—can be found.

Athletic performances are already beginning to reflect just that kind of research.

*   *   *

A few years ago I had a spinal anesthetic for some minor surgery. I woke before the spinal had completely worn off, and discovered that while I was getting some feeling back in my legs, I couldn't yet move them. I determined to do so.

The job was to force neural signals through several gauzy layers of unfeeling, to get the muscles to work. I began concentrating. At first I was afraid to try very hard, because I assumed that if I did move my legs, they might hurt—a mistaken assumption based on the really strange information I was getting from down there. Eventually I convinced myself—intellectually, anyway—that movement was safe, but that didn't enable me to move my legs.

The job of concentrating was so difficult that I can't describe it: it took an effort, pure and simple, that brought beads of sweat to my forehead. But it wasn't muscular effort, not at all, only an effort that started at the mind—whatever that is—and went, via some round-about route that I couldn't imagine, toward the feet. I assume that a great portion of that route was through the spinal cord, but I certainly wasn't capable of consciously directing any neurological traffic in that direction.

Finally I did move my legs—the dissolution of the effects of the anesthetic was racing to meet my fumbling powers of concentration. I would flop my legs an inch or two at a time, rotate my feet from pigeon-toed to slue-footed positions beneath the sheets. The effort was simply exhausting. It wasn't muscles that were being exhausted, there didn't seem to be any great consumption of muscle glycogen or ATP or any of that physiological stuff. I didn't get out of breath. What was tired was my head, my consciousness. Later, I heard that paralysis victims are told the mental effort required to reestablish disturbed linkages with their limbs is very similar to the mental effort one goes through when trying to recall a name, one that's right there on the tip of the tongue. That's another metaphor, of course, but it seems close to what I experienced.

I presume that this exercise of will—pushing neurological messages through partially downed physiological wires—is what is required of athletes in the last stages of maximum effort. It is the concentration that Dr. Costill speaks of near the end of marathons and in the preparations that weight lifters go through. Costill told me that in the five or six post-wall miles that wrap up a marathon he discovered that he had to decide how to run, and then instruct his muscles how to do it, virtually for every step.

(Is there a training method here? Could an athlete improve his neurological hookups by straining against a pharmaceutical interruption of his circuitry? This is the kind of suggestion that drives the purists wild—with good reason, now that I think of it. The very idea gives me the creeps.)

"It is a happy coincidence," say physiologists Per-Olof Åstrand and Kaare Rodahl in their *Textbook of Work Physiology* (McGraw-Hill, New York, 1970), "that the nerve cells which finally control the skeletal muscles (the motoneurons) are the most studied nerve cells in the animal. Consequently, these events are fairly well understood. (The physiology behind the capacity of the nerve cells to store information for future use is, on the other hand, a well-kept secret.)"

And memory—how about *that* for a mystery. Does memory require measurable physiological energy? Does it use up oxygen and liberate carbon dioxide to remember something? Can you remember more if your circulation improves? I find myself momentarily excited with what seems a startling series of questions. Then *I* remember: an elderly aunt, whose last years were fogged over with senile dementia, blamed on hardening of the arteries that supply the brain. Of course. To be so startled by the notion that a phenomenon as nebulous as memory might require nutrients and generate wastes merely demonstrates what a pernicious habit of thought the mind-body dualism is. I keep forgetting (maybe the circulation is impaired) that the brain is a physical system too.

*   *   *

It is tempting to say that for athletic purposes, no sensory receptors are more important than the proprioceptive organs, giving as they do such wonderful information about body and limb position, muscle state, acceleration and deceleration. Then I recall an acquaintance who was very close to being legally blind, who could still beat me at table tennis playing almost entirely by sound. Clearly, the requirements of sports are so broad that the more and better sensory information you can get, of any kind, the better you can perform; it is beside the point to attempt to single out one attribute or capacity that overshadows all the rest. The sensory receptors gather information, the sensory cortex processes the information, the effectors act on the information. The athlete needs all three parts of that procedure as sharply tuned as possible. The athlete simply needs *more*—of everything. Put more in, get more out. The difference is in rate: the athlete requires a different pace.

That overstates the case. Within the neurological richness that serves the normal senses, the problem is not to get more information, but to get more accurate information, successfully selected out of the swarm of sensation bombarding the organism. Sensorily speaking, discrimination is all. It is also apparent from that richness that restricting the human senses to the traditional number of five is gross oversimplification. There are, for example, five different kinds of sensory information coming from the skin surface alone, each with its own distinctive form of receptor, all lumped under the catchall category of "touch." Our skin is perfectly well equipped to distinguish easily among heat, cold, pressure, pain, *and* touch (as in contact), even if our language doesn't give it credit for it. I don't think this is semantic quibbling: refining the definitions helps refine the discrimination with which we interpret our sensory information.

For the most part the physiological understanding of the senses is full of fine detail and delightful trivia. The sensory organ in the skin that recognizes cold is known as the *end bulb of Krause*; the one that picks up warmth is the *corpuscle of Ruffini*. The receptors for touch generally take the form of disks, corpuscles, or bulbs—nerve endings that are encapsulated, one way or another, in connective tissue. One exception is the free nerve ending wrapped about the base of each hair follicle (making us sensitive to many touches that never even reach the skin).* Another exception is the pain receptor. It is a bare nerve ending, a metaphorical live wire buried in the skin and mucous membranes, which has the distinctive and often distressing capability

---

* Each follicle also has its own tiny muscle, the *arrector pili*, which can cause the hair to stand on end. The same muscle pulls the surrounding skin into "goosebumps," of course. And it is supplied with effector nerve, neuroeffector junction, actin and myosin fibrils, the whole nine yards.

of refusing to adapt: once stimulated, it keeps firing, refusing to grow accustomed to the stimuli that set it off. It can continue doing so even from a single initial stimulus. Gives me a toothache just to think about it.

We can taste things because we have a type of sensory ending that responds only to chemicals in solution; the information we receive therefrom is often modified, even overwhelmed, by information from another type of sensory ending that responds only to chemicals in their gaseous state. We can distinguish only four tastes (salty, sour, sweet, bitter)—or is it six (alkaline, metallic)? The rest of the flavors —apricot nectar, eggs Benedict, Big Macs—come from olfactory overtones, of which there are so many that any attempt to classify them has always created more confusion than it has cleared up: one man's Dom Perignon being another's Diet Pepsi. Tastes are categorizable because scientists have been able to identify four different areas of the tongue, each with a special capacity to taste one of the four basic flavors, and to tie chemical similarities within each of the four basic flavors to those areas.

No such clear distinctions have been found with regard to odors and the sense of smell. Although almost any smell can now be reproduced artificially by duplicating its chemical structure, the chemistry is too complex to allow the same kind of classification that is possible with tastes.

Hearing is also bafflingly complex. An elaborate set of physical linkages takes the variations in air pressure which constitute sound waves, and converts them into mechanical motions (in the lever actions of the small bones of the middle ear), then into wave motions in the fluid of the inner ear, then into vibrations of the fibers of the basilar membranes, finally into movement of the hair cells in the organ of Corti, where the physical motion is converted into electrical potentials which can be interpreted by the brain as sound. Exactly how all this takes place has not yet been positively settled, although theories abound, of course. That the sense of hearing can make fine distinctions in pitch (the speed of the sound waves), amplitude (the depth of the waves), and timbre as well (the complexity of overtones within a given pitch and amplitude) may help explain why a single comprehensive theory is hard to come by.

Hearing can provide another kind of fine distinction, one that probably helps the athlete more than all the others. See my table-tennis-playing friend, who does so well because he can hear *where* the ball leaves the opponent's paddle and *where* it hits the table. Our hearing is stereophonic; the space between the ears gives a sizable advantage in interpreting, by triangulation, the direction and distance from which sounds are coming. When the source of a sound behind our head is moving, for example, we are able to tell the moment when it clears the angle that allows sound waves to enter the ear directly, rather than bouncing off other structures. (Most animals are better at this than we are. The ordinary house cat has articulated ears, each of which can be pointed like a radar antenna at a source of sound. That's what enables the cat to spring toward a sound that is out of sight and still score a direct hit.)

The athlete relies heavily on this capacity. In football, when a wide receiver "hears footsteps" (from approaching defenders), he has perhaps developed the faculty too finely—and starts dropping passes. The basketball player who seems to have eyes in the back of his or her head is relying on every possible sensory input to keep track of the other nine players on the floor; the aural faculty is probably more important to that skill than the player realizes. Athletes even get subtle aural signals—echoing rebounds—to warn them away from running into walls and other obstacles. Enthusiastic crowds can leave an athlete feeling wrapped in cotton batting, engulfed in crowd noise, deprived of the quieter information needed to play the game. It is particularly hard on visiting teams, who get no compensatory psychological lift from all that cheering. And it is not to be taken lightly: the noise can literally be staggering. It can keep the inner ear so busy, so overwhelmed with neurological stimulation, that the other half of its job—preserving equilibrium—is swamped.

Also in the inner ear, behind the mechanism that processes sound into nerve impulses, is the complex network of canals and chambers that processes information about static position with relation to gravity, as well as such changes as rotation (around any of three axes), acceleration, inertia. Some of these chambers are filled with fluid; when the fluid is caused to move, it displaces flexible sensory organs that jut into the chambers—like rowboats tied to the bank of a tidal inlet, which swing back and forth to indicate the direction of the tide. The movement fires afferent nerves, notifying the brain. Another set of nerve endings terminates with hairlike tufts in the *macula*, a sensory area on the wall of the chambers. The macula is coated with a jellylike substance which contains small, relatively heavy particles called *otoliths* ("ear stones"). When the athlete's head changes position, the otoliths respond to gravity and pull the gelatinous covering with them; this in turn moves the hairlike nerve endings that extend into the macula, firing nerve impulses which tell the brain of the changes in position.

Most sports are played on foot; those that aren't usually insert some equipment, vehicle, or animal between athlete and playing surface. It's difficult to say which circumstance requires more balance. (In many sports that aren't played on foot, merely keeping one's balance —as in cycling, kayaking, hang-gliding—is a large part of the challenge.) A considerable amount of other information comes in from the rest of the organism—proprioceptors in the ankles and legs, pressure receptors in the feet, visual references—to assist in maintaining equilibrium. But in the end it is in the inner ear where all that information comes together, where the automatic processes make the split-second decisions that keep us from falling down. Remember Nadia Comaneci on the balance beam at Montreal; imagine the neurological fireworks going on in *those* inner ears.

*　　*　　*

Vision is, inarguably, our overwhelmingly dominant sense, the "king of the senses" (never mind my aurally talented table-tennis player). Eyesight is so intimately involved in almost every athletic task that superstars are often credited with what amounts to an unfair visual advantage: Ted Williams' vaunted hyperacuity of eyesight, Bob Cousy's off-scale peripheral vision, are the stuff of sports legends.* Yet what the eyes of us nonlegendary mortals can accomplish—in the day-to-day business of living and seeing—is in itself almost unbelievable. Grollman summarizes it succinctly: "The eye is a device by which the energy of a light pattern is converted into the energy of a nerve impulse that is conducted by the optic nerve to the visual cortex of the brain for interpretation as a visual image. The eye acts as a transducer for the specific purpose of converting light energies to the electrical energies associated with the nerve impulse." That it does all this with the speed and accuracy necessary, for instance, to

---

* Visual perfection is not required for superstardom. More and more modern athletes discover visual problems in the course of their careers, seek help, and markedly improve subsequent performance. See Bob Griese, the bespectacled quarterback of the Miami Dolphins.

guide the coordination of all the gross skeletal movements required to swing a baseball bat to meet a ball traveling at near 100 miles per hour, that's when credulity gets strained.

The mechanics are fairly familiar. The cornea admits light to the eyeball; the iris controls the size of the pupil (the aperture through which the light passes). The lens, behind the iris, focuses entering light on the retina, a displaced piece of brain tissue packed with over a hundred million sensory receptors per eye, which forms the back of the eyeball. The lens is controlled by muscles which change its shape to change the focal length within the eyeball, permitting close-up and long-distance vision. Internal fluids under slight pressure—aqueous and vitreous humor—maintain the shape of the eyeball.

The receptors are of two types, cones and rods. Cones, which make up only about 5 percent of the total, are responsible for *photopic* vision: image detail and color discrimination. Rods are responsible for *scotopic* vision: differentiation between dark and light. Sparing as the cones are in number, they are densely packed in the *fovea*, a spot at the back of the retina where images have the highest attention value. It is where we focus images for close inspection, where we have the greatest visual resolution. Rods have much less resolving power for detail but are much more light sensitive; they help us see in limited light. They are color blind, and therefore at night and in dim light, so are we. For color vision we need enough light to fire the cones.

The eyes move constantly, making momentary fixations, then moving on. It is assumed that the brain interprets visual images in similar "time frames" of about 100 milliseconds. By various scientific techniques, experimenters have succeeded in holding the eye perfectly still, damping out all movement. When this is done the subject temporarily loses *all* vision, demonstrating that what the eye actually responds to is not the steady image but changes in the patterns of light.

Each rod and cone is one end of a nerve cell, the other end of which synapses with a layer of nerve cells in the retina, which cells synapse with yet another layer of cells in turn. The last layer is made up of ganglion cells, the axons of which form the optic nerve, connecting directly to the visual cortex. Nerve cells from the left eye lead to both left and right hemispheres of the brain, just as do the axons from the right eye. The field of vision of the respective eyes overlaps by quite a bit, blending the images of our binocular vision, giving most of us superbly sharp depth perception.

In the rod cells there is a dark purple molecule, *rhodopsin*, which breaks down when struck by light. When this reaction takes place— the result of light bleaching the purple rhodopsin to yellow—electrochemical energy is released, sending a signal to the visual cortex. The brain is able to interpret the signal as light or dark and use it to create a visual image, by means we don't yet fully understand.

(I've always been dissatisfied with the quality of newspaper photos and television images, made up as they are of mere dots of light and dark. I want my visual images whole and continuous, "the way the eye sees." It is disconcerting, therefore, now to discover that the eyes —and the brain—get their images in dots too, one dot per rod, one per cone. Worse yet, we also get those images discontinuously in time, in flickering images not all that much more sophisticated than the frame-by-frame presentation of movie film.)

After rhodopsin is broken down, an enzyme works on the by-products, reducing one of them to vitamin A, which is stored in the liver. The next time the eye is in darkness, the retina resynthesizes rhodopsin from the vitamin A. Vitamin A deficiency causes night blindness: the eye can't resynthesize enough rhodopsin to recharge the bleached-out rod cells. When you enter a darkened theater in the afternoon, you are blinded because all of the rhodopsin has been bleached out of your rod cells, not because your iris is slow to let in more light. You must wait until the darkness lets you resynthesize enough rhodopsin to allow dim-light vision before you find your seat. When you come out of the theater, you are loaded up with rhodopsin from your time in the dark, and the bright light fires too many signals to the brain, making you painfully sensitive to light for a few minutes. It's not because your pupils are dilated from the darkness, although that is also the case.

There are several theories about cone vision, none of them totally satisfactory. Most posit that each cone has one of three substances in it. One of these substances makes the cone react to the long waves of red light, the second causes it to respond to the medium-length waves of green light, the third sensitizes the cone to the short waves of violet light. We see yellow when the red- and green-sensitive cones fire, blue when green and violet combine. When all three types fire simultaneously we see pure white. It is to be assumed that the firing of these cones takes place as a result of a photochemical reaction similar to that of the rods. Color vision is sharpest near the fovea, where cones predominate, and gets markedly less accurate on the periphery of vision. So, of course, does visual sharpness, fine focus, perception of detail. At the edge of vision, about all we can pick up is movement—but that's enough to alert us, to make us swing toward the movement and bring it to our center of attention.

The adaptability of our visual sense is immense. In one famous experiment subjects wore prisms that inverted everything they saw. (Reinverted them, rather, since the images on the normal retina are already upside down.) After a relatively brief period of accommodation, the subjects began seeing things right side up again, re-reinverting the images in the brain, and could function as before. When the prisms were removed the subjects again perceived everything as upside down for a while, until de-adaptation took place. In the same way we color the black-and-white images we get from the periphery of our vision, fall for optical illusions every day, adapt so quickly to failing eyesight that we don't notice what we are beginning to miss.

My first ride in a long-bodied Boeing 707 took place at night in rough weather. I sat at the rear of the plane, on the aisle, and grew transfixed by the pitching and yawing of the plane, as I kept watch up that amazingly long aisle toward the nose. Finally I realized I was getting absolutely zero information through my eyes about any motion of the airplane. It was dark outside, I was in a fixed position inside, nothing could possibly indicate—visually—that the plane's attitude was changing. Every reading I was getting about attitude change was arriving, sensorily, from my rear end—that is, from pressure receptors in buttocks and back—and from my inner ear. (Flying, literally, by the seat of my pants.) Yet no matter how carefully I kept telling myself that, my brain insisted I could "see" the change of attitude. Nerve impulses from back and butt were being interpreted by the brain as nerve impulses from eyes. It still happens, no matter how plainly I "know" better. I "see" the nose of the plane pitch and yaw.

* * *

Coded bits, says Jonathan Miller: "the information moving within the nervous system is conveyed in coded bits." Arriving—here's the part that's difficult to swallow—in discontinuous bits of time. According to the theories of vision, we see, and in some senses we therefore experience, in hundred-millisecond bits. Separated by . . . non-experience? It is only a step from this to the even more bothersome assumption that consciousness itself might be similarly discontinuous. Bite-sized.

Physicists (and mystics, fascinated by the small-particle revelations of the physicists) have always enjoyed teasing us with the discontinuous nature of what we regard as solid matter. If the space between the bits were properly conceived and understood, we'd tremble as we stood on solid granite, afraid of falling through. In the atoms that make the molecules of granite, electrons are as far from nuclei, in scale, as earth from sun, and so on. Quantum theory says that energy, also, comes in bits, just as matter does.

I can handle discontinuous matter only marginally better than I can handle discontinuous time, discontinuous experience—but then I've had more time to get used to the idea of a material world made up of nothing but jittery bits of whizzing electricity. Now the introduction of the idea of gaps in conscious experience leaves me floundering in my imagination, trying to conceive not of the gaps but of the bits themselves. Little pieces of time? I immediately get the image of interrupted slo-mo replays, as when there is trouble with the TV picture. That's only my own video brain damage at work. But do we really move in freeze-frame discontinuities even when, for instance, we glide smoothly across the ice on skates? Feels smooth to *me*.

My friend Billy Salter points out that it all depends on how fine the grain is. Anything finer-grained than you are, you will perceive of as continuous, and vice versa. I never thought I'd congratulate myself on my own coarseness, but it's too late for me now to start getting comfortable with jerking discontinuities in the smoothly beautiful motions that have given me so much pleasure, all my life, from sports and from a lot of other kinds of experience as well.

There's a clue here to how the physics of the Sweet Spot Theory might actually work. If 100 milliseconds is the minimum (human) time frame for sensory reception, then to hit the sweet spot in time is to put an action—the point of the action, the instant of percussion, for example—within that 100-millisecond segment. Or perhaps the superior athlete is one whose discriminations are based on that minimum time frame, while yours and mine slough over, hundreds of milliseconds off in one direction or another. As a matter of fact, I'm sure that the Sweet Spot Theory slips right into this notion without a tremor, but I'm not able to think about that just yet. I'm too busy hanging on—somewhat desperately—to the continuity of my own experience.

CHAPTER 8
Grooves

I close my eyes and in my imagination run an old newsreel of Babe Ruth at bat. From the first inch of windup in the bat's motion, the utter smoothness, the singularity of the plane of action, the perfect fluidity is shockingly clear. The motion is, as the athletes say, "grooved." It is as recognizable a movement as any in the history of sports; the groove is so glaring. Why? What *is* that groove?

Early morning: I roll paper into the machine and begin to type. My hands don't follow the orders from my fuzzy head. I make more errors than usual at first. Then, a few lines into the task, as I concentrate harder on what I am trying to get said rather than on the typing of it, the skills unaccountably improve; I pick up speed. Lewis Thomas speaks of the process:

"Working a typewriter by touch, like riding a bicycle or strolling on a path, is best done by not giving it a glancing thought. Once you do, your fingers fumble and hit the wrong keys. To do things involving practiced skills, you need to turn loose the systems of muscles and nerves responsible for each maneuver, place them on their own, and stay out of it. There is no real loss of authority in this, since you get to decide whether to do the thing or not, and you can intervene and embellish the technique any time you like; if you want to ride a bicycle backward, or walk with an eccentric loping gait giving a little skip every fourth step, you can do that. But if you concentrate your attention on the details, keeping in touch with each muscle, thrusting yourself into a free fall with each step and catching yourself at the last moment by sticking out the other foot in time to break the fall, you will end up immobilized, vibrating with fatigue."*

In other words, typing—the skill—is *there*, somewhere within the organism. It needs only to be summoned up and turned loose, set to work. Here, one part of my brain would seem to be saying to another, Why don't we let typing do this? Take this thought over and run it through typing, will you?

We know perfectly well that we can learn new movements, new skills (although we often resist doing so). We can pick up a dance step, a ski technique, a tennis serve. We absorb "it"—this movement, this idea, this notion of a motion—into our mental-physical makeup. We put "it" somewhere; we can bring it back into play later. There are difficulties; we acquire the new skill incompletely at first, inaccurately. But we know we can do it. What it is, how we acquire it in the first place, where we put it, how we bring it back, are questions that speak to the profoundest mysteries in human understanding: memory and learning theory.

One article of faith in our understanding of sports is that the athlete picks up a new skill more quickly and more accurately than the nonathlete, that he or she somehow absorbs the physical requirements of the motor task more easily. Occasionally we see an athlete exceed our expectations, usually by some marvelous demonstration of "ability" (first in a series of extremely vague attributes to come) that falls outside his or her narrow area of athletic specialization. When we do, we speak of such things as "body control" or "coordination." We can only project that for the athlete the whole process of learning a new motion must be easier than it is for us. Just look: watch Lynn Swann do that unfamiliar thing, so smoothly, so easily,

---

* *Lives of a Cell*, Viking, New York, 1974. Incidentally, we "vibrate" with fatigue because the motor nerves stop firing in steady, machine-gunlike fashion and start firing in waves. These nerve impulses, arriving in salvos, set up waves of contraction which give the muscle its tremor. The rock climber, pinned for hours to the rock face, surveying the next exhausting muscular commitment necessary to continue upward, is sometimes stricken with muscular tremors so severe they threaten to shake him or her off the rock face. Climbers call the phenomenon "sewing-machine knee."

so unconcernedly *well*. It would be maddening if it were not so wonderful to watch.

But bring Lynn Swann to the laboratory in the attempt to analyze that ease of accomplishment, break down into discrete categories those attributes that permit him such quick access to new motor skills, and they disappear on you. Or more to the point, bring in ten athletes of that caliber (if ten such even exist) in search of the single attribute that makes acquisition of motor skills easier, and you'll end up with ten answers—or twenty, or two hundred. About the only identifiable across-the-board advantage that good athletes seem to have over the rest of us is the quality of their attention. They pay attention to the task at hand a little better than you and I do.

(Learning theorists and psychologists explode into disagreement over just what "attention" is. In one sense, the argument can be made that it is sheer motivation: the direct expression *of* motivation. The more highly motivated individuals are the ones who pay closer attention to whatever they are motivated to attempt. Which raises chicken-and-egg questions of the most perplexing sort. A psychologist named Rosenzweig, discovering that the ability to estimate time spent at a task varies with the level of internal tension with which the task is approached, coined the term "need strain" for this psychological force that drives us. The term conjures up for me the image of the gradual filling of an emotional bladder. Don't take the strain off your need or you'll lose the ability to estimate time. Or lose your will to exceed. . . .)

Mysterious or not, there is a neurological argument to be made that acquisition of a motor skill does in fact cause a physical change within the organism, that there does develop some kind of groove— a wiring diagram, a magnetic affinity, a set of internal neurological connections, *something*. Some *thing*. If this is true (and it is generally assumed to be so, never mind the difficulty in locating or measuring or defining it), if an athlete can encode a skill within his or her body, then there must be room to improve the encoding. In the chinks and gaps among the swarm of factors identified as influencing the acquisition of skill there must be points of access. Exploring those points of access will contribute to the performance revolution to come.

*   *   *

Perception is the first requirement for learning to move with skill. And movement, conversely, surprisingly, is necessary for accurate perception. "Movement seems necessary to add substance to reality and to afford an accurate impression of size, shape, and depth," says Bryant J. Cratty, in *Movement Behavior and Motor Learning* (Lea & Febiger, Philadelphia, 1973). In a later version of the famous inverted-vision experiment, two subjects are fitted with prisms that invert the images their eyes receive. One sits in a wheelchair, the other pushes the wheelchair. The one who does the pushing adapts quickly enough to the inverted images; the one who is pushed, who does not use his own motor facilities to explore the inverted world, does not adapt at all. No incoming motor information, no restructuring of perception to reinvert the distorted world.

(This is a recurrent theme in physical education. Speaking of the contribution of the proprioceptors to *stereognosis*—"shape knowledge"—Arthur H. Steinhaus points out that if you've never held a sphere in your hand, you necessarily perceive the moon as only a disc. "It is probably safe to guess," Steinhaus says, "that many unlearned persons who work much with their hands often exhibit a high grade of 'common sense' because their concepts are richly supplied with this 'muscle sense' ingredient. On the other hand the unexpectedly naive judgment often displayed by persons educated too much in the rarefied air of books and abstract ideas may well be due to a shortage of this ingredient in their mental life." * Antiintellectual biases aside, the point is probably verifiable by experimental means.)

Certain measurable capabilities or talents vitally affect perception. Perceptual *selection* is the ability to pick out the significant elements in a given sensory frame. Perceptual *speed*—the ability to make rapid perceptual judgments, very likely a sizable component of reaction time—varies from person to person. Some of us have more perceptual *flexibility* than others—the ability to shift from one perception to another within the same sensory framework, to shake up or recast incoming information for greater understanding. Psychologists test the individual's ability to create whole perceptions out of partial or fragmentary sensory evidence, or perceptual *structuring*.

All of these perceptual components are predictive enough of ability to warrant further investigation, particularly for athletics. One study

* *Toward an Understanding of Health and Physical Education*, Wm. C. Brown, Dubuque, Iowa, 1963.

has shown, for instance, that the ability to pick simple geometric forms out of more complex patterns is a useful predictor of how quickly a tennis player can prepare his or her racket to meet returning shots! A similar test is rumored to be used in Eastern Bloc nations to uncover latent gymnastic talent. In it the subject is given a paper with numbers printed in random order and location all over the page, and is asked to search out and touch the numbers in order, as rapidly as possible. Good performance on this simple pencil-and-paper task is believed to translate into high gymnastic potential (assuming other factors such as size, weight, and strength are also suitable). The possibilities for more sophisticated versions of these tests, eliciting much more specific information about perceptual capabilities for athletic performance, would seem to be immense.

But perception is only the beginning point for performing a motor task, and vision is only one beginning point for perception. In fact sensory information arrives in so many forms, from so many receptors, and the receptors are so closely linked with each other, that the individual is aswim in a sea of information. There are broad-band receptors which respond to the general nature of a stimulus, and narrow-band receptors which pick out specifically applicable stimuli. One receptor can augment or inhibit another; one portion of the brain can damp out or overwhelm the receptivity of another part. Singling out discrete perceptions is valuable for establishing the elements of the mosaic in which the athlete must operate, but those single elements must not be assumed to represent the whole picture. Reality, for the athlete as for anyone else, is a universe of perceptions.

At the same time that judgments are being made about all that external information, the athlete must also be perceiving himself or herself within that universe. Proprioception literally means "self-perception," and the earliest work in motor learning was done to try to discover what, in a motor sense, man could perceive about himself. Working from the simplest of beginnings, early physiologists began to study movement. An early experiment, for example, consisted merely of handing small weights to blindfolded subjects, attempting to determine the smallest weight differential that could consistently be detected by sensory judgment alone. Hundreds of similar experiments were devised. What is the smallest movement that an individual can make? The smallest that one can detect? At what point does motor discrimination begin to occur? What are the finest discriminations that can be made in estimating speed, time, distance?

From these early experiments the fundamental structure of human movement began to be understood. Much of the information gained helped define what the proprioceptors are and what they can do. It was determined, for example, that when someone else moves your limbs, your hip and shoulder joints can pick up this passive displacement more quickly and more sensitively than can the other joints of your body. The joint receptors let you detect passive movement of a limb long before you can determine the direction of movement. Flexion movements (bending the knee) are much more easily detected than extension movements (straightening the knee). If your task requires that you make accurate movements, you'll do a better job if the movement takes place directly in front of you, in the space that is accessible to your vision, whether you use vision in the task or not (probably because we use vision to do most tasks, and therefore get more practice making accurate movements within the field of vision).

Some of these determinations seem self-evident, but many are not. Outward movements are more accurate than inward movements; short movements tend to be overestimated, longer movements underestimated. Judgments about movements made close to the body are more accurate than judgments about movements made farther from the body. In general, errors in the extent of movement are greater than errors in the direction of movement. Most skills that are used in sports involve ballistic motions—those motions discussed in the sweet spot theory, which are launched with an initial force, then use momentum to be carried to completion. Once initiated, such motions tend to be guided rather than powered, and correction while under way is almost impossible.

A lot of sports traditions find their origins in this early research. When the batter swings a weighted bat before going to the batter's box, he's not only cranking up his stretch reflexes and warming up muscles, but also taking advantage of *kinesthetic aftereffect*. You very likely have done the same as a child, as a kind of parlor stunt: you stand in a doorway, press the back of your hands hard against the sides of the frame for a few moments, then step away and feel your arms start to rise, seemingly of their own accord. That too is kinesthetic aftereffect. It doesn't actually improve performance. Your arms don't really rise by themselves, but they seem to want to. After the weighted bat, the regulation bat seems lighter, the batter feels as if he can get it around more quickly. The batter will take any edge he can get, of course, even if it is only a ghostly "feeling."

Visual phenomena produce less predictable results than do the purely kinesthetic studies. Subjects fitted with prism spectacles that make straight edges look curved report that those straight edges also feel curved to the touch. Movement will be spotted more quickly if it occurs near the periphery of your vision than if it is near the center, even though focus is much sharper at the center. An object moving vertically seems to be moving faster than one moving horizontally at the same actual speed. The larger an object is, the slower it will seem to be moving. Some people are velocity-susceptible—the faster an object moves, the more their judgment of its speed will be in error; others are velocity-resistant, their judgment less affected by increasing velocities. Good athletes, needless to say, tend to come from the latter group—especially good hitters.

Ted Williams, who could see at twenty feet what "normal" athletes see at ten, has always claimed that hitting a round baseball with a round bat is the most difficult motor task in sports. Visual tracking is the largest part of that job, and not even Williams in his .400-plus prime could track a fastball closer than about ten feet from the plate.

The mechanics of that skill are fascinating. A 90-mph fastball should reach the plate 0.4 second after the pitcher lets it go. The batter has about 0.1 second to pick up the incoming pitch visually and "recognize" it—discern whether it is a fastball, curve, or slider, and where it is likely to be headed in relation to the strike zone. (During that tenth of a second the pitch travels almost one-third the distance home.) The batter has another 0.15 second in which to decide whether or not to swing (or whether to get out of the way of a wild pitch). He loses sight of the ball thereafter—it is almost two-thirds of the way home—but he has another 0.15 second in which to start his swing and guide it to the spot where he thinks the ball is headed. To hit a fair ball he has to meet the ball within about 15 degrees to either side of a dead right angle to the direction the pitch is traveling, which means within about 24 inches of the bat's total travel. That means he has to have the bat there during the time the ball is passing that 2-foot arc. This passage takes 0.013 second. One study indicates that if the batter does not have the heel of his forward foot raised by the time the ball leaves the pitcher's hand, he's already missed the pitch. Ted Williams may be right.

(Also, for all that elaborate, falling-down, arm-twisting, knock-your-hat-off follow-through of the pitcher, the ball has left his hand before that hand passes the pitcher's ear!)

Visual tracking is more difficult on the horizontal plane than it is on a vertical plane, and requires more illumination. One study has shown a positive relationship between exercise and visual functioning; sedentary subjects who began getting into shape enjoyed an improvement in visual acuity of as much as 45 percent.

Another study found that high-level soccer players tend to have wider-set eyes—more distance between the pupils—than the statistical norm, a bit of self-selection which should mean they have better depth perception. Yet another study showed that motor skill performance is less affected when the central vision area is blotted out than when peripheral vision is restricted; obviously we rely heavily on peripheral vision to move comfortably in the world. (That faculty must contain a considerable athletic advantage. Bill Bradley, a basketball star for Princeton and the New York Knicks, later senator from New Jersey, has 15 degrees more peripheral vision on the horizontal plane and 28 degrees more in the vertical plane than an anatomically "perfect" set of eyes. That may give him no advantage as a senator, but it had to help him on the basketball court. Bob Cousy of the Boston Celtics is reputed to have greater peripheral range than that.) Perhaps the most interesting perceptual finding for athletic purposes was a study done in 1960 which showed that high scores in visual acuity predicted high scores in the faculty of balance—and balance scores gave the best predictive index to ability in sports.

In general, good athletes tend to score better than the norm in depth perception, visual apprehension, peripheral vision, sensitivity to depth cues, visual reaction time, resistance to ocular fatigue, and so on. That is, good athletes have scored well on visual tests in all these areas, in one study or another. But for every study that has shown such an advantage, there has been another study showing no significant differences. The design of experiments to prove one point or another in this huge and complicated area is very difficult, and consistent results almost impossible to secure.

More important, there have been great athletes who have been measurably deficient in one or more of these visual characteristics.

They are individuals who have compensated—with experience, with better visual-motor coordination, with superior motor response (with pure damned meanness, for all I know). Attempts to run down the specific physical or neurological advantages of great athletes are terribly frustrating. We keep expecting them to be off-scale in one faculty or another, to have some obvious huge advantage, since they have so huge an edge in performance. More often than not they may turn out to be simply closer to the norm—in *all* their faculties—than the rest of us. That could mean the difference: all faculties spot on the norm, and thus better balance, better coordination for the lack of a distorting single faculty on which to learn to depend. All those perfectly normal capabilities, fine-tuned to work with each other better than normal. The Walter Mitty in me says that this makes sense.

*   *   *

The Ford Motor Company conducts a nationwide "Punt, Pass, and Kick" competition, selecting national champions at ages 8 to 14 in the performance of these three skills. We generally see the finalists demonstrate some of their skills at halftime of a pro football game near season's end. It's a very nice promotion for Ford, and more than one preteen winner has gone on to make a professional athlete of himself. But it should not be construed to be any kind of accurate measure of athletic skills. The competitors are developing so rapidly in that age range that there are vast discrepancies in their performances from week to week. What Ford is really sponsoring is not a competition in punting, passing, and kicking, but a hormone race.

When I was in that age group my hero was Eugene Cox, a star on the Sweeny, Texas, high school football team. He would occasionally deign to participate for half an hour or so in our daily sandlot touch football games. He drove me to worshipful despair: he was only a few inches and a few pounds larger than we were, but he was so much faster, stronger, quicker, that to compete with him at anything was like going up against an extremely agile tree. He was a perfectly nice guy, but in the use of his own athletic skills, and in the utter frustration of my attempts to use my burgeoning skills against him, he simply humiliated me. He had moves I just could not deal with. I was not quite 14, and from the gap between our respective capabilities I tend to remember Eugene as being about 28. He must've been 16 or 17 at the time.

I would later know the additional humiliation of going up against individuals of my own age, size, and weight who nevertheless had just as much athletic advantage over me as Eugene Cox had. It's a familiar sensation: it makes you feel 12 years old again.

I would also come to know what it's like to slip the shoe onto the other foot, of course, to play athletic games with younger kids, to be able to toy with them and dance away as Eugene had done to me. It wasn't much fun. It makes me empathize with the athletically gifted who have that kind of advantage throughout their youth, be it hormonal or otherwise, who must search hard to find other athletes of similar capacity against whom to test themselves.

When Bill Walton came into professional basketball as an established star and also something of an antiestablishment radical, he was outspoken about capitalistic injustice and the need for reform throughout a decadent society. A sports reporter asked him about the inconsistencies in accepting a huge salary for playing games to entertain that decadent society while holding those beliefs. "Yeah, well, the thing is, I just really do like to play basketball," Walton said, "and the thing you have to realize is that here in this league is really the only place I can get a game."

*   *   *

For most of us, I suspect, there are ghosts of old playmates looming over every professional playing field. The superstar makes a certain move in a certain way, and suddenly there comes old so-and-so, who used to get by you regularly in eighth-grade basketball, faking and juking into your memory. (When I see Nate Archibald make a move that recalls eighth-grade embarrassments, I get a glimmer of why I couldn't handle such moves decades ago—and a glimmer of new respect for old so-and-so, the kid who used to put those moves on me.) But it isn't just idiosyncrasies of movement that so jiggle the memory, it is whole styles of play, characteristic bodily attitudes. The exercise physiologists have tried to classify these movements, to understand what makes them characteristic—to discover, in effect, what made Babe Ruth's swing so distinctively his own. If they can define the differences in movement, there is a chance that they can then teach movement more effectively.

The analysis necessary to accomplish this is reductionist in the extreme, of course. As a result a lot of commonly accepted notions get dissolved completely away. For instance, in the discussions I've had with athletes and coaches over the years, the generally accepted explanation of the star's superior athletic skills has always been "coordination." "Coordination," we assumed, was the quality that allowed the good athlete to pick up a new skill quickly and easily, to perform an assimilated skill more smoothly and efficiently, to improvise entirely new movements for unusual situations. It was something like "star quality": coordination is to an athlete as charisma is to a politician or movie star. We never defined it any more clearly than that.

There really isn't any such thing. There is coordination of hand and eye movements, there are capabilities for performing two or more disparate skills at the same time, there are capacities for performing complex motor skills while keeping an unusually high level of attention focused on the contest in progress. But general coordination, as some kind of athletic capacity that makes everything easier, seems to be something of a myth—a product, perhaps, of our own wistful longings to excel. One study that attempted to capture this elusive characteristic finally decided that "well-coordinated" individuals actually have one or more of three specific explanations for their seeming advantage at motor skills. Such individuals do have clear, specific qualities going for them, qualities as measurable and unmysterious as speed, reaction time, or strength. Or for reasons that may range from cultural expectations to the ready availability of opportunity, they happen to have put in a great deal of practice at a lot of different activities. Or their personal needs have given them so strong a drive for approval for their motor abilities that they work harder at acquiring skills than do their less "coordinated" contemporaries. (One might even say they have greater "need strain," in Rosenzweig's terms.)

Attempts to find a generalized key to skilled motor performance keep running aground on specificity. The small advantage one may have in performing this or that skill turns out to be the result of a measurable advantage in the specifics one needs to perform just that skill—and very little of those specifics translates to any other skills. Arm strength and maximum speed of arm movement, for example, have been found to be independent of each other. Limb speed and limb reaction time are likewise unconnected; arm mass and speed of movement are similarly unlinked, and so on.

Because of this specificity, research tends to come up with more applicable considerations, rather than fewer. It is as if when you start to study coordination it explodes on you into more and more different skill characteristics. Performance in gross motor skills has been found to be affected by at least ten different identifiable factors: strength, dynamic strength or energy, ability to change direction, flexibility, agility, peripheral vision, general visual acuity, concentration, understanding of the mechanics of the motions required, and the absence of conflicting emotional complications.

Athletic skills have been organized into three clusters of abilities: the accurate utilization of space; the maximum and immediate use of force and balance; the ability to move rapidly. Within these three broad areas, six primary motor ability traits have been recognized. If you want to compare the basic athletic capacities of members of a group, you might do well to devise tests to measure these six particular capabilities:

1. Speed of change of direction—the quick propulsion of the total body in running tasks, a capacity that is believed to be related to the ability to mobilize energy quickly.
2. Gross body equilibrium—both static balance (the length of time an individual can balance on a narrow beam, for example) and dynamic balance (skill at walking such a beam).
3. Balance with visual cues—a separate balance factor, evaluated in static balance tests with the eyes open.
4. Dynamic flexibility—the ability to make repeated trunk and limb movements quickly; that is, testing speed of movement through a wide range of body motion.
5. Extent flexibility—measuring the range of motion of the back and trunk. While dynamic flexibility measures speed of repeated motion, extent flexibility is concerned only with the amount of motion available.
6. Speed of limb movement—measuring leg and arm speed. These were once thought to be separate, but are now considered a single performance quality.

*   *   *

Check off high scores in items one through six, and you'd have a profile of a perfect running back for football. It would be a description written by a computer (or a physical educator), however, lacking the poetry that is an inescapable part of the running back's art. I keep thinking of Walter Payton of the Chicago Bears: at every touch from a would-be tackler, Payton's body somehow reacts as if stung, snapping away with a rubbery quickness that seems to make the whole figure proceed in a glow of hyper-energy: motor trait #1, "speed of change of direction," I suppose, although those cold words don't begin to portray the marvelous aliveness of that particular individual at work. Or maybe that aliveness is what the physiologists are talking about in category #4, "dynamic flexibility," which does sound a little more like what it is that I think I see Walter Payton do. But it doesn't capture the demonic joy.

Or the joy of watching him. As I began working on this book, I kept seeing a television commercial that opens with a woman and a man playing racquetball. It was not a good ad, as an ad—I don't remember the product—but the pitch is to women. The woman player, coming directly at the camera as she pursues the ball, reaches back to just about the day before yesterday to begin her swing, puts everything from her socks up into the smash, just *powders* that unsuspecting racquetball. It is a moment of startling physical force—we don't expect that from a woman—and of great physical joy. I suspect that tiny clip of film, of a woman really teeing off, physically, did more for the women's movement than it ever did for the product. I think it did more for the cause of women's rights than a dozen commercials showing men doing the laundry or immaculate women in executive roles.

That joy is important, and it comes to all of us in watching anyone perform with energy and verve, going all-out—abandoned, for the moment, to the motion. We forget, watching professional sports, that the effort expended at that level is almost always close to all-out (despite the grumbles about spoiled-brat pros who allegedly only show up to collect their paychecks). It takes only a brief exposure to lesser effort, to the tentative, the halfhearted, the timid, to illustrate the difference. That's why it is absolutely impossible for an artificial sporting contest, acted out for the camera, to look anything like real: when the athletes don't mean it, it shows. It demonstrates by glaring contrast how hard real athletes play their games. There's a pointer for would-be pros in all this: the peculiar eye of the camera exposes the uncommitted. Watch it.

Particularly in slow motion. Curious development. For some time now, entertainment film—the action thriller, the teevee movie—has used super slow motion as a gimmick to indicate its real-world opposite: extremely intense, high-speed action. See the ending of *Bonnie and Clyde*, which may have started the fad. This has become part of the grammar of film, a shorthand convention as trite now in its way as the wavy dissolve to signify the passage of time. Super-slo-mo = high-speed action, on the *Six Million Dollar Man* or in any Charles Bronson flick of the past decade.

It was the slow-motion instant replay in television sports that made this into a film cliché. TV uses slo-mo replays to show the significant points of action, the "big play." In the big play, the athletes are operating at maximum, all-out intensity. It shows: it is clear, during those replays, that here are a bunch of athletes really putting out. We have become so conditioned to equating slow motion with athletic intensity that the moviemakers can now use the gimmick to create artificial intensity. Sports' contribution to "art." (Eat your heart out, LeRoy Nieman.)

Never mind what Bronson & Co. have done with it, however. I suspect that the development of slow-motion filming techniques has given the general public a greater and clearer understanding of the workings of the human body at maximum effort than anything else in all the previous years of sports history.

*   *   *

It doesn't seem unnecessarily unfair to say that as far as identifiable athletic characteristics are concerned, research has not discovered a great deal that is of crucial significance in understanding athletic talent. The researchers have come up with a greater and greater proliferation of possibly significant athletic attributes, and finer and finer divisions of the components of motor skills. But at the same time that each of these components seems to contribute to athletic accomplishment, none of them quite turns out to be requisite. Fine athletes keep turning up who are woefully lacking in one or more of the traits. These are components that clearly help, but their lack does not necessarily handicap athletic achievement—which has a way of o'erleaping requisites, anyway. The human organism is too flexible, too resilient, to be contained in the lines and forms and standards that the researchers dream up.

Frustrated in the attempt to uncover some kind of philosopher's stone of athleticism within the motor skills, the researchers turn elsewhere, looking for other individual differences that might explain athletic excellence. One area of research that has been as frustrating for the researchers as for the suffering athletes is that athletic nightmare, the slump. There have been attempts to explain slumps by linking them with such variables as the individual's stage of learning of the task, particular personality types, simple versus complex tasks, absolute levels of skill, practice time or the lack thereof. About all they've learned is that slumps—temporary declines in performance levels—are a lot like the common cold. Everyone gets one now and then, at just about any skill level, under just about any conditions that can be conceived. Good performers get them but no more severely than do poor performers (the contrast in levels of performance is just more startling when the good athlete goes sour). There does seem to be some slight connection with learning plateaus.

Once research went beyond motor skills in the search for keys to athletic ability, it ran smack into an endless series of nature-vs.-nurture controversies, in which no measurable difference can quite be pinned down to either cause or result. Sex differences, for example, have been the source of endless investigation. Little boys, age 3 to 4, outperform little girls in motor activities that require force or speed; little girls score better if the tasks require precision and accuracy. By age 7 these differences have been diminished considerably; then as physical maturation sets in, the differences begin to open up again. Even though females mature two years earlier than males, the males have more muscle tissue and more strength per unit of body weight —even before testosterone begins exaggerating the difference. By adolescence there is a clear relationship between motor performance and level of physical maturity in males, but not in females. Girls who could outperform boys in preadolescence stop doing so by about age 14; they do not even perform up to their own physical potential anymore, beginning about that age. As the Harry Chapin song lyric says, "Why do girls grow up crippled while little boys grow up tall? Boys are taught to tumble, girls taught not to fall."

It is generally agreed that cultural expectations, peer pressures, lack of suitably athletic role models, and the like play a large part in forestalling female athletic development at the onset of puberty. But the argument is also advanced that the same external forces are responsible for the early sex differences in performances even at age 3 and 4. The recent upsurge in female participation in sports—aided by Title IX and further stimulated by the commercial successes of women's tennis and golf—is almost sure to diminish the differences we now accept as "normal." It'll be interesting to see if these same developments give us some measure of the strength of the cultural effect of the past.

Age differences in motor skills have not been studied as thoroughly as sex differences. As a general pattern, motor performance improves gradually from birth until midadolescence, but seems to pause there and doesn't resume until early adulthood. At about age 20 the rate of improvement of motor performance picks up again—now a product, it is assumed, of experience rather than of increasing physical capacity. The late maturity of some performers, however, particularly in endurance sports such as distance running, cycling, and cross-country ski racing, would seem to indicate that there can be gains in stamina and strength well beyond the late 20s.

The interruption in improvement of motor skills during the most excruciating period of adolescence is fascinating, with immense ramifications for sports programs. It is the period when most young people are most enthusiastically involved in sports, when they want most earnestly to improve their skills, and therefore must be a period of extreme frustration for them. In our culture it is also likely to be a time of intense sexual frustration. I have been unable to find any studies of this rather obvious linkage.

During most of adulthood, motor performance and motor skills are relatively stable. After about age 48, reaction times and other physical measurements usually begin to drop off. There is some indication that balance declines with age, for example, with acrophobia as a developing side effect. We can compensate for the lack of balance with experience, but it catches up to us when we are exposed to heights, and we may suffer vertigo as we get older. (Aging skiers may notice they no longer enjoy skiing steep slopes, particularly when visibility is bad.) Cultural expectations and even class differences play a large part in determining when and how fast our physical faculties decline, of course. A 65-year-old corporation president may feel much more inclined to the vigorous life than his 65-year-old assistant bookkeeper—and may have less energy to spend than a 65-year-old stevedore who has maintained an active physical pace all his life.

In the study of individual differences in motor performance, no area is more controversial, none more clearly loaded with sociocultural biases, than race. The agility of the athletes is as nothing compared with the agility of the researchers in dodging any hard and fast pronouncements of physical differences between blacks and whites, for instance. Differences do exist. Measurements have shown that adult American blacks tend to have longer legs compared with total body length, with shorter thighs and longer lower legs, than whites. Young blacks tend toward lighter torsos and heavier limbs, smaller lungs, and less body fat for a given body weight than whites of the same age. Studies of competitors at the 1960 Olympics confirmed that these racial comparisons held up irrespective of the athletic event considered, even when weight lifting, which can grossly modify physical measurements, is included.

Where motor performance is concerned, the testing gets dodgier. One study has indicated that black children, age 5, outperform white children in throwing distance, running speed, grip strength, and balance; another seemed to show that black kids could run faster and could follow complex rhythm patterns better than white kids—the last a test that sounds biased in its very conception.

Experimental design flaws crop up throughout all of these tests and studies. It is simply impossible to balance out all of the sociocultural factors that can affect the outcome. Even the seemingly bulletproof objectivity of purely physical measurement is hopelessly skewed by such things as the cultural forces that affect black participation (and white participation) in activities that enhance or retard physical development—to say nothing of the effects of diet and living conditions.

No scientist worthy of the name wants to contribute to racial biases in any direction. But whatever the alleged causes of the alleged differences in performance between blacks and whites—be they innately physical, sociocultural, or simply individual gifts that shine through—one set of numbers is inarguable: 19 percent of major league baseball players, 42 percent of professional football players, 65 percent of professional basketball players are black athletes. (Management positions in these sports fall shockingly far short of those figures.) Of 31 U.S. track and field medals at the Montreal Olympics, 22 were won by blacks, as were all our gold medals in boxing.

Scientists may be nervous about examining racial differences, but the athletes themselves seem to be perfectly comfortable—and good-humored—about them. When CBS Sports concocted its abortive "Slam-Dunk" contest to fill in at halftimes of NBA broadcasts, superstar Rick Barry opined, "There ought to be a separate contest for us white guys, who can't *jump*."

* * *

Other areas have been investigated in the attempt to explain differences in motor performance. Numerous attempts have been made to link motor skills, as well as personality types, to physique. (Attempting to determine characteristics of movement or personality or anything else from physical body type is called *somatotyping*; it's a pet theory of running guru and best-selling author Dr. George Sheehan.) Mesomorphs are expected to be sprinters or quarterbacks, ectomorphs to be high jumpers or distance men, endomorphs to be . . . students. Or musicians. Excuse the lame joke, but it makes an important point about expectations, I think. Although the techniques for somatotyping are sound, their implied predictions about motor performance seem to be culturally generated. "Expectations," says kinesiologist Bryant J. Cratty, "not only revolve around stereotypes about how people with various physiques are expected to perform physically, but also about how they may be expected to behave in a total way." The physical appearance that you present determines to a great extent what the world expects of you in the way of motor skills, and your performance tends to measure up to those expectations. The same may be true for personality. (One curious study of body-builders suggests that they alter and reshape their bodies so radically in an unconscious attempt to stabilize their own personalities!)

Nobody is quite willing to say that left-handers make better athletes than right-handers do—an observation that is perfectly obvious to us southpaws—but there is evidence that overwhelming right-hand and right-foot dominance is less prevalent among good athletes than among the general population. "Superior athletic performance is apparently *not retarded* by left-handedness," is the arch way one report puts it. (Emphasis supplied by a left-hander.)

Motivation is crucial to individual motor performance. Hypnotic suggestion, for example, indicates that we are capable of doing much more, physically, than we usually manage, and higher motivation can help make up the difference. Hypnosis has been used in attempts to enhance athletic performance, with mixed results. It works in rather left-handed ways. If you want to improve the steadiness of a hypnotized subject in a difficult manual task, for example, you get better results if you suggest that the subject relax than if you suggest that the subject be more accurate, bear down harder, be steadier. (Coaches please note.) There are inhibitory factors to motor performance, particularly as we grow older, and hypnosis can help remove those inhibitions. Rather than suggesting that the subject will be stronger, the hypnotist gets better results by suggesting that the "pain" associated with maximum effort will be reduced or go unnoticed. Work capacity, resistance to fatigue, and other measures of endurance seem to be more accessible to improvement from hypnotic suggestion than do such capacities as strength or reaction time.

Hypnosis and various other externally applied remedies have been used to try to bring the athlete up to the proper state of arousal for maximum motor performance. There is an optimum level of arousal, which tends to shade into tension. ("Arousal," as I'm using the term here, is of attention level, emotional state, the sensory receptors. By "tension" I mean the upper end of the arousal curve, manifesting itself in overt muscular contraction. "Anxiety" is the hyperemotional state, from whatever causes, that manifests itself in increased muscular tension.) In preparation for motor performance, tension can be helpful, but too much tension can be a sign of anxiety, which reduces motor performance. Anxiety damps out some of the cues that the individual uses to guide performance. This, too, can help at first—the individual is able to avoid distraction by cues that are irrelevant to the task at hand. But as anxiety increases, the individual begins to lose relevant cues, and performance deteriorates. Motor performance is more susceptible to this kind of anxiety-based deterioration than is either sensory or intellectual performance. As learning progresses, the tension that accompanies highly motivated motor performance diminishes.

Properly used, tension is a valuable tool. As there is an optimum level of arousal, there is also an optimum level of pretask tension. If the athlete can learn to reach this level of tension going into a task, reaction times are reduced. If the tension level peaks too early or too late, reaction times increase and the performance falls off. A lot of the meditative psyching up that weight lifters do seems to be aimed at properly timing this kind of arousal.

An even more graphic example is provided by high jumpers, who are given two minutes to prepare for each attempt. Former world record holder Dwight Stones is noted for spending that time in a virtual trance state, arousing himself with mental images of making the approach and soaring over the bar. He concentrates so fixedly on these images that his head actually bobs—you can see it from the sidelines—as he "watches" his own imaginary form through every galloping step of his approach run to come. Sometimes, he says, his image knocks off the crossbar—and he will not start an actual jump until he sees his ghost form succeed.

*　　*　　*

A few years ago I took a course in "Centered Skiing" with Denise McCluggage. It is an approach to learning to ski better that is based loosely on, among other things, T'ai Chi and the martial arts. We worked indoors each morning before going onto the slopes. One morning Denise had us close our eyes, sit still, and in our imagination "ski" down our favorite slope. She talked us along, almost hypnotically, through the experience, which became surprisingly realistic. I was enjoying the exercise when, on an imaginary left turn, my mental image fell down.

Out on the slopes I had developed the bad habit of leaving one ski pole planted too long, which dropped my weight back to that side and put me off-balance. In my mental imagery I continued making precisely the same mistake, just as I'd been doing on the hill. My image fell down. I burst out laughing so hard I disrupted the class.

*　　*　　*

We don't know if there is any difference between the way we learn movements and the way we learn anything else, although there is some evidence that there are differences. We don't know how experience is stored in the nervous system, although we are almost sure that it is stored in some as yet undiscovered anatomical or biochemical way. We don't know the difference, if there is any difference, between memory and experience.

Once we learn a motor skill we retain it rather better than we do other kinds of learning. "It'll come back to you," we say of long unused skill. "It's like riding a bicycle." That in itself is taken as evidence that motor learning causes a different sort of physiological change than other kinds of learning—and that when we recall a motor skill we "bring it back" from some other place, by some other mechanism. As motor skills are learned, they seem to require less and less conscious thought—indeed, as Lewis Thomas points out, conscious thought can become a positive hindrance to their performance. (This almost seems to fly in the face of The American Way —not to mention what it does to such notions as "need strain." We know perfectly well that we must concentrate harder, keep conscious control, pay attention, supervise every detail, make more effort. Don't we?) It is all a puzzlement.

One attempt to penetrate the puzzle has encouraged researchers to look to the single nerve cell as the key to motor learning. Using sophisticated lab techniques that include biofeedback training, it is possible to teach an individual to fire a single motor unit, even though the subject can feel no obvious muscular response from contraction of so small an aggregate of muscle cells. To do so requires sending a discrete signal to a single nerve cell. The subject can learn to fire the motor unit continuously, or to raise or lower the rate of firing. Although there are great differences in learning rates for this peculiar skill (athletes tend to learn it more quickly than nonathletes), it has been taught to retarded subjects and very young children (age 3 to 4). The ability to learn it varies with the amount of attention the subject is able to bring to bear on the process, but once it is learned the subject can perform it in the face of rather startling amounts of distraction. Benumb the limb that contains the motor unit even slightly, reducing the amount of sensory information the subject gets during the training process, and the learning is markedly slowed.

If motor learning involves the single nerve cell, as this test seems to indicate, then it is assumed that learning makes physical changes in the cell that is "taught"—changes that allow it to fire more easily, more quickly, more efficiently. "It is clear," says Bryant J. Cratty, ". . . that human retention depends on traces of the activity residing somewhere in the cortex, which become deeply ingrained and resistant to forgetfulness after a period of time has passed." (Among other influences detrimental to memory—along with drugs and electroshock treatment—is "massed practice." That is, long practice sessions with very high numbers of repetitions may actually reduce retention. Tennis and ski coaches please note.) The traces of the activity—the grooves—may be the result of structural or chemical changes. There are theories to support each, and the two possibilities are not mutually exclusive.

One structural change that has been proposed is that learning simply increases the available area for transmission of nerve impulses at the synaptic junction—a larger contact patch, so to speak. Experiments have also shown that nerve fibers swell as they transmit impulses, and the swelling can last for days, even years, indicating some structural change. Lab animals reared in "enriched" environments, with more stimulation, develop more dendritic branching than animals reared in "impoverished" environments—and in fact neurons from the brains of older persons show more extensive branching than neurons from the brains of younger persons. There is also evidence that learning does improve synaptic conductance; it is theorized that this results because the postsynaptic membrane somehow becomes more sensitive, with learning, to acetylcholine.

The last finding is more chemical than structural, and indicates the direction of more recent research. The great advances in molecular biology in recent years have focused more attention on the chemical, rather than structural, neural changes in learning. The brain of a trained animal has been discovered to be chemically different, for example, from the brain of an untrained litter mate. A body of research is developing that indicates that learning causes molecular change in the neuron, and that these changes store information in coded form.

Ribonucleic acid (RNA) is now believed to be the substance in the neural system that is modified in learning and that stores the new information. Certainly it has enough capacity. An RNA molecule consists of thousands of subunits, and any rearrangement of subunits creates an entirely different RNA molecule. The mathematical possibilities for distinctly different RNA molecules are astronomical. The RNA molecule acts as a kind of template or mold for the synthesis of protein in the cell. Each different RNA molecule synthesizes different proteins. The function of cells is controlled by proteins, so control of the synthesis of protein in effect controls the function of the cell. Since neural activity alters RNA, which alters protein synthesis, which alters cell function, RNA has been designated as the "memory molecule."

There have been tantalizing experimental results growing out of these theories. In the most spectacular, RNA has been extracted from trained animals (flatworms at first, rats later, trained to respond to light cues or clicking sounds) and injected into untrained animals, which have then shown definite signs of training. The implication is that the memory, the training, is contained in the substance that is transferred from animal to animal. (Here, take this spoonful of click-recognition.) Similarly, RNA has been administered to elderly human beings, who have then shown some degree of improvement in memory. These experiments have not proved easily replicable, and there is a great deal of controversy surrounding them. But there does seem to be some indication that learning and memory might eventually be boosted by biochemical additives—if we want to risk that kind of meddling with mental processes. If we do, there is a logical, perhaps even inevitable, use in sports, in the application and retention of motor skills. Considering past history, the first semiexperimental applications of such "improvement" might be expected to occur in sports. It is also conceivable that attempts to do so might come to be regarded as the chemical equivalent of psychosurgery.

* * *

Assume there's a problem confronting you, the solution of which requires that you acquire a new motor skill. What do you have to do to pick up the new skill?

For starters, you have to pay attention. You have to be engaged by the problem; you have to come at it with a level of mental and sensory arousal sufficient to pick up the stimulus cues you need for a solution. Next, you will probably examine the problem by comparing it with your own experience, scanning your past for similar applicable skills that might provide alternative solutions, assessing your own capacities and how they might apply. You make a series of more or less unconscious judgments about where your movements must take effect, about the speed of movement, the space, the force required. You will probably go through a certain amount of covert rehearsal, complete with spoken instructions to yourself—vocal or subvocal, depending on the complexity of the task.

Then you attempt the movement, running a constant comparison check between the motions you intend and the motions you are actually making, correcting the differences. As the discrepancy is reduced, as you grow confident that you can accomplish the movement you have in mind, you are able to reduce the monitoring and to let your attention go on to other things. This is where the movement begins to become a skill. In your first fumbling attempts—complete with instructions to yourself—the higher brain centers are in almost total control, leaving very little for any other controlling mechanism to do. As you are able to stop consciously analyzing every aspect of the motion, the higher brain centers begin to tune out. In effect, you acquire a skill by taking the act out of your head and putting it away, neurologically, in your spine. (But not in your muscles, for all the coaches' talk about "muscle memory.")

Skill takes over. It is perhaps only a pipsqueak miracle that takes place; certainly it is mostly used for inconsequential tasks—brushing teeth, tying shoes, serving tennis balls. But it'll do, for small-scale wonder: watch as you tie your shoes, and you may not be able to believe what you see yourself doing—if you are able to continue, once you've become conscious of the complexity of the movements. As you stop comparing what you do with what your mental model says to do, as you are freed from the necessity of close monitoring of all available perceptual cues, then the speed and accuracy of your movements increase. You even decrease the amount of muscular tension in your system. "The ability to relax all but the necessary muscles is also an important element in skill," says physical educator Arthur H. Steinhaus.

(Thus the sports cliché: the wily veteran beats the upstart rookie in the closing seconds. The rookie overpowers in the early going, but at a level of energy expenditure that can't be maintained. The veteran husbands his resources, gliding along, keeping the score within reach by skill rather than force, waiting for the inevitable collapse. The plot may be corny but the physiology is sound.)

In a skilled act there are usually a time element (speed), an energy element (strength, force), and a quality element ("coordination," the effective combination of speed and strength, sheer accuracy of motion). It is fairly clear that the learner of a skill proceeds in segments of action. He or she breaks the skill down into groups of motions, mastering one group before going on to the next. Then the learner starts organizing the groups into larger and larger chunks of action, until the skill—the total motion—is complete. This kind of fragmentation of motions is particularly useful when the movement is so rapid or the sequence so long that the kinesthetic information coming in during the early attempts is more than the learner can comfortably handle.

We do learn the skill. We learn skills of immense complexity, with motions that simultaneously require the greatest delicacy and speed. Being unable to tie one's own shoes is a standard joke about the ultimate motor incompetence, but tying one's shoes is not a small matter when you look at the task from a mental-motor standpoint, before that skill is tucked away in the central nervous system. From shoe-tying to the skills displayed at the highest levels of performance is only a linear progression. Circus acts are often built around the manic presentation of some particular motor skill carried to near-absurdity: jugglers, knife-throwers, acrobats, who perform at levels of skill that seem to surpass totally the skills demonstrated by professional athletes. The circus performer has a tightly controlled task in a tightly controlled environment, however, practiced to perfection and performed in circumstances that require no rapid revisions of motor input. Compare the task of a circus juggler, for example, with that of a professional tennis player. The juggler has no opponent but gravity; the tennis player has to demonstrate motor creativity, has to come up with responses that are both varied and original. Nobody comes up with more motor creativity than Julius Erving.

*   *   *

In my youth I spent a couple of summers as a clown diver with a traveling water show, cutting didoes in the air for laughs. Our crew spoke frequently, familiarly, of a phenomenon we called "getting lost." It happened all the time. You would make your customary approach on the springboard, bounce high to launch some caper, and suddenly find yourself lost in space. All the kinesthetic cues would somehow fail you. Once the linear progression through your scheduled flips and twists was interrupted, you had had it; there was nothing to do but curl into the tiniest possible ball, hold tight, and wait for the impact with the water. It was probably no more than a failure of concentration, but it happened to someone every other performance or so. The next time you attempted the same stunt you usually could perform it just fine.

A more baffling loss of a motor skill happened to me a year or two earlier. I was the second-string kicker on the high school football team. I could punt the ball thirty-five yards, almost exactly, with very high consistency. Another kid on the team could consistently punt for fifty yards or so. The coach decided, not illogically, that I should learn to punt like the first-stringer, should copy his kicking motion. I did, immediately lost my consistent thirty-five yard punt, and never regained it. I could no longer kick the ball even fifteen yards. (I still can't.) I simply lost the motion. I was never able to figure out where I lost it or why. In my mind, even now, I can recapture perfectly the feel of the motion that would punt the ball thirty-five yards; I just can't perform that motion with my leg, foot, and a football.

Such a loss of a motion is perhaps not unusual—see high jumping in Chapter 1. Or baseball pitching. It is not too rare a development for a good pitcher suddenly to lose his control and spend months— or his remaining career—trying to regain it. It happened to a hot prospect named Pat Jordan, finally drove him out of baseball, and left him so bemused that he has since published two books about his own and others' efforts to recapture such lost skills.

*   *   *

Once you perform a skill to your own satisfaction you tend to stop improving. Yet the physiological limits to your performance of the skill may be a great deal higher. There's plenty of research about the early stages of acquisition of a skill, but little about the higher reaches, about skills as they are practiced at the most demanding levels. Science is just now beginning to recognize what circus performers have always known: that the upper reaches are virtually limitless, provided there is sufficient motivation to reach them.* When the performer or athlete begins to assault these higher levels of skill, there are continuing subtle physiological accommodations that occur to help sharpen the skills further. The eyes become more precisely linked to hand movements; tiny refinements begin to develop in muscular controls, in energy processing, even in hormone regulation. Subtle adjustments are made in breathing patterns to accommodate

* At this writing an aerialist is attempting to perform a quadruple aerial somersault on the trapeze—a dream of that peculiar art form for decades. Reports say he's close to success. Of course, some say the quadruple is physically impossible. I'm confident that it will be performed regularly in circus acts within twenty years.

more delicate motions. Brain wave patterns may even change. (Some bench marksmen are reputed to squeeze off their shots between heartbeats, in order to reduce bodily vibration that might deflect the shot.)

Researchers continue to look for a "general motor learning factor," some as yet undiscovered total capacity rather like that "coordination" we used to talk about so much. There are plenty of suggestions for why some people learn new motor skills more quickly and more easily than the rest of us. Quick learners are assumed to be more highly motivated, perhaps a little stronger physically than the rest of us, with a talent for grasping the mechanical demands of a task— and, very likely, with a lower level of residual tension that might interfere with learning. But no single other factor has yet turned up. Many students of motor learning still believe that such a factor exists and will eventually be identified. Cratty indicates where the search might focus: ". . . when measures reflecting the quality of movement that occurs during learning (including assessments of smooth accelerations and decelerations, appropriate build-up of velocities that anticipate sudden application of force, and similar data which may be collected by the biomechanist) are collected and compared, one may begin to confirm what is generally observed about those who tend to be rather quick learners and those who seem to be 'motor morons.' "[*] See sweet spots.

*　　*　　*

One more tired old joke: "How do I get to Carnegie Hall?" asks the pedestrian in New York, violin case in hand. "Practice," mutters the scuttling passerby. Practice indeed: no matter how seemingly miraculous the motor skills of the circus performer or the professional athlete, those skills are not even in the same league with those of the virtuoso musical performer. And the musician develops those skills by dint of practice, of a quantity, but more importantly of a *quality*, that makes the efforts of most other performers look positively dilettantish.

[*] From *Movement Behavior and Motor Learning* (Lea & Febiger, Philadelphia, 1973). This book has been my principal reference throughout this chapter, and I recommend it to anyone looking to go beyond the rather rough summary I've drawn from it. Cratty himself points out that the bulk of the research in these areas is now done by doctoral candidates in fulfillment of degree requirements, and therefore is hardly the extensive and systematic exploration that might be wished.

Our family pediatrician always used to say that a baby only has to do something one time to establish a habit. That charming old homily implies a blank-page vision of newborn neurological tissue that has a long poetic tradition behind it. But the pages of the rest of us are already pretty well scribbled up. While a single performance of a motion may start us on the way to learning a skill, may even begin etching some kind of neurological tracery that will make repetition easier next time, real skill requires that the groove be cut deeper. In the RNA concept of neural pathways, you have to keep sending impulses down the path to stimulate the brain to send more RNA to the synapses to reinforce the production of proteins that facilitate the passage of the signal. If that unproved theory doesn't quite apply, then you have to keep repeating the motion to reinforce whatever other neural changes do take place. Practice. All of our understanding of motor learning, theoretical or practical, hinges on that notion.

Unfortunately, here comes another mystery: we don't really know how best to do the practicing. A great deal of research has been done, of course. Massed practice has been compared with distributed practice (long versus short practice sessions). Rest periods between practice sessions have been varied from a few seconds to several days. Varying the numbers of repetitions has been exhaustively tested (as with strength training). Reducing movements to their component parts, as a practice method, has been compared with practicing whole movements and with stringing together sequences of movements. The results of all these tests are too inconclusive to establish firm principles. There is even confusion about the definition of the skills that practice is intended to enhance. Is the practice intended to eliminate errors? To increase speed? To increase accuracy? Each individual movement seems to require its own definition of what skill it is that accomplishes the movement. In short, the questions about practice are so broad and so numerous that it's surprising we still believe in it.

If no hard and fast principles emerge from the research, there are at least some handy hints. All else being equal—as in the attempt to learn a totally new and unfamiliar skill—it is probably best to start out with massed practice, then as the movement starts to become reasonably familiar, to switch to distributed practice, with rest periods as needed. If the skill requires rapid interaction with an opponent, as in the various net-and-ball games, there seems to be some advantage to breaking down the movement into parts and practicing the parts separately. Conversely if the skill requires no reaction to an opponent's moves, as in swimming or skating, then it is better to practice the whole motion.

You may learn more quickly if you can break a new skill into segments, give the segments descriptive terms, then "talk yourself through" the skill. In fact you may be able to improve your performance just by imagining the segments in order and repeating to yourself the names of the segments, in place of actual practice. Mental practice does seem to help. (That's what we were doing in the Centered Skiing workshop when I mentally fell down.) With equipment that measures the electrical action potential of muscle groups, researchers have found that when subjects mentally rehearse a motor task they fire the correct muscle groups in the correct order, even if they are actually motionless. One study indicates this mental practice also is more effective in the early stages of acquiring a skill than it is later, when the skill is assimilated.

But maybe it works for the experts too. Denise McCluggage told me of watching the BMW automobile racing team hold a mental practice session before a major race. The manager had all the drivers sit quietly, close their eyes, and start "driving" the course in their minds—taking the car up through the gears, braking at the proper points for the turns in sequence, and so on. Each driver would give a hand signal as he crossed the start-finish line in his mind. The manager was timing these mental laps: most of the drivers' imaginary lap times were within a few tenths of a second of their best times in actual practice.* At any rate, the more complex the task is, the more improvement is likely to result from mental practice. And motor racing would surely qualify as sufficiently complex.

I'm not sure how much any athlete thinks about such things as neural pathways, but the subject did come up once in a conversation with Boston Celtics center Dave Cowens. He's a great believer in strength training, with a basement full of weight machines. He initi-

* The anecdote is included in McCluggage's book, *The Centered Skier* (Vermont Crossroads Press, 1977, later issued as a popular paperback by Warner Books). *The Centered Skier* really isn't about skiing, it's about movement—it ought to be called *The Centered Athlete*—and I found it extremely rewarding.

ated his own weight-lifting program while he was still in college, seeking to develop more upper body strength and bulk to hold his own in the trench warfare under the backboards.

"I used to work out with weights before I went to basketball practice every day," he told me. "I wanted to work on shooting baskets after my arms were already tired, feeling tight. I thought that would help me develop more arm strength. My basketball coach caught me doing it, and made me reverse the order, shooting baskets before lifting weights. What I was doing was developing one set of muscles to use to shoot baskets when I was fresh, and another set to use when I was tired. I'd be training two sets of nerve signals, and then in a game, when I wasn't tired yet, the signals would be bouncing back and forth between the two sets. So my shooting wouldn't be as accurate." (Cowens may not be the best pure shooter in the league, but his averages are consistently high enough to suggest that his neural pathways can't be too far off the mark.)

It seems very likely that the confusion about the best ways to practice springs from the same source as our confusion about the real physiological basis of motor learning, and the same source as our confusion about building general muscular strength and hoping it will improve performance in very specialized tasks. The real source of the confusion is specificity again, the amazing specificity of our athletic plant. McCluggage says that the trouble with practice is that when you do it, you only practice what you are practicing, not what you may *think* you are practicing. Practicing bad motions does not build good skills. There is specificity of skill as well as of strength, of neural pathways just as of muscle fibers. An athlete must put his or her effort as precisely and accurately as possible into improving the specific task that the sport requires. That's what the physical educators mean when they speak of quality practice. Anything else may be teaching the physiology to perform worse, rather than better.

Or that's what the kinesiologists would tell us. Generalization is not possible, as far as their measurements go. And there is no generalizable characteristic such as "athleticism" or "coordination" or anything else that can explain why you are better than I am at any one of six widely different sports—including that new one that neither of us had ever tried until a few minutes ago. That's what they tell us, anyway. But I know a good athlete when I see one, and so do you. I still wonder if there isn't some way we can explain why.

* * *

I close my eyes and in my imagination run the old newsreel of Babe Ruth at bat again. I marvel once again at the perfect fluidity of that swing. Grooved. Wonderful motion, wonderful skill. Then it occurs to me how easily and vividly I can select that image—from somewhere in my memory—and run that old newsreel so surely. The act of running that newsreel is something that *I* have grooved. The same kind of groove. Neural pathways.

CHAPTER 9
Fuels

When it comes to nutrition for athletes, a couple of things are clear. The first is that athletes are consistently advised by the very best nutritionists in the world that for pure athletic purposes, nothing they can ingest will improve much on the standard concept of a balanced diet: a wide variety of foods, preferably unprocessed or lightly processed, taken in normal quantities. A tasty selection from the four basic food groups, every day, period. Nothing in excess: just what those grade-school health films always told them to eat.

The second thing that is clear about athletic nutrition is that the athletes don't believe this advice.

Beyond that, very little about nutrition and diet is very clear at all. It is maddening. What the athlete requires of a diet is the maximum amount of useful energy over the long haul, and reasonable maintenance of the physical plant. There may be special requirements— short bursts of very high levels of energy, maintenance or augmentation of body weight, special endurance capacities—and the athlete will certainly seek ways to modify diet to achieve them. But the basic requirement is simple: plenty of energy, easily obtained, without damage to the body. That's a requirement which can be fulfilled from a normal, balanced diet. So why are athletes always buying all these bee-pollen pills, protein supplements, electrolytic fluids, and other dietary exotica?

At the highest levels of athletic effort—as in distance running, for which top competitors put in well over a hundred miles a week of hard training—the individual either comes to some kind of understanding of personal nutritional requirements, or falls apart, unable to keep up the training pace. Not every competitor bothers to try to hit the nutritional nail precisely on the head, however. Some simply glom down sufficient quantities of food, in any form they can lay their hands on, to overpower the problem, to ensure that they neither run out of energy nor begin to consume body tissue to keep up. Bicycle racers, who put in prodigious training distances, are notorious for the latter approach to athletic nutrition. "They eat so much," one coach says, "that when they are awake, they're either on their bikes or on the toilet." The ranks of professional athletes have always contained fabulous trenchermen and trencherwomen, with legendary eating habits. Those whose sports provide a level of activity to burn off the excess intake may fare reasonably well; those whose sports don't require that kind of energy jeopardize their careers (and, eventually, their health) by their overindulgence. See Babe Ruth.

The same psychological stimulus that leads to overeating also leads to nutball dietary fads, with which sports abounds. The athlete is looking for *any* edge—in energy or weight or strength, just as in elapsed time or distance covered. No matter how logical the rationale for modest and balanced dietary habits, the athlete will want *more*. The fear is always that a rival may uncover some secret advantage, may have ingested some additional secret substance that will make a difference. Therefore so long as there is no obvious risk involved, the athlete will tend to ingest anything that might make fuel, that might reduce the amount of self the athlete has to spend.

That, perhaps, is the key to the psychology involved: the athlete does feel that he or she is "spending" substance, expending physical capital that has been painfully acquired in training. No athlete wants to feel that he or she has to use sheer willpower, endure pain, or risk physical damage to compensate for an advantage the opponent has gained at the training table. Dietary gullibility and overindulgence thus become part of the psychological warfare of sport. "We easily fall prey to difficult fads," says Philip C. Weiser, a 2:21 marathoner with a Ph.D. in physiology. "If it is not wheat germ, then it is vitamin C, and if it is not that, it is protein pills. But these fads come and go, and improvements in world records seem to occur at a steady rate regardless of what nutritional fad currently rises to the top." Whether the athlete believes in the fad or not, down the gullet goes the dietary gimmick: as with the praying atheist, "just in case."

Athletic nutrition, as any other kind of nutrition, requires nothing more than a proper balance of carbohydrates, fats, proteins, vitamins, and minerals. Of these, only the first three provide calories and thus are conceivable sources of energy—and protein is an energy source only in fairly desperate straits. For most of the past two thousand years or so, nutrition for athletes has been protein-dominated, perhaps even what might be called protein-crazed. That's still the most common and most drastic nutritional imbalance practiced. But trends change. For a few decades there we became rather vitamin-crazed; some of us still are. Now, we seem aimed headlong into a carbohydrate craze. It is one rather dubious development out of the growing mass popularity of running—with the help of some utterly misleading popularization by the likes of Erich Segal and ABC-TV. We can probably expect minerals to be next (and, indeed, proponents of mineral-dosing are already bleating in the public ear). Fat, you may be sure, is due for its turn as our dietary savior. Dr. Nutball's Super-Grease Diet is just around the corner.

Nature combines carbon, hydrogen, and oxygen into organic compounds known as carbohydrates. We get carbohydrates in our diet as sugars, starches, and cellulose. The sugars, in more or less complex molecular forms, are eventually broken down into blood sugar, *glucose*, and burned directly for production of energy, reconstituting the ATP after it has been used to power muscular contraction.* The starches are more complex carbohydrate molecules which the digestive process breaks down into *maltose* (one of several complex sugars), and then into glucose. Cellulose (plant starch) is fiber, indigestible in human beings but useful in speeding the movement of wastes through the system. Carbohydrates make up about 45 percent of our dietary intake in this country, and as much as 90 percent of the diet in many developing countries.

Glucose that is temporarily unused is converted into *glycogen*, which is stored in the muscles and the liver for reconversion to glu-

* Arguments rage over which form of sugar is healthiest—hence the honey advocates, the brown sugar adherents, the fruitarians, etc. "Although much has been written concerning the benefits and disadvantages of different types of sugar molecules, to the best of our knowledge they are all delivered to the muscles as glucose," says David L. Costill, in *A Scientific Approach to Distance Running* (published by Track & Field News, Los Altos, Ca., 1979).

cose and production of energy later. (Only the glycogen in the liver is reconverted to glucose; the glycogen in muscle is almost entirely converted to an intermediate in the same pathway—glucose-1-phosphate.) Once the muscles and the liver are fully loaded with glycogen molecules, excess carbohydrates are converted into fat and stored that way. The ability to store energy as glycogen is the crux of the nutritional process for athletes and is the single part of the process that so far can be successfully manipulated for improved performance. One cause of fatigue in endurance events is depletion of blood sugar, which happens when the stored glycogen is used up. The infamous "wall" in marathon running is partially the result of glycogen depletion; that's when the runner's system starts digesting the runner, consuming body tissue to produce enough energy to continue running.

Fats are also composed of carbon, hydrogen, and oxygen, but have much more hydrogen and much less oxygen than do the carbohydrates. During digestion fats are broken down into glycerine and fatty acids; it is the fatty acids that are used for certain amounts of energy and to repair and replace some cellular elements. At low levels of oxygen uptake, near resting levels, fat is an important energy source, but when oxygen uptake increases, the body stops burning fat and starts burning glucose. If you are breathing hard, you are burning carbohydrates, not fats. (Frustration Number One for dieters: you can burn fat to produce energy at resting levels, but you don't burn it off fast enough to do any real good—and then when you pick up the pace to try to get rid of substantial quantities of fat, you stop burning the stuff. With special techniques you can vary these proportions somewhat, as we will see. To do so carries an energy-producing benefit, but doesn't do a thing for weight loss.)

Fat serves several other purposes in the body: protection and support of various internal organs, maintenance of body heat, formation of the protective sheath around nerve axons, and the like. Get too little fat in your diet and you can't properly use the fat-soluble vitamins A, D, E, and K. But get too much and you not only gain weight and unsightly love handles, but also may induce fatty deposits in the major arteries of the heart: *atherosclerosis*, which increases your risk of heart attack. That risk is also raised by high levels of *blood triglycerides*, caused by the release of one of the forms in which excess fat is stored throughout the body (more of a danger for the overweight and underexercised). A typical American diet provides about 40 to 50 percent of its calories directly from fat; nutritionists feel a healthier proportion would be closer to 25 percent.

Proteins, too, are made of carbon, hydrogen, and oxygen, but they also contain nitrogen and trace amounts of phosphorus and sulfur. Twenty-three known amino acids are the basic building blocks from which all the proteins are formed; thirteen of these can be synthesized by the body, the other ten must be obtained from the diet. We use protein everywhere in the body; not only does it form the actin and myosin filaments which are the contractile elements of muscle, but various forms of protein make up the cell membrane and parts of the nucleus, the oxygen-transporting mechanism in the blood (the *heme* in hemoglobin), most of our hormones and digestive enzymes, our skin, hair, and fingernails. Protein is the essential constituent in all living matter, and is important to us in growth and repair of the body, in resistance to disease and infection, in proper digestion and elimination of waste. But it is *not* a significant source of energy. (It does help control the rate of production of energy, and can be used for energy when other sources run out. But we've known since 1866 that it is not a useful day-to-day source. Nevertheless some texts still speak of it that way.)

We eat too much protein, much too much—especially the athletes among us. There are a lot of rather overblown explanations for why athletes gorge so on protein, going back to the primitive practice of eating the lion's heart to gain its courage, and other such dimly understood rituals. Whether or not the pregame steak started with the gladiators, it is a long-established tradition. Unfortunately, it is directly counterproductive. Heavy loads of protein slow digestion, which means that by game time, when the athlete needs energy, the blood that should be carrying it to the muscles is busy elsewhere, processing food in the stomach. (Fat also slows digestion—and that pregame steak may be 40 percent fat, no matter how lean it looks. Both fat and excess protein, which over the long run is converted into fat, add useless body weight that requires more energy just to cart it around.) Excess protein overloads the kidneys, tends to dehydrate the body, and can cause metabolic troubles later. We don't need anything like the quantities we consume, even for strenuous athletic participation: a healthy diet can contain less than one gram of protein per kilogram of body weight daily. That's a couple of ounces a day for a 150-pound individual. But in the attempt to explain our gross overconsumption, what all that anthropology and psychology overlook is how good protein tastes, at least to us addicted Westerners. (Actually, the flavor is in the fat that comes with most rich protein sources; pure protein without fat is tasteless—or worse.) At any rate, our love of protein is only an acquired taste, conditioned by the culture, and we may yet learn to control it. Protein also represents the most expensive possible way to satisfy our appetites, of course.

Vitamins are necessary elements in the diet, but they provide no nutrition. They can't take the place of meals, don't even really "supplement," if what you are looking for is a little boost, more energy, some extra push. Vitamins are simply substances that must be present, in tiny amounts, to allow the system to make use of certain foods. They are useless without a sufficient intake of the proper foods to act upon. Specific vitamin-deficiency diseases are well known, but when they occur the body is suffering from not using the nutrients it gets. Sickness from lack of nutrition isn't a vitamin deficiency, it is starvation.

Some studies have indicated that heavy exercise may increase the need for B-complex vitamins (important in metabolizing fats and carbohydrates), vitamin C (contributes to the oxygen-carrying capacity of the blood and the manufacture of collagen to repair injuries), and vitamin E (an antioxidant that may help increase endurance). A lot of athletes take supplements of these and other vitamins. But heavy exercise also automatically boosts appetite to increase caloric intake, and as these vitamins—as well as all the others—are readily available in a balanced, normal diet, the increased intake of food alone should supply the required additional vitamins.

Mineral needs should likewise be taken care of by a normal diet. Minerals control the heartbeat and the contraction of all the other muscles, help conduct nerve impulses, and regulate body fluids. Athletic effort depletes mineral supplies. Athletes use up potassium more rapidly than the rest of us do, for example, in part because of the elevated body temperatures they endure. "Even in frigid temperatures," says Dr. Gabe Mirkin in *The Sportsmedicine Book* (Little, Brown, Boston, 1978), "every muscle that is being exercised produces heat. To keep from overheating, the muscle releases potassium into the bloodstream. This widens the blood vessels, increases the blood flow, and carries heat away from the muscle. The potassium is excreted from the body via sweat and urine. Thus an athlete must constantly be on guard to replenish his potassium supply." (A good replacement source: bananas.) Similarly, in the first couple of weeks of intensive training some athletes show a temporary iron deficiency, often referred to as "sports anemia." However, the recommendation is not to load up on mineral supplements, but to make sure that the diet contains the fresh fruits and vegetables, milk, eggs, meat, poultry, and fish that will provide the minerals in natural balance with the other dietary needs.

* * *

The muscles' main source of energy, glucose, is stored as glycogen in the liver and the muscles. It is possible to supersaturate these storage depots—increasing the glycogen supply and thus the endurance for any kind of prolonged heavy work—through "carbohydrate loading." This is the only known athletic dietary fiddling that actually improves performance. (Plenty of dietary fiddles will work in the other direction.)

It is not a pleasant process. The athlete begins preparing a full week before time for the athletic test. He or she first depletes the glycogen supply as completely as possible, making the system "hungry" for glycogen. The athlete goes onto a diet high in protein and fat, with little if any carbohydrate, while exercising virtually to exhaustion over three days.* The depletion process is rather like squeezing out a sponge in order that it may then absorb more water —the sponge in this case being the muscles and the liver. Glycogen molecules are literally consumed out of the specific muscle groups used in the depletion exercise. To ensure this, the task must consist of the same form of work the athlete will be doing in the event to come—running, cycling, rowing, or whatever. Most athletes find the depletion phase a murderous regimen, "highlighted" by fatigue, nervousness, severe depression, perhaps even a little nausea now and then.

* Bill Fink comments: "It should be pointed out that the overall advantage of these first three days of carbohydrate starvation is debated. It may not be worth the trouble. What is agreed upon is the bout of depletion exercise. The 'classic' procedure is as described, but our lab is inclined to modify that. Also, heavy exercise during depletion is not usually scheduled for each of the three days. Regimens vary but usually call for a long bout of exercise on the first day, and sometimes again on the third day."

Once depletion is accomplished, the athlete goes to light workouts and goes onto a high carbohydrate diet for the three days remaining before the event, loading up on pasta, pancakes, bread, sweets. Most athletes don't mind this phase of the regimen at all. The carbohydrate loading is continued right up through the pre-event meal, which should have little protein and fats that might slow the emptying of the stomach. The athlete is aiming for a pre-event meal that clears the stomach and upper bowel in the three to six hours remaining before competition. Pre-event tension can play hob with this plan. There is a marked decrease in blood flow to and from the stomach, and gastric juice production may be affected. Weird food preferences and strange cravings may surface. The athlete often becomes briefly, unaccountably ill. These "butterflies" may be purely psychological in origin, but that doesn't mean they are not batting their wings, in the form of gastric upset, against the stomach walls.

Carbohydrate loading won't work well for any event that takes less than about two hours of continuous energy output—although there will probably be some benefit, even in shorter events, from the ready energy supply in the muscles. The miseries of the depletion stage aren't the only drawbacks to the process. The body puts up three grams of water for every gram of glycogen, so there's a measurable weight gain. (It's sufficient to serve as a means of monitoring the loading process, says Dave Costill. If you haven't picked up from one to three pounds over your training weight by the morning of your event, you haven't picked up much glycogen.) The extra weight and fluids can cause an initial feeling of loginess, of muscle stiffness, at the start of exercise. Carbohydrate loading exaggerates the already startling weight losses that some athletes undergo during their events, by starting them out at artificially elevated weights.

Boxing, a sport in which weight limits are very carefully observed, has been the scene of some drastic abuses of this phenomenon. A well-trained fighter often finds himself forced to sweat off a few pounds to make weight just before a fight. He does it by "drying out" —by exercising hard, he dumps off three grams of water each time he uses up one gram of glycogen. (The water is exhaled as vapor as well as sweated off through the body pores.) The process leaves him "wrung out"—as well it might, since it burns away most of the carefully accumulated energy from the training period. "Drying out," being "wrung out"—the sponge metaphor again—are part of the language, familiar states to experienced fighters. All the old pugs know, experientially, just how this mechanism works, without having the chemistry spelled out. But knowing the chemistry might help a trainer keep in mind the energy loss his fighter will suffer if he brings him in overweight. Wrestlers have the same problem. Weigh-ins held the day before a fight don't give the fighter time enough to restore his glycogen supplies. A three-day restoration period might leave both combatants better able to muster maximum effort at fight time.

Sometimes the drying-out is much too drastic. A couple of years ago a promising young light heavyweight was found dead in a sauna in Denmark. He was trying to sweat off one and a half more pounds to make his weight for the Danish championships.

*　　*　　*

"I spent a week at a San Francisco Forty-Niner football training camp a few years back," says Dave Costill, "and I was appalled. They were feeding these guys almost no carbohydrates, and working their butts off. The athletes would load up with protein, and by the third day of heavy workouts they were on their rears. They'd depleted all the glycogen from their muscles, and there was no chance of their catching up again on that kind of work load.

"I told them it was silly to put a million-dollar athlete out there and then never see him perform at his best. You'll let him go and somebody else will pick him up and make a superstar out of him. The least you could do is make sure the athlete is functioning at his optimum level when you try to evaluate him. I told them they just had to get more carbohydrates onto the training table.

"The funny thing was, one trainer told me later they'd tried to change the training table diet, but the athletes themselves resisted it. The athletes have this ingrained belief that they have to have steak for breakfast, lunch, and dinner. It's criminal."

*　　*　　*

Costill has done extensive lab work with glycogen loading. For one project, for example, he collected muscle biopsies from glycogen-loaded and glycogen-unloaded tissue, so the actual glycogen molecules within the muscle fiber could be counted. Thus he is intimately familiar with the process on a scientific basis. He's also intimately familiar with it as a practicing marathoner—one who doesn't particularly care for the unpleasantness of the depletion stage. His research indicates that may be avoided; the athlete may be able to raise glycogen levels near enough to maximum simply by going on a long "depletion run," then eating a high carbohydrate diet and cutting back to a light training schedule two or three days before an event. The depletion phase, in this view, is too severe a strain, too disruptive of quality training, to gain too small an additional increment of glycogen loading.

Everyone is different, Costill assures me, and biopsies he's done on himself have convinced him that he personally must taper off training and eat more carbohydrates for five to seven days before an event to maximize his own glycogen stores. But other athletes will require different schedules. In general, Costill feels that the depletion stage can virtually be dispensed with among athletes who normally train very hard and who maintain high levels of glycogen. Other researchers warn that the full depletion/loading cycle should be undertaken no more than two or three times a year.*

Costill's work (examined in more detail in Chapter 11) has uncovered another dietary aspect of energy production. This one has stirred up considerable controversy, so much so that Costill sometimes wishes he'd never gotten into it. It has long been understood that fat could be used to produce energy, but only at low levels of metabolism. Costill proved that there is a way to keep the system burning fat for energy at much higher levels of output—and thus to delay glycogen consumption. The key is to make enough fat available to the muscle to keep it from switching over to glycogen consumption. To do so, the fat must be in the usable form of *free fatty acids;* the agent that can make this possible is caffeine.

Several other researchers, including sports physiologists in Eastern Bloc nations, have been experimenting with caffeine for some time —but without widespread dissemination of their results. (Eighteen

---

* Researchers in the highly specialized field of high-altitude medicine have long warned mountaineers against climbing above 8000 meters—roughly 26,000 feet, which is possible only in the Himalayas—more than once or twice a year, even with supplementary oxygen. Physiologists have traditionally warned marathoners not to run more than one or two of their races a year. Some physiological connection might therefore be inferred between the wear and tear on the body in climbing above 8000 meters and in running twenty-six miles at a racing pace. But in recent years top marathoners are racing every couple of months, and putting in 120 to 140 miles of training per week in between, with no apparent ill effect. And after putting in a great deal of ultrahigh-altitude training, a couple of mountaineers recently climbed 29,000-foot Mt. Everest without supplementary oxygen. The possibilities keep expanding.

months before Costill's caffeine research was picked up by the popular press, one American exercise physiologist told me, almost with a wink and a leer, "We think we may be onto something with caffeine —but please don't say anything about it in print.") When Costill's results were published, one segment of sports research immediately accused him of advocating the doping of athletes. Another segment of the same group just started drinking a lot of coffee before the start of the marathons they were entering.

The object of Costill's search was to find some additional way, beyond carbohydrate loading, to delay glycogen depletion during extended bouts of exercise. To move "the wall" closer, in effect, to the finish line. As Costill explained the mechanism in *Runner's World:*

"The body is much like an automobile with two gasoline tanks, capable of running on either high-octane fuel (glycogen) or regular (free fatty acids). The challenge to researchers has been to facilitate and then control the switch regulating input from glycogen and free fatty acids so that the 'regular' fuel can be used in longer-distance runs when the 'high-octane' isn't available in adequate supply."

Caffeine can control that switch. "The explanation for . . . enhanced performance following the caffeine is rather complex," Costill went on, "but is certainly directly related to a greater burning of fat. . . . Without the use of caffeine, our subjects obtained 22 percent of their energy from fat. After the caffeine drink fat contributed almost 40 percent of the total energy demands of the exercise."*

The dosage that produced these results was 4 to 5 milligrams of caffeine per kilogram of body weight, an hour before the onset of heavy exercise. For most athletes that is the equivalent of about two cups of black, unsweetened coffee. In Costill's tests this dosage increased by as much as 19 percent the length of time an athlete could exercise before exhaustion set in. Caffeine ingested two hours before exercise increased capacity for physical work by about 7 percent. Clearly, these are significant increments for competitive endurance events.

(*Burns away fat!* The phrase leaps out of the ad copy for every mail-order diet pill on the market. Dieters' frustration: it doesn't quite work that way. No matter how significant the burning of free fatty acids might be for the production of energy, as far as fat removal is

---

* "Coffee Makes Longer Easier," *Runner's World*, July, 1978.

concerned—as in spare-tire midriffs and flabby thighs—it's an inconsequential process. "You'd have to do the exercise and starve yourself at the same time to do that," Costill says. "But that doesn't mean there might not already be some caffeine in those diet pills anyway. Caffeine is a nervous system stimulant. It has some of the same basic effects, when taken in proper dosages, as amphetamines.")

There are several caveats about the use of caffeine for any purposes, athletic or otherwise. There are wide variations in individual sensitivity to it. Even if an athlete is not hypersensitive to caffeine, an overdosage with it will result in no improvement in performance and there may be some deleterious effect. Coffee is a diuretic, which can be a problem—particularly in hot weather, when dehydration is always a serious concern. Well-trained athletes already release considerable stores of free fatty acids into their blood; they won't realize as much improvement in their performance as the underconditioned athlete. And caffeine *is* a stimulant, a fact that makes some people nervous without even ingesting any coffee.

This is a difficult subject for Dave Costill. I talked to him about the time the controversy was beginning to stir. "I wish I'd never written about coffee," he said then. "I don't mean I'm backing down from the published results. The figures are valid. But after I wrote the piece in *Runner's World* and saw the turmoil it caused, I wished I hadn't. People seem to think I was advocating doping or something. That's the last thing in the world I'd ever be interested in.

"It's silly. Everyone reacts as if it's something new, but my God, they were doing it in the 1940s in the army. Soldiers were encouraged to drink coffee for long marches. All I meant to do was point out that while working on mechanisms for burning fat, we'd found that caffeine helped you burn free fatty acids for fuel."

Costill published a more formal recantation in *The Physician and Sportsmedicine* in January of 1979:

". . . I never anticipated that my comments would be interpreted as an advocation of drugging among athletes, and I feel that I used poor judgment in presenting our research findings in a manner that seemed to endorse the use of a stimulant (caffeine) to enhance performance. Obviously my error was not in doing the research on caffeine; it was in failing to face the ethical issues involved in the application of our findings to sports. It was never my intention to present sports physiology as a method to artificially alter one's physical capabilities."

Still, as Costill said, it's silly. Caffeine has been banned in international competition in the past, but isn't at present because it is, after all, a constituent of several very popular foodstuffs. Not even the ghost of Avery Brundage can make athletes stop drinking coffee, tea, and Coca-Cola, just for starters. We've been using coffee specifically as a pick-me-up—a nerve stimulant—for centuries; all Dave Costill did was study some additional effects. The entire controversy tells us more about the hypersensitivity of scientists on the subject of drugs than it does about the efficacy or dangers of caffeine. We'll get back to this subject in Chapter 13.

Meanwhile, the caffeine is out of the bag, so to speak, and Costill's or anyone else's disavowals aren't likely to steer endurance athletes away from the stuff. Dr. Gabe Mirkin once polled over a hundred top-level runners with the question, "If I could give you a pill that would make you an Olympic champion—and also kill you in a year —would you take it?" Over half of his respondents said they'd take the pill.

*   *   *

I suspect there's more mischief done, maybe even more public danger, from the nonsense disseminated about carbohydrate loading than from anything that's been said about caffeine. The earliest exposures were the worst. When ABC Sports was looking for a way to hype their marathon coverage during the Montreal Olympics, they turned Erich Segal loose on the subject. Segal put a discomfited Frank Shorter on camera—the 1972 Olympic marathon winner and our best hope in 1976. Shorter was seated at a table loaded mostly, it appeared, with sugar. I gathered that he assumed the footage was being shot mostly to demonstrate what carbohydrates are, and that runners eat them. But all Segal could talk about was these amazing quantities of food. The implication was that Shorter would bolt down several stacks of pancakes, some slices of cake, half a dozen or so chocolate bars, and then zip out the door and win the marathon. Carbohydrate "loading" seemed to refer to massive gluttony. For months afterward I caught myself rationalizing that extra bowl of ice cream slathered in butterscotch sauce with the code words, "gotta get my carbohydrates." But then perhaps I am just suggestible. Anyway, carbohydrate loading refers to the proportions of carbohydrate, protein, and fat in the diet, not to the quantities. Overeating before competition is asking for trouble. Overeating is asking for trouble.

* * *

There's one other component of the athletic diet that needs mentioning, and as it happens, Dave Costill has also done much of the most valuable research about this one. The component is water. The simple truth is that the athlete needs much more fluid intake than our tired old athletic traditions ever recognized. When I played high school football in the late 1940s, in Texas, in August and September, we were forbidden any water on the practice field; during games we were to rinse our mouths and spit. By the mid-1950s these practices were recognized as a form of potential manslaughter, and the estimates of fluid requirements for athletes have rapidly been revised upward ever since.* It is now felt that a moderately active young person expending 3000 calories a day needs three quarts of water to go with the calories; a larger, more active athlete—an interior lineman in football, for example—may need two or three times that much. Dehydration is hazardous to the athlete's health, and may be the most significant limiting factor to performance as well. Dr. Mirkin explains why:

"Water is the main component of cells, urine, sweat, and blood. When you are dehydrated, your cells become dehydrated and chemical reactions in the cells are impaired. The cells can't build tissue and can't utilize energy efficiently. You don't produce urine, and consequently toxic products build up in your bloodstream. You don't sweat, so your temperature rises. Your blood volume decreases and you have less blood to transport oxygen and nutrients through your body. The result is that your muscles become weak and you become tired." †

Costill's research, keyed to the intense demands of distance run-

---

* And yet, and yet—a study published in late 1979 in *The Physician and Sportsmedicine* surveyed 75 coaches and trainers. Nineteen percent allowed only one water break during practice sessions and athletic contests, 7 percent provided water only in hot weather, and another 2.5 percent still provided *no* water to their charges during practice sessions or events. ("Diet, Fitness, and Athletic Performance," by Angelo Bentivegna, E. James Kelley, and Alexander Kalenak, October, 1979.)

† *The Sportsmedicine Book*, Little, Brown, Boston, 1978.

ning, indicates that the temperature rise itself represents the greatest danger. Sweat losses of up to 8 percent of body weight are not unheard of in a marathon. After a loss of 3 percent of body weight, rectal temperatures start to rise. Temperatures in the body core of over 105°F have been recorded in marathoners, even when competing in cool weather. It is almost impossible to drink enough fluids to offset the losses incurred in a marathon—but every little bit ingested helps counteract the drastic effects.

The subject is serious enough that the American College of Sports Medicine has issued a position paper, prepared by Costill, that sets guidelines for preventing heat injuries during distance running. There are suggested limits for the ambient temperature and humidity in which it can be considered safe to hold a distance event. The college recommends that runners be encouraged to drink from 13 to 17 ounces of fluid 15 minutes before the competition starts, and that watering stations be set up every 2 to 2.5 miles in races of 10 miles or more. (Until recently international regulations actually *forbade* a watering station within the first 10 kilometers—6.2 miles—of the start of a race, a ruling that in hot weather could lead to heat-exhaustion deaths.) The college also charges race organizers with the responsibility of providing plenty of fluids at regular intervals throughout the race, and even spells out a formula for sugar and electrolyte content in those fluids: "less than 2.5g glucose per 100 ml of water and less than 10 mEq sodium and 5 mEq potassium per liter of solution." Race officials are proposed to watch competitors for signs of heat distress and to reserve the right to stop any runner exhibiting signs of heat stroke or heat exhaustion.

The careful competitor will consider the problems of fluid replacement a little more deeply. For maximum stomach emptying—which is the limiting factor in fluid replacement during heavy exercise—the fluid supplied should have the above standard for glucose, or *less*. It should also be cold—about 40°F. In cold weather the glucose content might be increased slightly; during hot weather, when the athlete needs water replacement more urgently than carbohydrate supplementation, the glucose should be cut back. It takes a minimum of 15 to 20 minutes for the glucose to get out of the stomach and into the system anyway.

Electrolytes seem to have come and gone as what might be considered a scientific fad. They have been added to athletic drinks with the intention of quick replacement of the minerals lost during heavy exercise, to restore ion balance in the cells and ensure proper transmission of neural signals. They were originally touted as "scientific" thirst quenchers, since it was assumed they allowed quicker rehydration of depleted cells. There are even electrolytic chewing gums on the market, alleged to quench thirst or prevent its occurrence. (For very heavy exercise, that's not too good an idea. If you wait until you feel thirsty before you start trying to replace fluid losses from exercise, you're already three to five glasses of water down, too far behind to catch up without stopping exercise. So artificially allaying thirst, if it worked, could be dangerous.)

The development of electrolytic replacement fluids was extremely valuable, if not quite in the way expected. After the initial hoopla, a major licensee for marketing one of the athletic drinks asked Costill's lab to find out what was really happening with their products and the human body. Costill found that the problem is not to jazz up the fluids that the athlete ingests, but to find ways to speed up the absorption of those fluids from the stomach—and the best way to do that is generally to reduce, rather than increase, the electrolytic *or* carbohydrate content of the replacement fluid. The controlling factor, again, is the rate of emptying of the stomach.

Athletes sometimes find, for example, that under extreme conditions the sweet, or salty, or otherwise jazzed-up replacement fluids may be nauseating, difficult to get or keep down. A lot of experimentation with mixtures still goes on, usually in the direction of heavy dilution of commercial mixtures. Some hardy souls still drink tea, beer, or decarbonated Coca-Cola during the course of heavy exercise, but the practice says more about individual differences—some would say perversion—than it does about scientific training methods. Besides which, Costill's research also carefully measured all the minerals and salts removed from the body during heavy exercise, and found that a normal diet will more than replace the losses, will replace them in the proper balance, and will replace them just about as fast as they can be replaced with the commercial products. Nothing, it turns out, works all that much better than plenty of water and a balanced diet. The sponsoring manufacturer, who had been supportive and totally noninterfering throughout the project, took the news with good grace, Costill says. The products are still on the market, and athletes continue to use them.

The great value of the development of electrolytic replacement fluids came in the selling job they did with coaches. A lot of coaches, far removed from the research centers, were still not getting the message about the drastic and urgent necessity of replacing fluid losses on the playing field. The appearance of Gatorade, Gookinaid E.R.G., Body Punch, and the like on the market seemed finally to convince coaches—*most* coaches—that it was "scientifically" acceptable to let the kids have a drink. In that sense the commercial products probably save a lot of lives—not because of the space-age adjuncts they add to fluid intake, but because they also contain a lot of good water.

* * *

It shouldn't be surprising that the old pugs have always known about sweating off weight and the resulting energy loss, the "wrung-out" feeling. Or that science is now analyzing the mechanism, coming up with the numbers, that confirm what the old pugs have always, experientially, known.

A better example is the use of ice on sports injuries. That's been an established practice for decades now: when an athlete gets hurt, the trainer immediately slaps an ice bag on the injury to keep swelling down. Big-time athletic organizations, as in college and professional football, keep ice chests on the sidelines during the game, to make sure plenty of ice is always at hand.

I recently ran across a brief description of a medical paper that gave half a dozen other reasons for applying ice to athletic injuries, in addition to holding down swelling. This cold therapy reduces pain by slowing nerve conduction in the pain effectors, reduces muscle spasm by raising the threshold of muscle excitability, and so on. That's half a dozen additional very specific, very complex, highly scientific medical reasons for the trainer to apply ice to an injury site.

The old pugs, the experienced trainers, may take gleeful pleasure out of this, since it was already clearly established that the trainer was going to put the ice bag on the injury anyway. The trainer doesn't need the other six reasons—and may very well resist them as too complicated to think about. There is a point of view that says that all of this scientific research into athletics is repetitive nonsense, that basically we've known for two thousand years how the athletic body works, what it needs, what helps and what hurts. All the men in white coats do is come up with additional reasons for doing what we've always done. Pure water works better than electrolytic gizmos; the way you win is by training harder, trying harder, putting forth more effort than the other guy.

It is a point the scientists ruefully acknowledge: it is too easy to become enamored of the scientific approach, to expect the miracle pill that guarantees world records. (And scientific distractions and misinterpretations can indeed get in the way of training harder.)

But this doesn't mean there's no point in coming up with the other six reasons for applying ice. One of those six might provide a change of emphasis, a different understanding of the mechanisms of injury and healing that could shorten recovery time, diminish the severity of injury, reduce pain. Any of the six could open up new areas of improvement in athletic performance. To resist the proliferation of information about athletic processes is to stop looking for an edge. Old pugs to the contrary notwithstanding, it isn't about to happen.

Book II:
Schemes

CHAPTER 10
Slings & Levers

There is a bricked-up water tower on the Penn State campus which has been converted into a laboratory—a strange building, hexagonal in floor plan, with a peculiar domed top. Medieval-looking. It stirs fantasies: it is just the place to find a mad scientist practicing black magic. Go inside, however, and all is cheery bustle, computers clacking and young graduate students whirling from one printout to another. There is all manner of bizarre mechanical equipment stacked around the periphery, but most of the action centers around computer terminals—which is the way science does its work these days.

The magic we're talking about is not black, it is biomechanical, and one of the (perfectly sane) scientists who practice it best is Peter R. Cavanagh, Ph.D., a former racing cyclist, a marathon runner, a thirty-two-year-old Englishman seven years in the United States. In that time Cavanagh has helped make Penn State's name synonymous with the best work being done in this country in the curious discipline of biomechanics. He's done it by combining, among other things, a proper scientist's stringently conservative resistance to overinterpretation of his findings, with the audacity to adapt the best of modern technology—as in computer-produced animated films (cartoons, really, although there's nothing funny about them)—to make understandable to the lay person the sometimes abstruse findings of his research.

Biomechanics is an outgrowth of kinesiology, the study of motion; at one time it was only a small and rather mechanistic branch of that field of study. But owing to a technological boost from work with World War II amputees (and subsequent added impetus from NASA space programs), biomechanics became so fruitful an area of study that it has eclipsed its parent discipline. References to kinesiology have begun to have the ring of old-fogeyism.

Biomechanics is "the science which investigates the effects of internal and external forces upon living bodies," according to Richard C. Nelson, Ph.D., director of the Penn State lab. In Peter Cavanagh's first book, *The Physiology and Biomechanics of Cycling,** he expands that definition: it is "the use of objective techniques to analyze patterns of body movement, the timing of body movements, and the forces which create or result from movement." In short, it is the mechanics of animate structures.

Biomechanics' first contribution will always be in medicine, in areas such as orthopedics, for which it can be a valuable adjunct, for example, in the reconstruction and rehabilitation of skeletal injuries. But the possibilities for its application in sports are very large. Cavanagh's cycling book shows how. For example, in an attempt to understand better the muscle actions during pedaling, Cavanagh and his co-workers used electromyography—a technique for measuring the electrical activity of muscular contractions. The data they got, however, were fishy. Electrodes mounted on the major leg muscles used in pedaling a static bike showed patterns of activity that didn't make much sense. To pin down the anomalies, Cavanagh and crew added force gauges to the pedals themselves, looking for a more accurate measurement of effort than electromyography could give. (Electromyography, says Cavanagh, is a technique with serious limitations.)

What they discovered was that cyclists are almost whimsical about when and how they apply force to the pedals. In the extreme case a cyclist may do 40 percent more work with one leg than with the other, then—after 50 strokes, or 5 minutes, or an hour of pedaling—change the dominant leg, switching over and doing more work with the rested leg. Cyclists undoubtedly knew something of this, at

* Irvin E. Faria and Peter R. Cavanagh, American College of Sports Medicine Series, John Wiley & Sons, New York, 1978.

least on a subconscious level, but they could hardly have been comfortable with it. Logic told them that the goal must be a smooth, even, equally shared work load, leg to leg. (Smoothness is not to be construed from these results to be *bad*, says Cavanagh, cautiously. The experiment only showed that average cyclists are at times asymmetrical in their application of power.)

Cyclists are also coached in "ankling"—working to achieve certain advantageous angles of the foot on the pedal at different parts of the stroke, in order to generate maximum force. Cavanagh's studies showed that although this may be a nice theoretical idea, the angles prescribed bear little resemblance to the angles achieved when even the best cyclists actually push the pedals. There is much less ankling done in cycling than coaches had always thought. It isn't clear that more ankling would produce better results.

These discoveries demonstrate an important way that biomechanical analysis contributes to the understanding of sports techniques. Because the feet of a racing cyclist are strapped to the pedals, the legs move in a balanced, even manner and appear to exert equal force. There is no way without force gauges on the pedals to ascertain how unbalanced the application of force to the pedals normally is.

The case with ankling isn't quite as clear. Cavanagh says a careful eye should have been able to see that there was a gross discrepancy between what was being suggested in the literature for an ankling pattern and what champion cyclists were actually doing. Nonetheless it was by means of biomechanical analysis that the anomaly was picked up. And it appears, therefore, that some counterproductive coaching has been inflicted on aspiring athletes.

(New information does not instantly cure counterproductive coaching, in any sport. "If you combine the instrumentation we have," Peter Cavanagh says of the cycling studies, "with the computer programs we have developed, we have one of the most powerful techniques in the world for studying cyclists as they practice their sport. And what do I get when I approach the U.S. coaches about this? No response. Should I contact the Soviet Union about all this available data and technique? It's all just sitting on the shelf in our labs. . . .")

A similar case has to do with the start of swimming races. By analysis of high-speed film, biomechanists had shown that the "grab" start—in which the swimmer grips the starting block with hands as well as feet, in a lower crouch than the conventional, arm-swinging start—is about a tenth of a second faster over the first twelve feet of a race. This was the initial biomechanical contribution to the problem, and as a result the grab start became quite popular in competitive swimming. But coaches weren't sure how to coach it, whether it fit every racer's personal style, what was actually going on in the grab start. Should the swimmer stay tense or loose, pull hard with the arms, or what? No one was sure; no one knew quite how or where the tenth of a second was gained.

Penn State biomechanists used force gauges to measure what forces were being generated by the hands as well as the feet on the starting block. They determined that the grab-starters should build up prerelease tension in their legs by pulling on the starting blocks with their hands, in effect cocking the legs like the coiled spring in a jack-in-the-box. All else being equal, the grab-starters will then be faster from the sound of the gun until the feet actually leave the starting block. Beyond that—from the starting block to the surface of the water—old and new starting techniques turn out to be just about equal.

The improvement is tiny, but again, winning sports performances are made up of tiny advantages taken, minuscule bits of time or distance gained on one's competitors. (As in Valery Borzov's hundredths of a second.) In the case of the grab start the improvement is real, concrete, demonstrable—and the technique is well on its way to universal adoption. In the case of the cycling discoveries, the significance may not yet be clear, and the coaches are not sure how to turn the new information to the racer's advantage. ("In fact," says Cavanagh, "some coaches are not even sure whether they want to acknowledge our existence at the moment.")

Biomechanics has a way of coming up with answers to questions that haven't been asked, which can indeed sow confusion in sports. There's a larger danger, however, about which Peter Cavanagh takes a gravely cautionary stance. There is a tendency in biomechanics to leap to wrong answers, to see answers where there are no answers at all. If the biomechanist doesn't state the problem correctly, what seem to be valuable revelations may be nothing more than hunches, misperceptions, which can do more harm than good to sports techniques. The study of biomechanics requires great procedural delicacy, and it does not always get it. It is being touted as a miracle-maker for sports performance, but much too often its application is so superficial as to produce only misleading results.

* * *

The seductiveness of the biomechanical approach to understanding sports movement is irresistible. Its clarifying reductionism is what leads me to the Sweet Spot Theory, of course. Once one begins to comprehend human movement in terms of levers and arcs, the necessity, in sports, for *good* arcs—for true trajectories, accurate timings, impeccable meetings of subject and object—becomes apparent. It is inescapable.

I find myself thinking of athletic movements in two categories. There are those movements that anyone can do—running, jumping, striking with an implement—but which the athlete learns to do much better than the nonathlete. ("Nonathlete" is a dubious category, but let it stand for now.) There are also those athletic movements that not everyone can do, that only the athlete learns to do, and only after considerable effort. Then the superior athlete goes on to do these extremely difficult things—as in the outer reaches of gymnastics and diving—with grace and beauty.

Watching Baryshnikov or Julius Erving, one sees impossible moves made easy. Those moves must be extremely difficult, one thinks, and it is only Baryshnikov's genius that makes them look so effortless; even he must be straining to pull them off. Except that he couldn't do them that way if they were not in fact easy—easy for a Baryshnikov, easy after he has invested his massive skills in acquiring them. For him the strain must be only to expand the moves, to perfect, to amplify.

At age sixteen, in 1948, I was a would-be competition springboard diver. The one dive that symbolically represented the threshold into competition was what we then called a periwinkle: one-and-a-half forward somersaults with one full twist. (Nowadays they do the same dive but add two more full twists.) All serious divers did the periwinkle (rather easily); very few Sunday afternoon show-offs did. My ambition was to graduate from the Sunday afternoon show-off category into seriousness.

The dive gave me endless grief. For whatever psychological or motor-learning complexities, I couldn't seem to learn it. The movement eluded me; it was too difficult. I spent a frustrating several weeks doing various complicated versions of the belly-flop. When you miss a dive you hurt something—back, front, legs, testicles, whatever. I bruised a lot that summer.

Then in one unaccountable moment the breakthrough came; I "got it"—discovered how to perform the motion I'd been struggling with—and acquired the dive. What had been too difficult a moment before, instantly became almost uncomfortably easy. Thereafter it was possible to work on form, on performing the motion more clearly and cleanly.

The changeover was shocking in its suddenness. I'd been repeating an error, and all it took was to omit the error to make the dive fall into place. I kept climbing back up and doing it over and over again, unable quite to believe I had it. Every time it worked, I was surprised anew. The suspicious ease of the movement—so unlike what I'd imagined the dive to require—was almost more than I could take in. This difficult dive that was going to elevate my stature as a diver was suddenly robbed of its difficulty. I had a Groucho Marxist reaction: once they let me into that club, I was disappointed that the admission requirements were so low.

I've since gone through similar learning processes with parallel ski turns and various other athletic movements—experiencing each time the wonderful moment when the difficult suddenly becomes easy. There's still a shock, each time, but increasingly it is the shock of recognition. It will never be my fortune to practice any physical act at Baryshnikovian levels, but I treasure the tiny glimpses I've had of what is involved in these learning experiences. Still, when I watch Baryshnikov, I can't believe that the learning of any movement is ever as difficult for him—with those gifts—as that bloody periwinkle was for me.

*   *   *

When I arrived at the Penn State biomechanics lab, Peter Cavanagh and Keith Williams, an associate pursuing his doctorate with Cavanagh, were in the frantic closing stages of a major project. They were putting in all-night work sessions in the attempt to extract from over ten million pieces of computer information, gathered over the previous several months, the material that could be put into comprehensible form for a lay person. The subject was the golf shoe and the forces at work therein. Not too surprisingly, nobody had ever thought to ask what really goes on in a golf shoe during a golfer's swing.

Cavanagh's procedure for ascertaining these forces is a model for biomechanical investigation in almost any direction. Several subject golfers were asked to drive golf balls for science. In the lab where they were to perform, four separate movie cameras were aimed at a single target area, the tee from which the golf shots were to be made. The cameras were aligned with the help of an elaborate precision gridwork so that movements anywhere within the target area could be measured to within a fraction of a millimeter. The golf shoes—and in a few cases, the bare feet—of the golfers were marked with multiple reference points which would show clearly on the film.

The subjects were filmed driving with irons as well as woods. Film of their lower legs and feet, shod and unshod, made it possible to track with maximum precision every component of motion in the lower extremities. The golfers were also standing on force plates which measured the amount and direction of forces generated between shoe and ground while they swung.

The filmed information was coordinated with the force plate data and fed into computers, which cranked the information back out in the form of graphic representations of golf shoes, frozen at intervals of two-hundredths of a second, throughout the golf swing. Additional graphics traced the movement of the center of pressure underneath the shoe and, with large colored arrows leading out from the edges of the sole (in the graphic representation), showed the amount and direction of shear forces working within the shoe. Finally, a head-on, full-length, composite stick figure of a golfer going through his swing was also produced by the computer, tracking the motion from start to finish at the same two-hundredth of a second intervals.

Put together into a single piece of animated film, all this information gives a remarkable set of images. A stick figure goes through a composite golf swing, as a continuing reference to where the clubhead, arms, and upper body are positioned in relation to the feet. Beside this figure there is a see-through, three-dimensional picture of a golf shoe moving gracefully through the same swing simultaneously. The right shoe rolls up on one side of its sole for the backswing, cramps at the toe as the golfer raises the heel; the left drags slightly at the toe during the follow-through, and so forth. At the same time, brightly colored force-arrows swirl about the perimeter of the sole, showing where and in which directions the force is being applied. Always with the little stick figure to relate foot position to golf swing at any moment in the swing.

It is a breathtaking piece of film, even at the early and incomplete stage at which I saw it. I am not a golfer, but I ski; my immediate reaction to the film was to wish for a similar production showing the forces at work in a ski boot during a turn. If only we could simply dial up such film footage, instead of having to go through the thousands of hours of the computer equivalent of hand labor required to get the data together. The technology to do so is not yet available, but don't bet that it can't be developed.

This particular research was done on a grant from the Charles A. Eaton Company, makers of the Etonic golf shoe, and will likely go toward designing shoes that for the first time will positively aid the golfer in his game. It was immediately apparent that the film would be as valuable as a teaching aid as it is for product research. This sort of instructional backup should help a good teacher work wonders in teaching the golf swing to neophytes. I'd think that the manufacturers of other kinds of sports equipment may soon be applying similar techniques not only to assist in the design of new equipment, but also to help instructors teach their customers how to enjoy the equipment more by performing better with it.

The computer is able to produce the little animated stick figure so clearly because of the Sweet Spot Theory. That is, for purposes of computer analysis the human figure is reduced to levers, torque arms, fulcrum points, crack-the-whip segments of linked motion. These can be reproduced clearly and simplistically by the computer to demonstrate every bit of motion that the figure goes through. Such a stick figure doesn't tell you anything about how muscles work, what efforts must be made to control extraneous motion, how much force must be used at which point to accomplish the motion. But it does show you the motion that results, and the relationship of body parts at every point in the motion, which can be extremely valuable in the analysis of sports techniques.

Of course, my Sweet Spot Theory develops out of biomechanics, rather than the other way around, and I couldn't make these small jokes about it if the biomechanists had not analyzed human movement in these terms for years. In one sense I am only putting into prose the somewhat mathematical body of work they have already produced. There is a great deal more to sports motion than my theory acknowledges, of course. For a single example, deceleration—how, when, and where you *stop* a given segment of motion, how the clamping of brakes on a motion multiplies the momentum that is transferred to the next segment—can be much more important for an athletic movement than merely accumulating acceleration.

As in the slap-shot in hockey: how, coaches wondered, do some wiry little skaters shoot the puck so much harder than their burly teammates? The slap-shot artist, it turns out, hits the ice, hard, with the blade of the hockey stick just before it reaches the puck. This stops the blade and lets the shooter build up much more force behind the stick than he could by merely swinging through the puck. As with the grab start in swimming, the arms, hands, and shoulders are in effect cocked for action. What's more, the hockey stick is bent, and therefore stores energy, just like the bow in archery. The stick is then released from the ice with greatly multiplied momentum, and it fires the puck with immense force. This is all ancient knowledge now in hockey, but it took biomechanical analysis to show how it happened, to make the slap-shot truly coachable.

The man who usually gets credit for the slap-shot findings is Gideon Ariel, Ph.D., head of a firm called Computerized Biomechanical Analysis, in Amherst, Massachusetts. Ariel has done more to promote these analytical techniques than anyone else in the field. Among other things, he has made a series of predictions in the popular press about ultimate performances in track and field: a 9.6-second hundred-meter dash, an 8'11" high jump, a 100-foot shot put. Ariel analyzed films of world record performances, computed the forces involved in each segment of those performances, and then extrapolated the forces onto biomechanically ideal athletic techniques, physical bodies, reaction times, and so on. He's also worked with real-world athletes. He told *Sports Illustrated* * that when he advised shot-putter Terry Albritton to quit bending the knee of his forward leg, Albritton quickly set a new world record of 71'8½". He also advised Mac Wilkins to put a new wrinkle in his discus technique; Wilkins says the advice was worth a quick seven feet over his previous personal best, and he eventually improved—on the way to another

* "Gideon Ariel and His Magic Machine," by Kenny Moore, Aug. 22, 1977.

---

world record—by over thirteen feet. Ariel has since been appointed by the U.S. Olympic Committee to the post of Director of Research in Biomechanics and Computer Sciences.

Ariel also uses a digitizer to break down films of athletic performances for his computer, as Cavanagh does. He then applies his own computer programs to determine the biomechanical forces at work throughout the performance. This way he predicts the theoretical advantage that could result from a change in any segment of the motion. "If a hammer thrower's elbow is in the wrong position at a certain time," Ariel says, "I can have the computer move it an inch or two and then recalculate the forces."

Peter Cavanagh is not so sure about this. "Right now," he says, "many seem to think that all you need do is point a ciné camera at a performing athlete, and then you're going to be able to understand the fundamentals of that athlete's movements and tell him what his errors are. That just isn't true. It's like looking at smoke to try to determine what's burning. It's worse than that. What really happens is, you apply a force to the body, the force causes an acceleration, the acceleration causes a change of velocity, and, finally, somewhere down the road, the velocity will cause a displacement of the limb segment. So if you're looking just at the displacement, you're so far away from what causes the movement that you can't really tell much. Look at what we found in cycling. The difference in the forces applied with each leg could never be found by looking at ciné film."

I asked Cavanagh about Bob Beamon's long jump at Mexico City in 1968, when, in what track and field experts have called a "mutation performance," Beamon jumped 29 feet 2½ inches, a full two feet farther than anyone had ever jumped before—and a distance that no one has yet come within a foot of matching since. That performance, I proposed, was surely an instance of an athlete putting together all the sweet spots.

Cavanagh resists my sweet spot terminology, particularly in application to the body: "Beamon was able to produce a combination of optimal motions," he says. "There are maybe a hundred variables that apply, and he must have hit a lot of them in that jump, an awful lot of them. What's more, though, the environmental conditions must've been just right, the psychological conditions, and so on. That's why the problem gets so complex. Who knows whether there are two hundred or five hundred variables in that situation? Beamon's history in the previous month, week, year, somehow had to be just right. Perhaps someone said something to him that morning, or on the runway, that enabled him to hit another variable or two. I don't think that kind of performance can be explained in purely mechanical terms—even though the end result of all those things was that he was able to optimize the mechanical conditions and get them just right. But again, film of Bob Beamon's jump is never going to tell us the answer to this. You just can't redesign peoples' sports techniques on that basis.

"Nevertheless," says Peter Cavanagh with a measured smile, "there is available out there, in any sporting movement, the equivalent of a Bob Beamon long jump. That's one of the things that makes sports such a seductive activity."

*   *   *

It is not too surprising that Cavanagh, a marathoner himself, has done much of his most productive work with the human foot, with running and the running shoe. In fact if he is not directly responsible for the great proliferation of running shoes on the market (roughly 160 different models from 20 manufacturers, last time I counted), he is the force behind the quantum leap upward in quality in those shoes in recent years. A few years back, *Runner's World* magazine wanted to do a special shoe issue, and was looking for a way to judge quality. The magazine commissioned Cavanagh and the Penn State lab to develop testing methods for running shoes. Cavanagh has been expanding that testing program—for what has become an annual shoe issue of the magazine—ever since.

The problems are more complex than one might expect; the foot will not be understood quickly. It is the platform from which most athletic motion is launched. It is a sensor that tells us where we are in relation to gravity and the ground we stand on.* It is the lever we use to propel us into action, to change direction while in action, to brake us when action must be slowed or stopped. For purposes of either motion or stability it is, simply, the major interface between

---

* Cavanagh doesn't entirely agree with my description. I'd told him earlier that I'd once broken my foot. When he saw this depiction of the foot as sensor, he wrote, "Perhaps your broken foot has developed some marvelous accelerometric powers, but I think it is an overstatement to say that the foot will tell us where we are in relation to gravity. Certainly there are many proprioceptive mechanisms in the foot." That's what I meant.

the body and the environment. It is capable of supporting over five times body weight and of launching split-second motions, gross and fine, in an infinite number of directions. That it evolved with twenty-six separate bones and, as running guru Dr. George Sheehan has described it, "four times as many ligaments, and an intricate network of tendons which act as guy-ropes or slings," is as much a tribute to the complexity of its tasks as it is to the manic originality of the evolutionary process.

During a running step the foot first acts as a very flexible sensor, reaching out to find out where the ground is. As the body weight is rolled more firmly onto the foot, during the middle half of the step, the foot functions as a semirigid weight-bearer and an aid to balance. In the last quarter of the step, as the weight goes up onto the toes toward toe-off, the foot becomes a rigid lever to propel the body forward. To go from flexible sensor to rigid lever in every step, the foot must go through some amazing biomechanical complexities. If any of the transitions is mistimed, the likelihood of injury to the foot —or the knee, the hip, the lower back—is greatly increased. The forces at work during foot strike can be three times body weight or more; an hour of running is five thousand steps. For a 150-pound runner that's twenty-five hundred 450-pound blows to the bottom of each foot, the resulting forces then transferred right on up through all those bones, joints, guy-wires, and slings. Any imbalances, structural or functional, will only serve to multiply the forces further. It is the running shoe's job to contain, align, absorb this pounding. Thus the significance of the orthotic shoe insert, helping to make up for both the running shoe's inadequacies and the wearer's misalignments.

Because of Cavanagh's research, good running shoes have changed markedly in recent years. They have acquired heel counters sufficiently well designed to stabilize the heel as the foot hits the ground. The cushioning of both forefoot and rearfoot has been improved to deal with those repeated 450-pound blows. And most of the shoes now have enough forefoot flexibility to allow the foot to go through its necessary structural shifts without transferring forces to the wrong parts of the foot. Insufficiency in any of these areas can lead to injury. The testing program has also helped establish minimum standards for wear, for weight, for quality control. Shoes that get low-rated in either design or manufacture are usually quickly fixed

—or are withdrawn from the market for serious runners. Those supermarket Formosa Flyers have to come from somewhere.

The rigors of proper biomechanical research have sometimes been frustrating, at least to the athlete in Peter Cavanagh. "Sometimes I feel quite sterile," he says. "Here's all this work that we're doing, and yet we still have just a rudimentary understanding, for example, of the most important factor in running, which is efficiency. We work hard, we've developed techniques that no one else is using, we've got nice ways to display the data, and still, we don't know much about running.

"So the running shoe work is one thing we've done that rescues me from this sterile feeling. Our work on running shoes has had more effect at the level of the user than anything else we've ever done. You go into a shoe store now and you see wall charts of twenty running shoes, with results of how they performed on our tests. That gives me a very warm feeling. We're now doing something which some of those twenty million runners out there can get some good out of, which may help some of them choose a better shoe. It might help some of them avoid injuries.

"Up to now we've just been concerned with understanding the external mechanics of running. What is the force environment that the feet are going through? Basically, we've been saying here is what is happening, let's find out how they do it. We haven't been trying to make it better. That's the next step.

"We did one interesting experiment that points in that direction. We took a group of runners, put them on the treadmill, forced them to change their preferred stride length, and measured their oxygen uptake. We found out, as we expected, that to change their stride length even a slight bit increased their oxygen consumption. But we also found that eight out of ten of them had already located their own optimum stride length. The curve is U-shaped—if you look at stride length versus oxygen uptake, the chosen stride length gives the minimum uptake. If you shorten or lengthen the stride, the oxygen uptake goes up. The body knows. The body has found the optimum. This held true when we tested Bill Rodgers, incidentally—change his stride length and his oxygen uptake goes up, just like anyone else. The surprising thing is not that Rodgers is at his optimum, but that Joe Runner is also.

"There are two possible explanations here. One is that you could take any stride length, do it long enough, and the body would adapt to it. That's a possibility, but I doubt it. The other possibility is perceived exertion. The runner has gone through a process of learning, perceiving his own exertion, realizing that he's using too much oxygen at this stride length or that one—most likely by a subconscious process. By moving up or down in successive stages, he has located the most efficient stride length.

"If you change the stride length, you change the action of virtually every muscle in the body. A tiny little insignificant, innocent-looking change is really powerful as far as what its consequences are in the muscles of the body. It's a very satisfying kind of experiment, where you make a mechanical change and look at the physiological costs. You're not just making a mechanical change and then saying this probably causes that, and you're not making a physiological measurement and saying look, this has increased and it's probably because of that. Instead, you are completing the circle. You've got the whole cycle, the whole chain together. You make a change and you look at the result directly in terms that are meaningful to the runner."

Despite the satisfactions of so neat an experimental result, Cavanagh is quick to point out that the information about stride length vs. oxygen uptake does not solve many problems in sports technique. "Technique is another matter," he says. "It's difficult. I don't really know if five years from now we will be able to suggest changes that would improve the running style of a Bill Rodgers. We picked up some unusual features in his style, but we're nowhere near being able to recommend that he change anything. We simply don't know enough about how these various things interact to produce a good running technique. Progress is going to be slow. Anyone who thinks different is deceiving himself.

"It doesn't work, for instance, to tell the novice to imitate Rodgers," says Cavanagh. "Running style, or performance in any sport, eventually boils down to the way you adapt to your own anatomy, your own physiology, to the peculiarities of your own body. One of Bill Rodgers' legs is shorter than the other. One of his arms swings way out to one side as he runs, in some form of dynamic compensation for what's happening to his lower extremities. That wouldn't be good for you, you don't have that problem. Okay, we do away with those peculiarities, and then, probably, fundamentally, there are patterns of movement that remain, and these are what we assume are 'right.' At least that's the assumption that people have used until now. Take a good performer and then try to imprint his movements onto the others.

"But we studied twenty elite runners a few years ago, a group of the best runners in the country. We found that the variability in patterns of movement among the elite runners was even greater than the variability among a control group of college runners. So that isn't going to work either. There is no magic pattern for a marathon runner. You can't take the runner and put his limbs into this or that set pattern and expect that to make him win marathons. But in sports, the pressure to say that you *can* do these things is immense.

"If there's one position I'd hate to be in, it's that of the coach. To gain and keep the respect of the athletes, the coach has to be ready to answer questions about technique. If the athlete asks a question about technique, the coach has about fifteen seconds in which to give a convincing, reasonably balanced answer. And he knows in his heart that he really doesn't know. Nobody does. He's got to come up with an answer because he's influencing athletes in other important ways. He's motivating them, he's keeping them in training. And if they ask him a question, if one of them says, 'Coach, should I flex my leg more to get it through faster?' he's got to say something like 'Oh, no, you're just about right the way you're doing it'—and he knows in his heart that he's being fraudulent when he says it. I'd hate to be in that position. I'd always have this awful sense: God, I really don't *know*."

*   *   *

The alacrity with which novices adopt the tiniest moves and mannerisms of their sports heroes is wonderful. Millions of kids diligently learn to spit between their teeth like Reggie Jackson, to pump the elbow before swinging the bat à la Joe Morgan. They stuff great wads of miscellaneous materials into their cheeks to distort their faces like Rod Carew. Not a few young basketball players must have dreamed of shaving their heads when the spectacularly bald Slick Watts, sweatband jauntily cocked over one eye, was helping spark the Portland Trailblazers in the playoffs on national TV.

When I was sixteen my maximum hero was Tommy Ortiz, a fellow diver whose aerial maneuvers were so cleanly precise that it was as if he were practicing some other skill than we were. Tommy, a couple of years older, was simply miles ahead of the rest of us. He happened to affect a pinkie ring, a gift from a girl friend, and before each dive, as he stood quietly on the diving board concentrating on the complex movements to come, he would wriggle his little finger, twisting away at the ring. Before very long I realized I'd picked up the habit. I'd studied Tommy's every move so carefully that I'd learned that one, too, and I'd catch myself, as I prepared for a difficult dive, twisting away at an imaginary pinkie ring. I am sure I blushed with embarrassment every time I noticed myself doing it. Half a dozen other kids, most of them considerably younger, hung around the pool that summer. I spotted most of them repeating the same mannerism at one time or another, which only deepened my mortification.

Did any of us ever consciously suppose that that talisman finger-wriggle could possibly help us pull off a dive as masterfully as did Tommy Ortiz? I don't think so. I think we imitated what we could of his movements, and if we couldn't duplicate the important part—the marvels he accomplished in the air—well, then we would settle for the peripheral rituals. It is no wonder to me that athletes get caught up in strange behaviors, superstitions, allegiances to quacks. They are dealing with far too many unknowns to leave everything to rationality.

Thirty years later, when faced with a difficult physical maneuver, I still sometimes feel—like a nervous tremor—the ghost of that inane little finger-wriggle. It doesn't have to be an athletic movement: it might be the prospect of skiing a difficult pitch, but it can just as easily be the necessity of scrambling over a roof edge to reach a TV antenna. The finger seems to want to wriggle. I don't *think* I am invoking the muse of Tommy Ortiz. I think I am using that little neurological signal to help me cut through the environmental distractions, to make me concentrate on the movement I have to make. I think it is a useful signal to myself, a cue: pay attention, now. That doesn't mean I don't still blush when I catch myself doing it.

* * *

There is nothing condescending in Peter Cavanagh's recitation of the simple realities of athletic specificity. It is so elemental a truth in athletics—yet so easily lost sight of in enthusiasm for novel approaches to the athletic task—that the best sports scientists must keep repeating the reminders to themselves. But Cavanagh is obviously restless to get on to more challenging matters.

On his office wall there hangs a striking blue-line print of a very lumpy shoe sole, a shoe sole that has sprouted mountains. It is a three-quarter view, on which computer-generated graphics have created three-dimensional representations—elegantly smooth hills and valleys, in perfect perspective—of the distribution of pressure on the bottom of the shoe at one point in the gait. In many senses that drawing represents the future, as far as biomechanical research is concerned.

It was generated by a subject walking slowly across a flexible mat made up of a matrix of small force gauges, transducers which measure and record pressures at each point in the grid. Every bit of pressure applied downward toward the earth can just as well be understood as upward pressure, the earth pressing against the foot. That's the way the computer pictures it. The drawing shows the shoe sole as if it were a sheet of rubber: each area of pressure makes a raised hillock, its height representing the amount of pressure. "This technique has a tremendous advantage," Cavanagh says, "because although it is quantitative, it is also visual. There's no leap of faith required. You can look at it and say yes, this is happening and that is happening, I can see it. It's a technique that I think could be the basis for something quite far-reaching.

"The next step would be to get the transducers inside the shoe. If we could do that it would have tremendous implications, not just in sports but throughout orthopedics, throughout the field of physical medicine. If we knew the magnitude and distribution of the pressure exerted on the sole of the foot during walking and running, it would be extremely valuable in the classification, diagnosis, and treatment of any number of disorders of the lower extremities. Right now when orthopedists try to discern what's wrong with the movement in their patients, the only analytical tool they have is the eye. I think they could use more powerful techniques. Getting the transducers into the shoe is the way to provide those techniques. The technology is quite close. If the National Institute of Health agrees with me, we'll have it in two years.

"What's interesting about these ground reaction forces is that people have opinions about them, opinions that may be right and may be wrong, but nobody knows. And yet people act on these opinions. It happens in sports more than in medicine, of course. It is perfectly possible for some folk tale to be carried on as if it were true, for people to coach according to it and to train according to it, without anyone ever knowing whether there is any basis for it in fact.

"People have always believed, for example, that when you are running slowly, you hit the ground first with the back part of your heel. But nearly everybody we've ever tested hits the ground with some part of the outside rear edge of their shoe. Hardly anyone hits the ground with the heel first. There aren't any true heel-strikers. There's no such thing as a true heel strike in running. You can confirm this simply by looking at where the wear is on everyone's shoes.

"So the wrap-up heel design they've now put on just about all running shoes is almost purely cosmetic. The shoe designers have spent a great deal of energy trying to make the shoe better in the rearfoot area. They've been trying to provide better cushioning at the rear, they've put huge amounts of material under the rearfoot, and until recently left the forefoot almost paper thin. Partially, this was to provide a wedge shape, since we generally function better with the heel higher than the forefoot. But they also virtually ignored the forefoot of the shoe because they thought it was unimportant.

"Then our force platform studies started turning up forefoot strikers—people who touch down first with the forefoot area, no matter what speed they run. For the forefoot striker, in level running, it is the forefoot of the shoe that must do everything for him. More important, we found that the forces in the forefoot are larger generally, even for rearfoot strikers. The forces under the forefoot are the greatest that the runner experiences, no matter how his feet hit the ground. If you ignore the forefoot area of the running shoe, you're doing the runner a disservice. The manufacturers are now responding to these findings, putting a lot more forefoot protection into their shoes."

So far Cavanagh's work with shoes has focused entirely on protection. His studies have been aimed at influencing the shoe manufacturer to provide the runner with a shoe that might not be the fastest in the world, but that would let the runner run longer—injury-free. There's been considerable improvement in this direction since the shoe testing started, but he'd like to see more before proceeding to the next step.

That step is toward increased efficiency in the shoes—toward energy recovery. Cavanagh would like to investigate the possibility of shoes that could give you back some of the energy that they have stored on impact. "What you would like to do in running is maintain a constant velocity," he says. "That way there would be zero metabolic energy simply going into fluctuation. You have to burn up metabolic energy to make changes in kinetic energy. If I walk a mile but do it in ten-yard slow-downs and ten-yard speed-ups, I'm probably using twice the metabolic energy just to keep changing the amount of kinetic energy.

"In running, every time your foot hits the ground you do the same thing. You slow down as your foot hits, then accelerate as you push off. There's no way you can run without contacting the ground, so the objective in running has to be to minimize the changes in kinetic energy each time you touch down. You want to make your contact just a fleeting touch, so you minimize these peaks and valleys of kinetic energy. That is the theory so far, anyway."

Cavanagh conceives that with sufficient research it might be possible to design a running shoe that enhances this fleeting touch, that is both safe and superefficient. But he isn't likely to be the one to do it. "Those two qualities—safety and efficiency—may be directly conflicting, particularly for the elite athlete. The elite athlete seems to be willing to sacrifice anything for superior performance. I'm not. I'm not likely to get into that area of super speed, because I don't think for the general individual it has that much relevance. I don't care if I run faster tomorrow than today, as long as I get out of running what I want from it for myself. I think most people—apart from the elite athletes—feel that way."

Cavanagh's vision of the future for biomechanics is in line with his cautious approach to radical change in athletic techniques. "The most immediate contribution we're liable to make to sports is in equipment," he says. "It's something we're reasonably good at. It's not as difficult as the other problem, the movements of the human body. I think we should see quite dramatic effects from biomechanics in the equipment for several sports. Nobody had ever studied the golf shoe before we did, for example. When you think of how many people play golf, that's incredible. And that's not an isolated example. The same thing was true with running shoes when we started studying them. There are lots of sports out there that are yet to be studied in detail. Sports don't just use equipment, they *depend* on equipment for successful performance. And the number one contribution that we're likely to make, at least in the short run, is to that performance.

"It's too bad, but physical education has never been regarded as a proper academic discipline, perhaps quite rightly. Therefore people have basically ignored the research that has been done in it. What sports has had to rely on for research has been someone like the individual who is a mechanical engineer and who also happens to be inclined toward sports, perhaps, who does a bit of research in his spare time. And while he might be a good engineer and amateur sportsman, he still isn't likely to have the insight to solve the biological problems.

"But what we're seeing now is the growth in numbers of people coming into the field who know physiology, who know biomechanics, who have the broader feeling and who have the analytical techniques. They're people who can do the mathematics, the computing, the engineering themselves. So now we're seeing more competent people in the field who can solve the problems that stumped researchers in physical education before."

Since Cavanagh does a considerable amount of globe-trotting, I asked his assessment of sports science and biomechanics in the Iron Curtain countries—these sports juggernauts who, the popular press assures us, will soon sweep all before them with their sophisticated scientific methodology. "My feeling," Cavanagh says, "is that they are probably ahead of us in realizing that this has to be applied in some way, and they put a lot of their effort into applying what they do know rather than finding out what they don't know. At least that's my impression from the literature that's passed my way.

"One Eastern Bloc sports scientist told me, 'You know, my bosses just want gold medals.' He is a very nice man and a good scientist, and he's under tremendous pressure to produce results. 'They don't understand that we have to go toward this in a steady way,' he says. He recognizes, just as I do, that you have to approach these things step by step. But he's got this fifty-ton weight on his shoulders, saying produce, damn it, get gold medals. It's unfortunate.

"I think that what they demonstrate best is how to use whatever information they have. They aren't saying they know everything about how to produce a particular movement or how it's generated. They use what they have. And in some sports—weight lifting, for example—they have had very good results. Weight lifting is a fairly simple activity, and it's easy to study it using force platforms. Their athletes have had great success in weight lifting.

"But as cautionary as I've been about how much I think biomechanics can contribute to sports, I still feel a certain confidence about what is possible with these techniques. If someone said to me, 'You have two years, here are Frank Shorter, Bill Rodgers, Marty Liquori, and twelve other of the best runners in the world'—and if I had an opportunity to get some data on them now and at any subsequent time I needed it—then I think there could be some result. That's not the way I'd like to attack the problem, but talking about the Soviet approach makes me think of this in a different light.

"I'm sure there are some things one can say already about distance running. They're not fundamental, they're not far-reaching, they're not going to tell you the whole story. In a sense they're gimmicky. But I have to admit that given the athletes and the time to work with the data, I'd have some confidence about the outcome." Then Peter Cavanagh pauses as he searches for just the right scientific distance to put between himself and the self-described miracle workers who have popped up in his field. "Let me just say that there are some generalisms one could come to if one worked specifically on that topic."

*   *   *

The quickest way for biomechanics to get into trouble is for it to attempt to improve athletics by focusing the athlete's attention on *how* he or she does the movement, rather than simply on doing the movement, on the movement itself. If the motor-learning people agree on anything, it is that you learn to make the movement, you don't learn to contract the muscles required to make the movement. As one traditional kinesiology textbook puts it, "Many a coach has completely disorganized an athlete's performance by injudicious emphasis on specific muscle actions." I think that's what happened with my punting technique.

Or maybe what happened to my kicking career was from the second quickest way for biomechanics to get into trouble: from an analysis of the movement so complex that the mind fogs. Or as one biomechanist explained how to ride a bicycle: "You just adjust the curvature of your bicycle's path in proportion to the ratio of your unbalance over the square of your speed."

CHAPTER 11
Sweat

One of the better stories in physiology is one that the great research physician Hans Selye tells on himself. As a second-year medical student in Prague in 1926, he attended his first lecture on diagnosis. A professor of medicine examined five demonstration patients who had five different infectious diseases, diagnosing them one by one for the assembled students, flabbergasting the would-be doctors with the brilliance of his insights. "I cannot describe the respect and humility that I experienced in front of that great physician who could diagnose disease just by asking patients certain questions or looking for certain signs," Selye said. "I was awestruck."

Not too awestruck, however, to pose to himself the question that would lead to his most important discovery. "Why, I wondered, did that great professor never say one word about all those manifestations of disease that even I, in my complete ignorance, could see very well? He never mentioned that those five sick people, whatever their diseases or complaints, looked sick. . . . They all looked sick to me."

When he asked his teacher about this, the professor laughed. The same thing happened when he mentioned his observation to his fellow students. So he put the question aside for the next decade, while he pursued a career in research. It was not until 1936 that Selye returned to what he called the "syndrome of just being sick." He noticed that lab animals subjected to any number of very different stressors—from cold temperatures, for example, to the actual injection of harmful substances—reacted similarly. He discovered that they tended to develop the same general set of symptoms: enlarged adrenal glands, atrophy of the lymphatic system, peptic ulcers. From this he developed the revolutionary notion of a generalized physical response to stress. (The concept was so novel that he had to borrow the term "stress" from physics, and soon learned that it didn't translate very well—hence in the lexicography of international medicine we now have *le stress, der stress, lo stress, el stress,* and so on.)

Originally stress was only a negative concept. In his first public mention of it, Selye pointed out that harmful experiences could cause the same set of stress-reaction symptoms as harmful substances. Later he realized that stress can result from positive influences—joy, reward, excitement—as well as negative ones. Now, he says simply that stress is the "nonspecific response of the body to any demand."*

Selye's stress research quickly led to a larger concept, called the general adaptation syndrome, or GAS, which is the three-stage response of the organism to stress. The first reaction is *alarm*, which kicks off a response from the pituitary-adrenal system: the "flight-or-fight" response of increased heart rate, elevated blood sugar, dilated pupils, slowed digestion. The second stage, which we are most interested in, is *adaptation*, during which the acute symptoms of stress diminish and the body begins to repair the effect of its arousal. In the third stage *exhaustion* sets in, and the organism faces the onset of deterioration. Various diseases can develop.

Athletic training was invented, some say, in the sixth century B.C. by Milo of Crotona, when he began lifting a growing calf each day and kept at it until he could stand upright with a full-grown bull draped over his shoulders. Or so the legend goes. Athletes have trained diligently ever since. Yet in some senses, training—that small, common miracle—was never fully understood before Dr. Hans Selye codified stage two of the GAS. That's when we finally began to grasp the power of the body's response to stress. It might be noted of the GAS that stages one (alarm, panic) and three (exhaustion, deterioration) are generally negative, but stage two is quite positive. Stage two *is* training: the body's urgent drive not only to repair itself but to adapt and prepare for greater stress in the future. To

---

* The anecdote and quotes are from "They All Looked Sick to Me," by Hans Selye, *Human Nature*, February, 1978.

improve itself. If you make a muscle do more work than it is accustomed to doing, it will respond, in time, by increasing in size, strength, capacity; if you make the cardiovascular system do the same, it will enlarge its volumes, increase its efficiency, acquire the ability to do more. That is, training applies to all systems, to flexibility as well as to strength and endurance.

Athletes speak of it as "overload" rather than stress, but the principle is the same. They use it for everything from filling out their T-shirts more impressively to cramming their gullets with carbohydrates to provide the fuel for endurance activities. They also use it, of course, to prepare themselves for all of the off-scale accomplishments that take place out at the limits of human performance. Training is the great growth gift of the system, the means by which we can mold, structure, change our very selves. It is the principle by which we can treat our physical substance as a kind of clay, to be formed according to our own energy and will.

The way we do it is with work; work, or exercise, *is* stress—and whether it is a positive or negative stress depends on the nature of the work and the attitude of the worker, I suppose. (I have to confess that the quaintly Victorian—or neo-Nietzschean—tone of all this talk about work and will makes me nervous. But I also suspect that it is a set of attitudes, not necessarily moralistic, whose time has come—again. Motto for the postpetroleum civilization to come: Work works.) In some senses the work/exercise physiologists are the scientists who roam through the overarching structure of the GAS, explicating the details of its mechanisms. Stage two is their special province. They are the scientists of sweat.

Perhaps the best of them is Dave Costill. If you walk into just about any exercise physiology lab in the country, one of the first things you're likely to learn is just who on their staff has done training at Costill's Human Performance Lab at Ball State University. That's one quick indication of his stature in the field. Another is his past election to the presidency of the American College of Sports Medicine, although he is not a physician and the science he pursues is not really medicine. A third is the frequency with which his name and work crop up in any discussion of the science behind athletic performance. (This book being no exception.) It is unavoidable: he's done seminal work in just about all the available areas.

Costill is tall, skinny as a marathoner almost has to be, prematurely silverheaded; he looks like a younger (and more fit) version of Jacques Cousteau. He is disarmingly laconic, casual-seeming, in presenting his work to the public; and in that low-key manner is a clue to his effectiveness. He works hard at making the results of his investigations available and understandable to journeyman exercise buffs as well as elite class athletes, and he provides plainspoken guidelines for their application. His reputation in his profession is international; he globe-trots continually, tirelessly, campaigning for hard-nosed, fad-proof application of science to the human body at work.

The principle that fires Dave Costill's scientific curiosity is the capacity of the organism to improve itself in response to stress. "Certain aspects, like anatomy, you aren't going to change," he says. "No hundred-and-thirty pounder is ever going to win the Olympic discus. But the purpose of all this sports science is to make the most out of what you've been given. It's the trainability of the organism that makes possible the greatest changes you can induce.

"I've never been more impressed with this than in my own physiology. I was a sprint swimmer in college, a little better than mediocre. I could compete with anyone in the world for seventy-five yards, and then I just died. Unfortunately the races went on longer than seventy-five yards. So now to transcend my own athletic history and run a marathon is amazing to me. I'm never going to run a great marathon—I just don't have the physiology for it. But I can see how much I've adapted in that direction, and it's still incredible to me that the body is that plastic, that the body can adjust itself if you put enough properly managed stress on it. That you can gradually develop the system to the point that a marathon can even be run. I'm convinced now that anyone can run one. But when I started running about thirteen years ago I couldn't believe that I would ever run one mile."

One reason Costill began running is because in every experiment he is his own first subject: "If it's something you can't tolerate, then you sure as hell shouldn't subject anyone else to it." He learned to do muscle biopsies by removing bits of muscle from his own legs, under the tutelage of a physician friend. (Analysis of that tissue tells him he should stick to sprint events, rather than running marathons.) He is not so much heroic as just ruefully resigned about this approach to research. "One time I drank 350 cc's of corn oil," he says with a grimace. "We needed to put a concentrated bolus of triglycerides into the bloodstream. God, the thought of it gives me goose bumps even now. That's about a soft-drink bottle full of corn oil. First my gallbladder went berserk, and then everything else did. I was in cramps from one end to the other. I'm still hypersensitive—I can get sick just from eating a fatty meal.

"But one of the most interesting things for me about running is that as an exercise physiologist, I get to experience the very things I'm studying. I get a subjective, sensory confirmation of the very things I know scientifically. It may be that you develop intuitive theories that way—putting bits and pieces together, what you know as fact compared with what you're picking up from your own sensory equipment. If I have a particular sensation, then I know what the likely causes are. When I first started running I had never thought much about the physiology of exercise from a personal point of view. While I was running I would dissect every physiological system that came into mind. My respiration, for example: I'd think, my God, *feel* that respiratory drive, that heart rate response, the temperature rise. All the things I used to read about or observe in the laboratory were actually happening to me. It was wonderful. It still is."

That's not the only reason the marathon fascinates Dave Costill, of course. Frank Shorter has said he's convinced that running a marathon tears down the body in ways that we don't yet understand —and Shorter, too, has the subjective data, God knows. The challenge is irresistible: the marathon is such an overwhelmingly large chunk of exertion that the exercise physiologist almost by definition must be drawn to it as moth to candle. Because of that fascination, Costill has put most of the great distance runners of recent years through his lab procedures, gathering complete physical data on Shorter, Bill Rodgers, the late Steve Prefontaine, and many others. He's run them to exhaustion on treadmills, poked and prodded them, taken muscle biopsies, the full routine. The data were collected in the early and mid-1970s; other researchers are still publishing papers developed out of that data.

In those days the muscle biopsies were analyzed for slow- and fast-twitch fiber percentages, as described in Chapter 3; that study was the one that most clearly demonstrated the differences in muscle type between sprinters and distance runners. More recently Costill's biopsies are being analyzed in new ways, opening up new areas for investigation. He is using them now to search for the limiting factor in prolonged endurance exercise. "Is it a limit to the supply of oxygen to the muscle, or to the muscle's ability to use the oxygen it gets?" Costill asks. "Through biopsy we can measure the muscle tissue's top rate of oxygen uptake. Then we can bring that individual back in and get him to do a maximal test—isolate the muscle and work it with weights, find out what its maximal oxygen uptake is.

"Now we're getting a lot of people with widely differing capacities. We're beginning to get people who have good muscle and who are also good performers. With them you begin to see a relationship between the muscle composition and the muscle's oxidative ability. So we're dealing with a rather academic question, but we're also getting some very practical information that tells us something about the basic underlying premise for training. What do you want to train for? Train the muscle, or train the cardiovascular system? We can train them separately. We can overload one and not have to overload the other." The ramifications for the preparation of athletes for competition could be tremendous.

This trainability that so rivets Costill's interest is not limited to athletics. His first major project at Ball State—a National Institute of Health grant that enabled him to begin equipping the laboratory in the first place—studied the trainability of people with coronary disease. "I screened five hundred people, looking for the ones who had heart disease and didn't yet know it—the forty-five- to fifty-year-olds who were having chest pains." He located and tested such a population, and found they could be trained for better cardiovascular efficiency, reducing the load on the heart. (A local fitness program grew out of the study, using Costill's lab; it continues today.) He has studied knee injuries, using muscle biopsies taken before and after surgical repair to show that traditional rehabilitation has neglected endurance training. The knee depends on the surrounding musculature for stability. After surgery, if the leg muscles become fatigued, the knee loses muscular support and becomes liable to reinjury. Athletes with repaired knees were working at restoring strength but were ignoring endurance. Now, emphasis on endurance training during rehabilitation improves the athlete's chances of avoiding reinjury.

Costill has also done a great deal of work with body fluid balance, as related in Chapter 9, and with burning fat to produce energy. (That's the project that led to the great corn oil fiasco.) The whole subject of fuel for exercise has led Costill to work with diabetics, an area of research for which he has high hopes. "Diabetics not only have a problem with burning sugars," he says, "but also have trouble getting rid of their blood fats. We're finding and studying some diabetics who are distance runners. Handling their dietary needs and their insulin demands in a heavy exercise program is a critical problem. We figure if they know how to handle that, their treadmill and other data may tell us some things that can help other diabetics. That should tell us some things we don't know." *

*   *   *

Skill can't be trusted; effort can. Skills elude us. The delicacy of touch, the precision control that characterize the movement of the superior athlete may just not be possible for the likes of us to acquire. For the pathologically competitive among us, the fallback position is sheer effort. What we cannot accomplish by pure skill, we will try to pull off by overspending—of energy. We may not be able to beat that next tricky bastard, with all his shifty skills, but maybe we can grit our teeth and outlast him.

I suspect there's a lot of this curious rationalization at work in the fitness craze—particularly among the middle-aged, and more particularly than that among middle-aged males, of which I am one. I hate this grim-jawed competitiveness, hate it in others, hate it worse in myself, but I suspect it helps keep me fit.

When I find myself oppressed by this particular turn of mind, I take refuge in Jonathan Miller's wonderful book, *The Body in Question*, which obliquely suggests that the desire to understand our own processes is a more powerful drive than is competition. That understanding only began to be possible, Miller says, when we began to find metaphors for bodily processes in the mechanical world around us. "The moment when man first suspected that what he did was the result of hidden things getting done must have changed his whole view of the sort of thing he was. The suspicion that his effectiveness or agency was caused by something other than his conscious urge to be effective, and that he himself had no real control over this, constitutes an almost inconceivable leap of the imagination, and one can

---

* As this was going to press, The *New England Journal of Medicine* announced that sensitivity to insulin, and therefore the body's ability to utilize the substance, increases in direct correlation to physical fitness. Exercise may help diabetics fight their disease.

only conclude that it was largely the result of drawing an analogy between himself and his own technological artifacts," says Miller.

That notion may be taken a step farther. Perhaps it was not just the technological artifacts from which we began to draw our understanding, but the social and economic ones as well. I think that those of us who have grown up in a capitalistic society apply that metaphor to our physical processes. Notice "overspending," above. We have come to regard energy expenditure as a cost, somehow; energy replenishment—eating and sleeping—is gain, profit. (The same thinking equates exercise with pain, and regards effort as a product of superior moral fiber. This is the most tiresome single attitude the fitness movement can spawn.)

A more natural conceptualization would be to regard the income and outgo of energy as parts of a cycle as repetitive and unremarkable as breathing. If we don't think of exhaling as a "cost," why do we have to think of work, energy expenditure, as some kind of loss, a reduction of our capital? Only the periodicity is different. (Excuse me, I think I'll go compound the interest on that energy deposit I made at lunch, and take a nap.)

That's the pessimistic view of the fitness movement. I prefer one that is considerably more upbeat. I think this movement, like several others of the preceding decade, is nothing less than a change of consciousness. It is, in effect, a mass acceptance of responsibility. Hospitalization and "health" insurance are symptomatic of the previous consciousness. When you buy that insurance, you are attempting to hire health—to hire someone, some institution, to take the responsibility for keeping you healthy. To become fit is to take on that responsibility yourself.

Can the fitness movement be a kind of social coming of age? Maybe we are growing out of the nervous desire to drape that responsibility around someone else's shoulders? Certainly it is a responsibility that neither the "health industry" nor the medical profession has been very responsive to.

*   *   *

The first work physiology laboratory in the country was the Harvard Fatigue Lab, established before World War II, and in some senses fatigability is the opposite side of the trainability coin. I asked Costill just what fatigue is, and the answer I got was a short course in what exercise physiology is all about. "In the first place, fatigue takes several different forms," he told me. "For example, there's the fatigue you feel in running four hundred meters, there's the fatigue that occurs in a two-mile run, there's a completely different kind of fatigue that occurs in running the marathon.

"In the four hundred meters, the key component of fatigue is a disturbance in the intramuscular pH." (The symbol "pH" is used to denote comparative acidity or alkalinity. A pH value of 7 indicates neutrality; lower than 7 is acidic, higher than 7 is alkaline. The normal pH of human muscle tissue is about 7.08.) "What happens is that the interior of the cell becomes so acidic that it literally shuts down the operation. As you develop pH values lower than 7.08 you begin to get malfunctions in all the enzymes in the cell, in the ability of the actin and myosin to do their contractile jobs. So you get a decrement in tension capability. Finally you reach a very low level, around 6.4, and at that point the muscle just won't function.

"In a four-hundred-meter race you're accumulating lactic acid all the way through. Part of that accumulation results in a spin-off of free hydrogens, and the free hydrogen condition is very acid, dropping your pH. By the time you reach about three hundred meters, things start to shut off. When you come off the last turn rigor mortis sets in, because you can't generate enough tension—or the tension you can generate is limited, because you're groping, searching for muscle fibers that aren't already exhausted.

"This is a very acute kind of fatigue, but quickly recoverable—it passes in half an hour or so. You feel it as pain. Your system interprets it as pain because the acid in the system is stimulating pain receptors in the connective tissue—the acid solution is in the fluid around the cells as well as inside them. Everything is trying to shut down, and the way it does so, the way it protects itself, is by generating pain and dysfunction.

"As the distance gets longer, the exercise becomes more aerobic —you start the race running at a slower pace which allows the system more time to adjust. As the exercise becomes more aerobic you begin to shift over to other problems. You still accumulate acid, but you do so at a slower rate. In running a distance like the two-mile, you pace it even slower, you don't upset the acid balance so severely, but you're beginning to get into other problems. Now you have to begin to consider the need for fuel.

"In high-intensity exercise like running, the primary fuel is carbo-hydrates, and most of that comes right out of the glycogen that is stored in the muscle. As you move up to longer distances, one of the limiting factors can be depletion of this substrate—the stuff that the enzymes act upon to generate ATP. When you run out of substrate it becomes very hard to generate enough ATP, because although you can burn fat, you can't combust it fast enough to maintain the pace. The only way you can continue to exercise is to slow down. At a very slow rate the demand for ATP isn't so great, and then fat metabolism might be able to help you. But even at distances of four to five miles you're still burning glycogen at very high levels, using up blood glu-cose. Combine that with the pH disturbance, and you now have a complex cause for exhaustion.

"As you move up to the marathon distance, pH problems are no longer a factor—unless you go out much too fast. If you pace it right, if you start out slow enough, you may be able to burn fat in the early stages. The primary source of energy is going to be glycogen, and the object is to avoid burning the glycogen too fast. Most of the burning of glycogen occurs in the first fifteen minutes, so the critical period is the first thirty minutes of the run. If you're not careful you can burn off so much glycogen so early that you're already exhausted. That's when you have selective depletion of the muscle fibers—the ones you've been calling on to do most of the work. You have fewer and fewer fibers with adequate glycogen left, and it's an exhausting job summoning them up. It's when you have to do that that the gradual sensation of fatigue sets in—you may feel fine for a while, then you begin to shift over, you begin to count miles. That's the most exhaust-ing kind of fatigue of all."

A couple of threads wind themselves through any conversation about exercise with Dave Costill. One is simply trainability, the mar-velous plasticity of the organism itself; the other, closely related, another aspect of trainability, is muscle fiber recruitment. From his early work with muscle fiber types to the present, it is a subject that continues to pull Costill forward, ever deeper into the mysteries of the muscle cell. I asked him, for instance, about all the publicity generated by the manufacturers of the isokinetic and other weight-training equipment discussed in Chapter 4, some of which makes references to Costill's own muscle fiber studies. "Our interest is in how muscles adapt to training, not in comparing equipment," he told me. "Personally I don't think the muscle knows whether you've got $9,000 worth of equipment at the end of your hand or a tomato can full of cement. When you train for any activity, part of what you're training is the nervous system's control of that activity—which is specific to the activity.

"If you train for swimming by lifting weights, the weight lifting is never going to make you as good a swimmer as swimming will. You have to train the nervous system to recruit muscle fibers and muscle groups to coordinate your swimming stroke. What could do that better than swimming? You can't do that on any piece of equipment. The basic principle is to overload the muscle, so why not overload it doing the specific task? Of course, you can run into other difficulties —maybe there's a weakness in one component of the stroke. The advantage of a weight system is that you may be able to concentrate on a specific weakness—the long head of the triceps, say—and strengthen that. But the weight machines don't isolate specific weaknesses as clearly as they claim they do.

"The issue gets confused when the weight-machine people start talking about slow-twitch and fast-twitch fibers. Fast- and slow-twitch only refer to one characteristic, the speed at which the fiber contracts. When you talk about endurance, that's another characteristic entirely. That's not to say that a fast-twitch fiber can't have good endurance. You can train a fast-twitch fiber to have better endurance, and it may develop enough oxidative capacity in that process that if you biopsy it, it looks red—that is, it may look like a slow-twitch fiber.

"In fact when you train for endurance work some of the biggest changes that occur in the muscle occur in fast-twitch fiber. They're so low in oxidative ability to begin with that they have farther to go. They can improve tremendously. The slow-twitch fibers can't. Speed of contraction can't be changed, at least not very much—it's a function of the neurological impulse, not of the composition of the muscle cell. When you try to train for speed, what you're trying to do is condition fibers that you don't ordinarily use. It's like strength training—you try to learn to recruit more fibers, and to bring new fibers in with the proper timing. If you smooth out the recruitment pattern, you smooth out the whole function. You no longer have fibers working against each other; you get less internal resistance. So the biggest training effect comes in training the nervous system to do its job more efficiently, to recruit fibers that have the potential for doing work—and to learn to use them."

* * *

In the closing stages of the contest one athlete, faced with defeat, somehow manages to "reach way down," in the words of the sportscaster, to "find a little something extra," and wins. What he is reaching down for—the little extra that he finds—are muscle fibers with some glycogen left in them, or muscle fibers not incapacitated by accumulation of lactic acid. He's recruiting muscle fibers.

Every sports cliché is finally true. The clichés are quickly reduced to rote catch-phrases that athletes and coaches use to keep the devils (and reporters) at bay—or to avoid having to think about the sport—and we dismiss them as boring platitudes. But dig down into their meaning from the point of view of physiology, of our growing understanding of how the athletic body really works, and there is rich new meaning in them. They become true again in new ways.

(Most athletic instruction involves a search for the appropriate metaphor, an image vivid enough that the student can turn it into muscular movement. A ski teacher kept telling me, "Press down with your little toe." My feet were encased in rigid plastic shells almost to the knees; what effect could pressure with one toe possibly have? Yet I tried it and it worked. It put my mind into my boot; it made me get my weight into the right place; it caused me to relax other, interfering muscular effort. It made me think about what I was doing in a new way. It got my motor concentration working on the correct part of the problem. Metaphors make muscular movements graspable. The good instructor is the one who can come up with the metaphor that best fits the individual student's current level of understanding of the task.)

Anyway, nobody ever reached down any farther, nor came up with any more useful something extra, than baseball pitcher Tommy John. He virtually destroyed his pitching arm in 1974. One operation took a tendon from his right wrist and used it as a ligament to tie his left (throwing) elbow together. Another operation removed and re-attached his ulnar nerve, making it pass in front of, rather than behind, the disintegrating elbow joint—where it had become so inflamed that he could barely hold a baseball. He was told that nerve grew at the rate of an inch a month, and he had sixteen inches of nerve to regenerate.

He spent weeks lobbing a ball thirty feet—his maximum range—to his wife in their backyard. He went to spring training when all he could do was toss a ball against a concrete backstop, playing catch with himself like a kid on a stoop. At first he had to tape two fingers together and force the ball into his nonfunctioning hand to get a grip on it. Yet he came back, at a cost in pain and frustration that us civilians will never understand. He started a ball game in April of 1976, and won twenty games a couple of seasons later. And that, folks, is a major-league job of recruiting muscle fibers.

*   *   *

My visit to Ball State was in September of 1978, shortly before the New York marathon saw its first ten-thousand-runner field. In other words, it came just at the time when public interest in physical fitness seemed to be changing from a sizable fad to a swelling craze. The country seemed to be coming around to a vision that had long fueled Costill's work, Costill's lab. I asked him if he knew why.

"I think people are hungry to *know*," he said. "There's been a declining demand for physical activity in our society for decades, now. There's no physical demand in either our occupations or our life-styles. Someone put a pedometer on an ordinary office worker awhile back, and found out that in a normal day he walked about three hundred yards. Well, I think the human being is naturally an active animal, and this minimal demand for physical activity is unnatural. I think the fitness movement is really a recognition that we're leading an unnatural existence.

"We get people in the lab who might as well be in a body cast, for all the training values they show. But we now know how muscles adapt to physical activity, and we can prove that if a middle-aged adult wants to become physically active, he or she can adapt as well as a sixteen-year-old. The stuff we see suggests that people who literally haven't done anything in twenty years can come back. Compared to their peers, they can become almost superhuman. We find detrained middle-aged people, fifty and fifty-five years old, who put forth the effort and become better trained, in better shape, than the average twenty-year-old. The body is capable of greater adaptation than we ever give it credit for. People don't attempt anything because they think they'll fail. But in fact they can achieve more physical improvement than you can believe."

So what is the next step for exercise physiology? What is going to be happening in the near future, out there on the cutting edge of human performance? Costill-the-athlete defers to Costill-the-scientist: "We do want to optimize performance, so I suppose we'll have to continue to look at sport. We'll try to find out what it takes to be good, or to improve, in an activity, and then try to develop tests, methods of evaluating in those sports. So if a kid wants to be better in swimming or golf or some other sport, he will have ways of identifying his weaknesses, so he can train more specifically to overcome them, so he can improve. As far as sports are concerned, though, I'm not too interested in coming up with high-powered sophistication.

"In exercise physiology, what I personally would like to learn in the next ten years is a lot more about mechanisms. Why muscles adapt, what triggers them better after they are changed—those are Nobel-laureate-level questions. The triggering mechanism is probably related more to cellular function than it is to exercise adaptation. It's a very broad sort of cellular change in all areas. Exercise *is* muscular activity, so you have to start by asking what we know about muscle and its ability to sustain activity. We know a lot about how muscle contracts and how it functions, but maybe in total we've only scratched the surface. There's so much we don't know about how muscles make changes, what turns them on and off. They're pretty complex things. We don't have the technology for that yet. But it's what I'm interested in.

"I hope the trend is toward the incorporation of sports sciences into all levels of sport—not to make sports better, not just to win, and not just to sharpen the elite athletes, but to try to optimize every individual's talents, to help each individual get the most out of what he has. We need a little more cooperation from the sports scientists to try to bridge that gap. There's been a big change in that direction in the past ten years, and I hope that'll continue.

"But the direction and philosophy of physical education are still inappropriate. It's still stuck in the 1930s—they still teach the same philosophies that they taught forty years ago. The social trends, the needs of the population, are very different, but the physical educators haven't even approached that change yet.

"Just the other morning my daughter was all excited about getting to school because they were going to have gym that day—and my immediate thought was, it's amazing how quickly the public schools can kill that interest. Within a year or two she will be dreading PE. What are they doing wrong? Kids really enjoy playing. Every kid is an athlete. There's no reason why you should ever lose the joy of play. Unfortunately, people connect sport and competition with physical education, and that shouldn't be. The only joy in sport is like the joy in art, and it's the joy *you* see. Sport and play ought to be for you to enjoy, not for me to judge whether it's right for you to do it or not—and not just enjoyable when you win all the time. In PE the classes are arranged so that someone fails; they're competitive, and that destroys it for everyone. And it's the kid who fails who needs it most."

A gentle sentiment, I thought; did it mean that Dave Costill didn't believe in competition? "Oh, hell no," he said, "I *love* competition. I'm very competitive, in my work or running or anything else. Listen, half the reason you work your rump off in this business is just to outdistance your peers."

*   *   *

Chris remembers a pile of dirt—sod, really, probably intended to patch a lawn—that someone left outside the apartment house where she was growing up. The kids took it over before grown-ups could put it to practical use. They ran and jumped into this pile of dirt, climbed on and jumped off of it. They played king-of-the-hill on it, rolled down it, dug holes in it, threw pieces of it at each other, built forts and highways and castles in and on it.

It gradually compacted, lost any resemblance to sod, became part of their landscape. They rode bicycles, wagons, skates, scooters over it. It became a launching ramp, a base for hide-and-seek, a pitcher's mound, a crow's-nest atop a mast over a stormy sea. You never passed the dirt pile during daylight hours without finding a kid or two somewhere around it. Eventually it was worn completely away, but it served so well while it lasted that its location remained as an organizational entity in the neighborhood for months after there was no longer anything like a dirt pile to mark the spot. No playground designer ever designed any piece of equipment half so satisfactory. It remains in my wife's memory decades later: a pile of dirt.

"Every kid is an athlete," says Dave Costill, and waves of memory wash over me. I too remember particular dirt piles, ditches, hillocks, tree limbs, patches of grass, vacant lots. I remember the approach my friends and I took to any structure, piece of terrain, distinguishable portion of real estate or apparatus: what could we use this for? How could we best explore, then exploit, this piece of reality (before we were forever banned from it, as always seemed eventually to happen)? We wore out the world in those days.

And ourselves. I remember bursting out the door—the screen slamming back on its hinges—the moment I was set free, launched into the morning on a dead run, not to stop until it was no longer physically possible to continue. When we did stop it was from hunger, thirst (I seem to remember always being thirsty), or illness; we never admitted simple fatigue, preferring to stay out, away, free, even if we had to hide from the adults—or each other—to rest.

Or at least that's the romantic claim I am inclined to make: that we never did really get tired in those days. My actual memory is more accurate than that. I can summon up all too clearly the bone-ache of final fatigue, near the end of almost any summer day. And how it felt to drag myself up for one more giggling, floundering round of capture-the-flag at dusk, on the verge of hysterical tears from weariness.

And that, folks, was major-league physical education. That is, no PE class ever brought us to that edge: nothing they organized for us was ever fun enough to extract that kind of energy. All we were doing was stressing ourselves, living up to Dr. Selye's GAS, stage two. We were training. (Costill also says that everyone trains for his own life.) Our physiological reaction to that stress was, eventually, to grow up.

I don't know whatever gives me the idea now that I can get along without that kind of release and joy and, yes, fatigue—although I find myself trying to. Mostly I wish I could find another kind of activity that would support that level of energy investment. Another reason to get that tired for joy.

Or as archy the cockroach said of the moth who immolated himself on a cigar lighter:

> i do not agree with him
> myself i would rather have
> half the happiness and twice
> the longevity

but at the same time i wish
there was something i wanted
as badly as he wanted to fry himself

archy

CHAPTER 12
Science

It is a scenario of which Hollywood could be proud. Act I might be called "Humiliation in Montreal." There, at the 1976 Olympic Games, East Germany—a tiny nation of only 17 million souls—won an astonishing 40 gold medals. The United States, with twelve times the population from which to select our athletes, picked up only 34 golds. (The Soviets won 44.)

Badly psyched American coaches and athletes came away mumbling. The East Germans were, well, *cheating*, somehow—that is, they'd come up with the ultimate weapon for bluffing American athletes right out of their jocks: science. They were using science and technology to prepare athletes, and as Mary Shelley had discovered a hundred and fifty years before, rumors of science would support almost any horror story. The East Germans were assumed to be using supersecret scientific training methods under constant scrutiny of chemist and computer. The American press began implying that East German athletes (and those of other Communist nations) were being genetically selected, hormonally altered, doped, drugged, brainwashed, enslaved, maybe even surgically redesigned into superhumans. What chance did our poor playground-produced, free-enterprise mortals have against the laboratory monsters from the Godless Communist enclaves?

In the script for Act II, the American sports establishment was supposed to initiate a sporting version of the scientific push that followed the launching of the Soviet Sputnik in the late 1950s. Without compromising the American Way, great breakthroughs would be made. Good old American know-how would be applied to our athletes; they would begin to develop their own understanding of what is required, in the modern age, to compete in world athletics. In Act III, American science, technology, and athletic talent would prevail once again, and the Red Menace would be turned back at the final curtain.

Act III was scheduled to open at the Moscow Olympics in 1980, but along about the middle of 1979—long before talk of the Olympic boycott—it became apparent that the show was in trouble on the road, irrespective of political developments in Afghanistan. It is now being rescheduled for Los Angeles in 1984 (a chillingly symbolic date). Or maybe 1988. In fact there is some indication that Act II will not, as they say, "play"—and even Act I could use a little ex post facto revision. The scary stuff about science turns out to be not quite as scary as the political implications of how it is accomplished. What was supposed to be adventure drama now starts off as a tiresome propaganda vehicle—and then in the middle of Act II, however unintentionally, it turns into high comedy.

The East German effort is a multifaceted one, a widespread movement across the face of international sports, and in many ways is more of a social phenomenon than an athletic or scientific one. Its genesis was the conscious decision by that government to seek international prestige through sports—in the language of the 1960s, to co-opt the massive publicity machinery surrounding international sports competition, and use it to sell East Germany to the world. No bones about it: "When I run," one East German sprinter told *The New York Times*, "the first thing in my mind is the aim of strengthening the international reputation of the German Democratic Republic"—and other athletes echo those sentiments. Cuba has made similar efforts, and other small nations can be expected to attempt to use this propaganda tool. Humiliation of the superpowers is no small prize, even if it is only in boxing or track and field. Besides, sports provides a much cheaper way to thumb a national nose at the big boys than getting involved, for example, in another Vietnam.

American reaction to those startling successes is best demonstrated by the affair of the East German earlobes, mentioned in Chapter 5.

Just as East German women swimmers started knocking off world records right and left, nervous U.S. coaches discovered that East German trainers were routinely taking blood samples from the earlobes of their athletes after each competition and workout. What was going on? There had to be a connection, the Americans reasoned, but they remained mystified.

Then in a fortuitous bit of timing, Dr. Alois Mader, formerly on staff at one of East Germany's better swim clubs, defected to West Germany. He claimed to be the originator of the earlobe procedure, and explained the tests. Lactic acid buildup was being monitored, and workouts and race paces were individually prescribed on the basis of the results. The East Germans had found a way to keep tabs on the athlete's state of training without elaborate treadmill procedures (particularly inappropriate for testing swimmers—although the East Germans had also developed a "current canal" in which the swimmer could remain stationary while swimming against a regulated flow of water), and without analysis of all inhaled and exhaled gases, and other complicated methodology. With the earlobe technique it was possible to measure, immediately at the close of a given bout of exercise, just how intense that exercise had been for that individual athlete. Then succeeding workouts or segments of workouts could be precisely tailored to that level of response.

At this point shooting cracks began to splinter the frozen surface of the American sports establishment. The American Athletic Union, the national federation that controls swimming, had a committee on sports medicine, but that group had been virtually inoperative for decades. Now, with "science" as sports' newest buzz-word, it was time for the committee to come to life. Its new chairman was Dr. R. G. Greenwell, a former diver and promoter of a sports complex as well as a physician. Greenwell looked up Mader and brought him to the United States to present his methods to the AAU, figuring that rescue for the sagging American (women's) swimming fortunes was at hand.

Dr. Greenwell began selling the earlobe test, selling it hard. "Our approach to training has been to go till it hurts and then to keep going," he told *Sports Illustrated*.* Mader confirmed Costill: "According to Dr. Mader, the acid balance within the muscle cells, to which lactic acid is the major contributor, is the weakest link in the metabolic process. When acidity becomes excessive, the athlete can no longer produce energy efficiently, which is why limits should be set on training. All this has long been known to physiologists and biochemists throughout the world, but the East Germans were the first to devise formulas to determine limits. As I see it, this has been a major key to their success," said Greenwell.

As some other coaches saw it, however, it was not all that clear. For an AAU annual convention, Greenwell borrowed the instrumentation to conduct tests on live swimmers; unfortunately the combination of borrowed equipment and unfamiliar operators blew the test results, which took only a little of the wind out of Greenwell's sails. Some coaches agreed to give the earlobe method a try, at least for a while. (This also entailed promoting the equipment—roughly $40,000 worth—that the method required.) Others pointed out that American men swimmers, most of whom just trained till it hurt and then kept going—that is, trained anaerobically much of the time, ignoring lactic acid buildup—continued to dominate world competition, and it was far from clear that overtraining was the weak spot in U.S. training programs. In other words, the coaches went home still grumbling.

(Before the point gets obscured by the political maneuvering to come, it should be pointed out that American women swimmers have since rebounded considerably in international rankings. Most of the improvement has been credited to a heavy program of weight lifting.)

So split number one was among members of the AAU over whether or not to pursue lactic acid testing. Meanwhile, the United States Olympic Committee, the enormously wealthy organization that oversees U.S. participation in all Olympic sports, was attempting to revitalize its own sports medicine committee. The debacle in women's swimming and other dislocations in medal production were not the only problems in 1976. American athletes had been victims of numerous glaring training errors in other sports. Injuries had knocked out distance-runner Marty Liquori and several sprinters, and the implication was that these injuries were not so much random accidents as they were the result of poor coaching and inadequate medical backup. The U.S. program was in such shambles that even European coaches were suggesting to USOC officials that they should pull back and reorganize. The USOC wanted someone to straighten out not only American research in sports sciences, but also the quality of medical services provided U.S. athletes at future Olympic Games and trials. Dr. Irving Dardik, a New Jersey vascular surgeon and former team physician to the U.S. Olympic Rowing Team, was the man chosen.

According to *Sports Illustrated*, Dr. Greenwell requested that Dr. Dardik join him in assessing the lactic acid testing program, "at least until the whole Olympic program is worked out." Dardik demurred: "We do plan to review the lactic acid business, but I suspect you can find out the same things by measuring oxygen consumption or running treadmill tests, which we're doing. You can't take one thing and say that's the answer. The guy's a promoter." To which Greenwell responded that since we had already been taking oxygen consumption tests and running people on treadmills and hadn't gotten the kind of data that the East Germans seemed to develop, wasn't it time to try something else? Thus split number two, between the AAU and the USOC, Depts. of Sports Medicine. (No new development this, since those two parent organizations, plus the NCAA, have been feuding over any subject they can find to feud over for the past sixty years or so.)

Lest it appear that Dr. Greenwell is clearly established in this tale as either a farsighted hero or a self-promoting opportunist, or that Dr. Dardik is being unnecessarily recalcitrant, it might be appropriate to proceed to split number three—although these ruptures are presented here in no particular order. Split number three is among exercise physiologists, and concerns just what it was that the East Germans were trying to obtain from that lactic acid data.

On the one hand, there is the interpretation that the East Germans were developing the perfect method for maintaining training levels at the highest possible work load short of overtraining: the maximum training with the minimum breakdown. It is fairly clear that this is a use that is consistent with the data they were developing. In Dave Costill's cautious words, it is "a somewhat objective evaluation of the intensity of exercise."

In the best of all possible exercise worlds (which the East Germans are assumed to have designed) the earlobe technique could maintain a near perfect control of intensity. The blood samples taken after every bout of exercise are fed into a central computer that is programmed with, among other things, each individual athlete's total past exercise history. The computer develops the precise next level of exercise pace and distance to meet the criteria for accumulation of lactic acid. The athlete has only to follow the computer's instructions to maintain the best possible training program. (We're talking here only of activities that require repetitive movements at a relatively constant pace—swimming, running, rowing, cycling, cross-country ski racing, and the like.)

On the other hand, some exercise physiologists see a more ambitious intent and a larger gain in the East German method: raising the anaerobic threshold. The training effect should accustom the athlete to one pace of exercise, at which he or she should learn to tolerate the level of lactic acid in the blood produced by that pace (subdivision A of split number three), or produce less lactic acid for a given pace (subdivision B). In either case the athlete could then train harder without overtraining, and should be able to compete at a faster pace. The aerobic capacity has been increased.

Or how about subdivision C, in which the athlete deliberately trains in anaerobic territory? The carefully monitored lactate levels would be used to keep the athlete anaerobic, pulling the threshold along. As one exercise physiologist theorizes, ". . . a significant portion of training should be done at a pace which exceeds the current anaerobic threshold so that untrained muscle fibers would be recruited. This supra-threshold pace should be prolonged as much as possible and repeated often to provide the stimulus to increase the anaerobic enzymes in the appropriate muscle fibers so as to allow the selected nerve pathways to improve their function and to increase the number of capillaries supplying the appropriate muscle fibers. Changes in these enzymatic, nervous, and circulatory functions and structure must take place if the desired training effect is to be realized."[*] Which might be considered a fancy way of saying just go till it hurts and then keep going.

The problem with these interpretations of the East German program is that nobody on this side of the Atlantic has yet matched performance with theory. Dave Costill again: "We've looked at raising the anaerobic threshold. It appears that it moves a little bit, but the problem is that nobody really knows what 'anaerobic threshold'

[*] "Stepping Across the Anaerobic Threshold," by Ben Londeree, *Runner's World*, June, 1978.

means. It's one of those things that gives you some interesting numbers, but we haven't really decided what predicts it, what causes it. We have a number of different measures that seem to show that it could be characteristics of the muscle itself. But nobody's really positive, and there's still a great deal of controversy and fumbling on all that."

To be fair, exercise physiology as a field has pretty well agreed that the East German lactate tests were not leading to any miracle development in athletic training, although some researchers are still pursuing related approaches. And as mentioned before, the U.S. women's swimming program seems to be back on schedule, pursuing its own special training methods. But three full years after Montreal there was still residual consternation from a single aspect of the East German program in a single sport. And the beat goes on: at the 1980 Winter Olympics the East Germans won 23 medals, the Russians 22, the U.S. 12.

Imagine, then, what the rest of the East German rumors did to the American sports establishment. At a time when we still had world-class athletes who had to climb fences to get into athletic facilities to train, the East Germans had 21 sports clubs and 19 sports schools devoted to their national sports program. In the East Berlin club, which has an operating budget of half a million dollars a year, there are 600 athletes training under 32 professional coaches, with half those members of school age and attending the sports school next door, which arranges its studies to suit the training programs of the athlete-students. The Berlin club has gymnasiums for soccer, handball, basketball, and calisthenics. There are swimming pools, weight-lifting rooms, boxing rings, an indoor track, and an indoor skating rink "the size of a football field," according to *The New York Times*. There is no facility anything like it anywhere in the United States, even at the most jock-crazed university. And Berlin is only one of 21 such clubs—for 17 million people—and is not even the center of East German sports research; that's in Leipzig, where the Sports Research Institute employs teams of physicians, physiologists, biomechanists, biochemists, psychologists, and dietitians to dig up athletic intelligence which the sports clubs then apply.

One reason East Germany produces so many good athletes from such a small population is that its public schools function as a farm system. (So do ours, but much less systematically.) Physical education is compulsory, and teachers keep a careful eye out for signs of athletic talent, particularly in the 8- to 12-year-old range. It's hinted that there are bonuses for officials who turn up hot prospects. A precocious athlete may be spotted, tested by the sports scientists, and offered a place in a sports school at age 8. It's not compulsory, but the benefits are so large that membership in a sports academy is an offer that's hard to refuse. In some cases the government has resettled parents in distant towns just so they can be near the sports school where their child has been sent to prepare for an athletic career.

Information about the testing programs for young athletes is sketchy, and American scientists maintain that it's unlikely the East Germans have come up with any breakthroughs in spotting athletic talent at early ages. But rumors also swirl about the recruitment process. One source says that prospects undergo the following tests: bone x-rays to predict final body size; electrocardiograms to measure innate cardiovascular endurance capacity; anthropometric measurement and somatotyping; pulse rate measurement; muscle strength tests; blood tests; oxygen uptake tests; flexibility and range-of-motion tests; and general health, intelligence, and psychological stability testing.* There's some redundancy in the list—at least as we would administer the tests in this country—but it is a more complete battery than we are likely to give at any stage of an athlete's career. And the very thoroughness of the list, spurious though it might be, is just the kind of scientific psych-job that American athletes and coaches have been working on themselves ever since Montreal.

It's fairly clear that the testing of adult athletes in East German sports programs goes far beyond the taking of blood lactate levels. According to Brian Chapman blood is also tested for urea and creatine phosphokinase levels, which can give an indication of breakdown of muscle tissue, another sign of overtraining.† Performances are filmed and analyzed for biomechanical effectiveness. Athletes are tested regularly for muscular imbalance; and flexibility and weight training are prescribed to ensure that relative weaknesses don't develop. Training schedules are broken into six-week segments, at the end of which the athlete must pass a complete medical checkup

* "East of the Wall," by Brian Chapman, Runner's World, March, 1978.

† "Very nonspecific measures of 'muscle-breakdown,' " says Bill Fink, "and a nearly worthless indication of overtraining."

before being allowed to proceed to the next, harder segment of training.

Strength training is emphasized in most sports, followed always by stretching exercises and rubdown by a physiotherapist. (Runners, says Chapman, get two hours a day of weight training and flexibility exercises, and an hour of massage—"a luxury American runners either can't afford or find unnecessary." Elsewhere, however, Chapman says that East German runners train three days a week for endurance, and two days a week for strength, which schedule is in line with American training concepts.) The careful daily monitoring is only used during the month or so leading up to important events; during the off-season athletes are tested at somewhat longer intervals.

And then, of course, there are drugs. The East German sports scientists have quietly admitted that they've done research in the past with anabolic steroids (used in this country to add poundage to beef cattle and shot-putters) and maintain a discreet silence on the subject of blood packing (transfusing the athlete's own previously withdrawn blood to boost aerobic capacity). One must assume that the latter research has also been done. The U.S. press has regularly accused the East Germans of using steroids so extravagantly, for instance, that their women swimmers begin showing secondary masculine sex characteristics as an effect of hormonal upset caused by the drugs. One East German defector, a sprinter named Renate Neufeld Spassov, brought along some "vitamin pills" that she claims she was ordered to take as part of her training, which did turn out to be anabolic steroids. Only one East German athlete has been disqualified from competition by steroid testing at an event, as of this writing. Sophisticates say that means only that the East Germans are better chemists than we are—that is, they can beat the detection tests. The press has also accused Eastern Bloc nations of using drugs to delay the onset of puberty in female gymnasts, keeping them tiny and agile beyond their years. That charge, too, has not been proved.

Drugs and other kinds of cheating will come up again in Chapter 13, but the "magic pill" rumors abound, even when our own scientists insist flatly that no such drugs exist. I have to believe this keeps some U.S. athletes off-balance, emotionally if in no other way, when competing against Eastern Bloc athletes—even if the American press (and jock gossip) are more responsible for that particular psych-out than Eastern Bloc performances are.

*　　*　　*

Ah, the athletic imagination. The very idea of blood chemistry can support endless fantasies. Chapman uses the term "blood profile," which carries just the right note of design, or more or less nefarious calculation. Presumably the East German sports scientists maintain complete blood profiles on their athletes. Assume that the blood profile—a complete assessment of the athlete's blood chemistry—is taken at the time of the athlete's best performance. At the setting of a new world record, let's say. The next time a superior performance is required the coach can, with constant blood monitoring and computer support, train the athlete back up to the precise blood profile that obtained at the time of the best performance. Then at race time the coach can say okay, look, your blood profile is perfect again. Go for it. And the perfectly trained athlete, buoyed by a hefty dose of medicotechnological flim-flam, enters the fray in a state of indomitable confidence. Besides, he or she knows damned well that no excuses will be acceptable in the face of a perfect blood profile.

That is, the blood profile might provide a "perfect" training control for bringing the athlete up to competition pitch, for determining when that pitch has been reached, for chastening the lazy and encouraging the timid, for inspiring and for alibiing. And because of the placebo effect, it doesn't really make much difference if it works or not, so long as the coach and/or athlete believes it does. Just as baseball trainers, in a less sophisticated day, used to keep bottles of "base-hit pills" and "double-play pills" on the shelf. A couple of handy sheets of graph paper with some curves drawn on them could be all the training tool—all the science—that a shrewd coach needs to drive (or pull) athletes to superior performances.

*　　*　　*

So the U.S. athletic establishment set out to catch the East Germans on the sports medicine/science front. The USOC would launch a combined training center and sports medicine program, starting with a defunct hotel and real estate development in Squaw Valley, California, which became the first Olympic Training Center. A sec-

ond was established at Colorado Springs, Colorado; the prospect
of a third was dangled alluringly in front of Lake Placid, New York,
among other places. (Note the technique; it becomes important.)
The USOC's Sports Medicine Committee would survey sports medicine and sports physiology research throughout the world, and then
with big Olympic bucks would construct a better American version.

Oh rosy dream of empire! Before we watch the waves begin to lap
at the sand castles of sports science, it might be worth reflecting for
a moment on what that decision might come to mean. To start with,
the Olympic concept has, with the help of the media, superheated
itself out of any contact with reality. For example, being awarded a
future Olympic Games gives a city a guaranteed license to blackmail
that city's state and national governments out of huge buckets of tax
dollars, as we have seen at Montreal, Lake Placid, and Moscow and
may soon see again at Los Angeles. There is no reason for this except
that the Olympic Games as political events have so far overshadowed
the very sports that make them possible.

And because of this the International Olympic Committee and the
various national Olympic Committees have become powers in sports
in ways that have no connection with the sports they "govern." For
any given sport, its own world championship (if there is one—some
sports aren't organized that way) is a much more meaningful test,
usually eliciting better performances, than that sport's Olympic version. But the Olympic Games get the publicity, and have thus come
to represent a more significant sporting event. This means that the
national Olympic Committees are continually meddling with sports,
changing their nature (and resisting their development) in ways that
the governing bodies of those sports can no longer control. The
Olympic Committees are too powerful for them.

In the case of the United States Olympic Committee—as nastily
self-serving, elitist, and unresponsive an organization as exists anywhere outside the higher chambers of OPEC—this has resulted in an
immensely rich organization that maintains its power only by iron-
handed control of all matters pertaining to Olympic competition for
Americans. In some mysterious way, that has been translated into so
much prestige—or maybe it is just social status—that the USOC has
come to represent the tip of the pyramid of our world of athletic
organization.

When the USOC chooses to dispense some small portion of its

wealth among the frayed-cuff academics and coaches out there who are trying to accomplish something with the inexact sciences of sport, it sets a scenario for real trouble. Imagine, for example, exercise physiologist X, sitting in his lab at Sasquatch State U. with a treadmill and an ergometer, dreaming of getting his hands on some real athletes. Consider what visions spring from the prospect of an expense-no-object lab and the opportunity to work in the territory where world champions live.

Or, more realistically, consider the prospect of being on an Olympic committee, a working official with real responsibilities (and letterheads and expense accounts and chances to speak at committee meetings and a USOC title to tack onto one's name on future publications). Consider that selection to the committee would signify the top level of possible prestige within one's own chosen field of sports science. There is no higher position that one could aspire to reach.

Several did so aspire. The jockeying and campaigning for selection to the committee were intense, and the intensity was not reduced by the fact that selection was delayed and delayed again, for better than a year after the USOC announced that it was getting serious about what it calls sports medicine. When the selections came they were a mixed bag: some very prestigious scientists and physicians, some publicity-hungry lesser lights. With the appointees came some rather gaudy predictions, budget figures, and commercial tie-ins. The next steps were predictable. Members of the scientific sports establishment who were not selected began immediately to point out what was wrong with the way the committee was proceeding. Meanwhile the suppliers, subcontractors, and prospective employees started snarling over dispensation of the committee's goodies. Some of the most notable appointees resigned a few months after their appointment, recognizing the whole approach as untenable.

Equipment, some donated, some purchased, was set up in Squaw Valley, where a "complete" testing program was to begin. National teams in several sports signed up for a chance to come live and train at Squaw Valley for a short spell, and to have their athletes tested. They were eager to get some advice on more scientific ways to train, and maybe uncover a magic secret or two of their own. In all the publicity surrounding the establishment of both the Squaw Valley and Colorado Springs centers, the USOC press releases said that although the training facilities were fine, the real gains were going to come from the sports medicine research that went along with the training.* But more than one of those national teams came, tiptoed through part of the scientific testing process, and checked out: no thank you very much. At Squaw Valley the training facilities were adequate (if high-altitude training was applicable to your sport), but something was not altogether satisfactory about the scientific part.

It should be interjected here that modern American athletes are becoming quite sophisticated about the scientific approach, but at the same time they are growing increasingly leery of its demands. The testing procedures are often exhausting, always time-consuming, sometimes painful, interruptive of training. The scientists have a tendency to make lavish promises about very helpful results that the athlete can use in training, but once the testing is over, that's the last the athlete ever hears about it. One American ski jumper is purported to have given up muscle biopsies from his legs six different times over the years, and has yet to hear the first word of explanation or analysis of the results. (Some athletes are more resistant to this kind of fiddling than others, of course. They tell me it is worth your life to try to get even a finger-prick blood sample from a boxer; they don't want to give away *anything*.)

In the Squaw Valley program yet another small philosophical split developed. The people who were doing the testing wanted to build a body of data that might someday give us a meaningful baseline—a starting point for scientific training in 1984, 1988, even 1992. Rome wasn't built in a day, you know. The coaches and athletes, on the other hand, wanted to start cutting tenths of seconds off their times. They wanted information they could use right then, to get ready for 1980. But the equipment available wasn't sufficient for, nor the largely volunteer staff capable of, providing that kind of immediate information.

Worse, the program was running aground on that old athletic bugaboo, specificity, again. Athletes were being run through standardized tests, whether they were 98-pound gymnasts or 340-pound weight lifters, whether their sports required the explosive swiftness of slalom skiing or the gut-wrenching endurance and brute strength of rowing. The tests were not able to get into any of the specific require-

* This message is for the feds. It is virtually impossible to get a grant for sports research from the federal coffers, but if you can figure a medical aspect to your area of inquiry, you can hope to get research money.

ments of any particular sport. And there was still no appreciable feedback to coaches and athletes, so they could attempt to adapt their training to their measured physiological states. Check-out time, said the athletes. (As the 1980 Olympics drew closer this situation improved somewhat, and athletes and national teams began to utilize the Olympic Training Centers more fully.)

Meanwhile, the USOC powers on the sports medicine committee seemed to be growing disenchanted with the hard, slow work with treadmills and biochemistry. Biomechanics, they announced, was going to be the new savior: the labs at the Olympic Training Centers were going to be completely equipped for biomechanical analysis of sports techniques. New breakthroughs were just around the corner. For example, the East German women didn't win at Montreal through superior training or conditioning, according to one piece of USOC publicity, but because they *pushed off with their hands* from the starting blocks, and were thus half a second faster to the water. (Emphasis supplied.) This penetrating insight was obtained by biomechanical analysis of films. It may sound like an upside-down version of the Penn State work with grab starts in swimming (see Chapter 10), but it was the kind of discovery that pointed the sports medicine committee in a new direction. Victory margins in the longer races of over half a second seem to have been discounted.

Then there began to be rumors about the purchase of a couple of million dollars' worth of computers and other equipment for biomechanical analysis, equipment which the USOC has never quite been able to get working, somehow. That has been followed by a long period during which the USOC sports medicine program has been very quiet. Last I heard, there was to be a major regrouping—a rethinking, as it were—and right after the Moscow Olympics we are going to launch a major push in sports medicine and beat the Red Menace at its own game. As soon as we get the equipment working. Meanwhile, several prospective sites for additional Olympic Training Centers have mounted their own rather undignified dog-and-pony shows to try to win official designation—i.e., USOC dollars.

I suppose all this is inevitable. If you start out to build from scratch an operation to match that of the East Germans—as complete and thorough, if not quite as outwardly massive—just imagine the possibilities in that rickety new structure for mistakes, incompetence, graft, profit, waste, brother-in-law deals, overzealous free enterprise, manipulation of the press, abuse of the athletes, and so on. There is some evidence that as far as the establishment of the USOC sports medicine program is concerned, none of these opportunities has been missed. It's a story crying out for its own Woodward and Bernstein.

*   *   *

In these pages and elsewhere we are promised scientific breakthroughs in improving athletic performance. If that promise seems to be losing a little of its brightness along about now, that's intentional. There are some problems to be ventilated. It is in fact possible to apply scientific methodology to improving performance, despite the cynical tone of this chapter; it's just a lot more difficult to do than the publicity surrounding it would have us believe. In many areas the work that is being carried forward is spectacularly unscientific, because when the variables are as numerous as they are in sports, the scientific method is often the first casualty. It is very hard to "do" science about the athletic animal. (Even the business of taking exact measurements on a living body is something of a crapshoot: too much soft tissue. I asked a podiatrist about unequal leg lengths, source of endless structural troubles among runners. "It's hard to measure," he said. "Everything moves around too much." About the only way to get precise measurements is by dissection.) To make science work properly on human beings you have to push the problem into smaller and smaller corners—the cells, the nerve endings, the molecules of biochemistry—and the smaller the corner you find to work in, the farther from the whole, functioning, athletic human being is your place of business.

Our imagination leads us to expect too much from this kind of science. It's not entirely our fault; the imagination is constantly stimulated by an unfortunate relationship between the press that covers sports and a new breed of pseudoscientist/promoter who has started working the same territory. It's an interesting combination. Take a superficial understanding of modern sports events, mix in a dollop of Sunday supplement science and the public's fascination with all things medical, and present it to a reporter. The usual result should be labeled speculative fiction but isn't, and usually implies that if we will only put up the money and the warm bodies, there are scientists out there who will dial up any kind of athletic superiority you want.

One version of this story is about the Red Menace and how it's going to crush our kids. The other version is about how any moment now we're going to start computer-programming our own kids for Olympic gold medals, cranking them full of supervitamins, building up their muscles with space-age gadgets, in short doing everything to our own athletes that we've been scaring ourselves with in the rumors about East Germany.

It is the way these stories are generated that worries me. I understand how a perfectly reputable scientist, attempting to simplify a complex subject for popular consumption, might accidentally overstimulate a reporter's imagination. The scientist can't accompany that simplification all the way to the reporter's typewriter, swatting down overinterpretations. That happens; I don't doubt there's a fair measure of it in this book, although I have tried to run my speculations past more informed people than I, for checking. But there is a more dangerous version, in which the scientist/promoter, for whatever motivations, does the speculating first, before the scientific work has been done—and then proceeds to lead the reporter much farther down the garden path toward athletic miracles than the reporter would ever go alone.

My concern is not for the integrity of us reporters, which is our own lookout. The larger problem is that there are simply a lot of people out there ripping off the public through sports, and some of them are using science as their dodge. If you are doing research in muscle development, for example, it doesn't seem to be too difficult to find some manufacturer of a strength-building device who wants to underwrite your test equipment, your laboratory overhead, perhaps even the braces on your kids' teeth, for the "correct" experimental results. The same is true for researchers in any other exercise-related area, or for any scientists working so close to so huge a market as sports have come to represent. If the feds won't issue grants for sports-related research, there are manufacturers who will. There are commercial interests who could not care less about how research is done, so long as the results say their product is effective. So there are expensive athletic products on the market with extremely dubious scientific rationales behind them.

A lot of expensive athletes—amateur as well as professional—use these products, sometimes for the lucrative endorsement fees that are available, but also occasionally because the scientific rationale seems convincing. Athletes and coaches can be sold a bill of goods as quickly as you or I. So there's bad science (poor techniques, faulty reasoning, stupidity), and there's dishonest science (sold-out to outside interests). Two not entirely distinct cans of worms.

Wormier yet is the case of the scientist who at some point decides to manufacture his own product or promote his own methods or sell his own test equipment—or simply to sell himself and his expertise into positions of real responsibility and authority on the international athletic scene. The moment such a decision is made, any pretense of scientific objectivity becomes thin indeed. Research for this book has led me to some charming, entertaining, charismatic individuals who represent themselves—sort of—as scientists, but who are also selling something. They have a lot of startling ideas about what we will soon be able to do, scientifically, with athletes and sports. They scare me —because they can be so convincing, and because their own professional field as yet seems to have no effective way of policing itself, or of policing them.

Furthermore, the press, equally hungry for colorful personalities and for sensational stories about sports science, is particularly vulnerable to their blandishments. When we report on these people we unwittingly legitimize them; they use each bit of personal publicity to bootstrap themselves to the next. Frankly, we have already created too many of these figures, as we've created too much of a story about the Red Menace in sports. In a sense both are figments of sportswriters' imaginations. Unfortunately the world of sports tends to believe its own press, and treats them both as real.

*   *   *

I find this entire subject bleakly depressing, as I do most of modern sports' dismal failures. In focusing on sports' physical glories, I've deliberately ignored all that, and I'd just as soon continue to do so. I'm as appalled as anyone at what happens in the name of sports, from Little League fathers to spoiled superstars to franchise owners with plantation mentalities. The violence of professional football, hockey, and boxing is simply unconscionable. (Yet I admit I choose, however guiltily, to follow these sports—wincing.) The politics of sports seems to me consistently corrupt. I used to report regularly on some of that peculiar politicking; and in the dealings I've witnessed, the two most predictable characteristics of every single governing body, from the IOC right down to the local softball league, were hypocrisy and arrogance. The machinery that our society has set up for the administration, governance, and marketing of sports is an outrageous failure, and often, to the extent that that machinery deals with the lives of individual athletes, a public tragedy. One of sports' larger miracles has been to survive our mismanagement of them.

Nor would I want to pretend ignorance of the excesses that overtake individuals who find themselves swept up in sports, from the riots among fans to the physical and emotional damage suffered by overzealous participants in the sports themselves. There is a strange human tendency to turn sports into a nightmarish obsession that loses all connection with the best interests of the individual and society. (Just as burning precious petrochemical fuels to jet teams across continents in order to provide circuses for a jaded public—and profits for millionaire team owners—would seem an egregious kind of decadence.) These are problems that develop out of sports' very power, its vitality; they are diseases of overachievement, which may be a small comfort. I'd be more comfortable with a little moderation. I vote for human-sized sports.

*   *   *

Upon contemplating the National Basketball Association's adoption of the three-point basket, or Charles O. Finley's methodical dismantlement of a baseball franchise, or the latest installment of Dwight Stones' adventures with sports governing bodies, what I am likely to feel is black despair. When I do, I can always go Frisbee the dog.

Throwing a Frisbee (T. M. undoubtedly Reg.) is hardly a major-league athletic activity, but I would claim there is some small element of skill to it. (I can personally identify at least a couple of members of modern society who cannot yet successfully fling one.) That is, some throws are better than others; there is a certain smooth duration of flight to be strived for. A proper throw requires some muscular control, a well-timed flip of the wrist, a modicum of effort. By my late forties I find it worthwhile to warm up—to start easily and work my way up to harder throws, waiting for my arm to get ready for the effort. Once I am warm there is a considerable measure of satisfaction in snapping off a long throw, watching the sensual swoop of that silly plastic disk.

There is also pleasure in watching the headlong flight of the dog as she pursues the Frisbee. Her name is Evie, and she is a medium-to-large nondescript of immense but sly good humor. I used to believe that all animals of a given species were natural athletes of the same general level of competence, but I've come to know other dogs that make Evie look like something of a motor-skill retard. She's not really terrible at chasing Frisbees, but I would not say she is dogdom's Lynne Swann.

(I have a recurrent fantasy about teaching two teams of house cats to play soccer. A playing field the size of one side of a tennis court, tiny goalies, colorful little uniforms . . . never mind.)

Superskilled or not, Evie chases the Frisbee for her own pure pleasure, and that's why this activity is such an effective antidote to the damp, drizzly Novembers of sports. Her sprint start, for example, is simply joyous. I don't think she expends that burst of all-out effort in any large hope of catching the disk in flight (she averages about .615 in that category), but because she obviously likes to run fast—for short distances, anyway. She's middle-aged; it isn't puppyish exuberance. There just has to be an impulse, an instinct, to expend that energy, to pump out effort for the sheer joy of making the muscles work, of feeling her own animal power. She knows on some dim level what I with my allegedly higher consciousness keep forgetting: use it or lose it. Something tells her to move more rather than less, to forego the plodding, languorous line of least resistance. She *demands* exercise (poking me in the elbow with her nose every afternoon at 4:30). I count that a valuable reminder.

What's more, when she begins to sprint—when her head goes down and the muscles bunch up around her shoulders, when her center of gravity drops, when her long body alternately coils tightly and then lengthens out, reaching, driving for more acceleration— she is a biomechanical joy to watch, an object lesson in singleness of purpose. She is a demonstration of how gladly a body may be used when it is not distracted by my kind of dithering overconsideration. Reckless abandon, they call it; it leads her to occasional injury, which she evidently considers a small enough price. She heals quickly but not quickly enough, being as impatient at letting her injury rest, at staying off it, as any athlete.

She is not a pretty dog, but in action she is beautiful enough. Any animal is. You don't often see clumsiness in successful species. (I'm assuming that giraffes and other evolutionary geeks are not terribly successful, as their numbers keep dwindling.) Denise McCluggage often makes the point of how precisely a cat jumps onto a table, just clearing the edge, without any extra height in hand but also without any undignified scramble at the last moment, struggling for another inch. But I've seen cats miss, now and then. I think they know what they're doing; they're toying with the possibilities (as they toy with a captured mouse). They are making sport of the jump. I'm serious: I think they often choose to see just how close they can cut it. They wouldn't move with that silken glide, that manner that gives us the very term "catlike," if they didn't take huge pleasure in their own bodies, their own movements. They express that pleasure too clearly in their play to deny it elsewhere. When the cat slips up over the edge of the table like water running uphill, when the dog leans so hard into a running turn that divots of grass are thrown up by the centrifugal force, these are animals taking pleasure in their own athleticism. I swear it.

The pleasure isn't just for them, it's also for us (although I wouldn't claim for a moment that the animals give a flip about that). It's hard to watch any creature, human or otherwise, using its musculature for pleasure without a smile coming to your face. (Smiling, itself, is another way of using muscles to express pleasure, right?) That's got to be one reason we elect to keep these small hairy animals among us. They move so exquisitely well that it pleasures both parties. They keep reminding us we have bodies.

Anyway, I find that speculation about such matters leads much more directly to what sports are really all about than does the question, for example, of who decides to boycott the next "nonpolitical" Olympic Games.

*   *   *

Oh, yes, the Red Menace. From the viewpoint of the athletes and coaches it is substantial; from the viewpoint of the scientists it has been greatly exaggerated. Scientists who have traveled widely among Eastern European countries say there is not so much an athletic gap as there is an application gap. We know what they know, we're just not using it yet.

Costill says the Russians are lacking in sophistication in exercise physiology, but are making a sizable effort in biomechanics. Cavanagh says that their push for gold medals—instant results—is getting in the way of the basic biomechanical research that they need to be doing to advance the state of the science. Costill also says that the Russians are probably far ahead of us in sports psychology—the management of athletes' heads—at which we are terrible. Poland, Czechoslovakia, and the other Eastern European countries are far behind us in all categories. Other authorities concur with this assessment.

But the East German bluff continues. Remember the rumors of those standing computer banks with the complete athletic history of each individual, revised and updated at the close of every workout—and then *used* (which is where we slip up) in the further training of that athlete. It's hard to conceive that the rumors could be accurate; the cost alone would be astronomical. If the rumors are true, then the East German investment is even larger than we'd dreamed. But even if the rumors aren't true, the psychological effect on U.S athletes still seems to obtain.

Actually, the East Germans have about the same grasp of exercise physiology that we do—or, perhaps, that our better exercise physiologists do, which is not quite the same as having the same level of expertise operant among coaches and athletes. The East Germans have a little less of the technology required to push that knowledge ahead, particularly in computers. The one clear advantage that they do have is one that we don't want—yet: when they develop some scientific information about the training of athletes, they can simply require that that information be applied in training. We can't—and that might make all the difference.

Our athletes desperately want to have the kind of scientific backup that their East German competitors have, but they want it on an advisory basis. Until it is provided for them—organized, financed, and made "official," somehow—they aren't going to get it. In the meantime they make do with what they can pick up, do their own research, adapt what they find to their own experience. And grumble about the lack of organized sports-medical support. Or they find a scientist/doctor/guru/coach of one stripe or another, and follow that individual's advice with a kind of nervous faith—nervous because our athletes have been burned so often and so badly by the con men of athletics that they are extremely leery of trusting anyone. Meanwhile, the inability of exercise science to police itself and its interface with the world of athletics allows new athletic con men to spring up out of the weeds every day, looking for new talent upon which to try their experiments.

We are blessed with a nation full of superb athletes, who have developed out of various bona fide programs, collegiate or otherwise, or out of their own fierce urge to succeed. For purposes of maintaining a healthily balanced attitude about the relative importance of sports, that may be the best all-round solution we could have. But until we find some way around the current state of disorganization, the legitimate athletes and the legitimate scientists of sports will too often find themselves facing each other across a great gulf of missed opportunities, while the better organized programs of other nations run off with a lot of international prestige. That, too, may not be the greatest tragedy in Western history, but it is maddening as hell to those who are consumed with the desire to explore the limits of human performance.

It may not be possible, within the definitions of human choice and freedom that we cherish, to bridge this gulf; it may be a gulf not worth bridging. But if it ever is bridged, I'll guarantee you one thing: the bridge builders aren't going to be the NCAA, the AAU, or the USOC.

CHAPTER 13
Alchemics

The men's field events followed their familiar pattern, with world records being broken in obscure meets where there were no tests for anabolic steroids. Distances were always several meters shorter at major events where athletes were tested.

That enigmatic little paragraph was buried in the text of an end-of-season wrap-up of the 1978 track and field year by United Press International. There, in among the news of Henry Rono's amazing four world records in distance events and Mike Tully's 18-foot 8¾-inch pole vault, was the UPI's anonymous judgment that chemical cheating in field events was the rule rather than the exception. "Everyone" is using steroids, of course. Everyone knows that.

Everyone, that is, except the officials whose job it is to keep athletes from taking drugs. Those worthies, expert by their own definition, know a lot of interesting things. They know, for instance, that anabolic steroids do not enhance athletic ability, because that's what it says right there in *The Physician's Desk Reference* (a compendium of information totally supplied by drug companies, with no editorial judgment applied). They know, in effect, that athletes do not use drugs because they, the officials, have told the athletes not to. They also know that no drug-taking athlete can escape detection through their infallible drug-testing procedures, although a lot of the testing procedures for specific drugs are too expensive and too time-consuming to be bothered with, and the administration of the testing program almost always breaks down in practice.

The athletes know some interesting things too. They know that at past Olympics they could have been disqualified—four years of training and an athletic career junked on the spot—for using Vicks Throat Lozenges or Visine Eye Drops. But at some meets if the athlete is female and claims to be on birth control pills—which are in themselves steroids—she can be excused from testing, and therefore can go ahead and take all the steroids she wants. (Which could be one explanation why women's strength-event records are advancing faster than men's records, although there are plenty of other good reasons for this improvement.)

In short the athletes know that the drug-testing procedures are a whimsical crap shoot. Yet many of the athletes are confident they can spot drug abusers in their own ranks pretty much on sight, just from familiarity with the characteristic physical signs brought on by the drugs. If the athletes themselves can spot users in their midst, imagine how angry it must make them to see the officials fail so consistently to spot those users—and how doubly maddening, when the crap shoot actually catches someone, that the penalties are so severe.

During the psychedelic sixties, when drug experimentation was a national hobby, an acquaintance told me about a major drug conference in Washington, D.C. Government expert after government expert was paraded through an auditorium full of kids, testifying to the horrors of drug use of every kind. Finally one street-wise kid got to a microphone. "Look," he told the experts, "I know from taking drugs myself that most of what you people are telling me here just isn't true. So do the rest of these kids. You don't understand—we've done these things. We *know*. If you lie to us about stuff we already know, how can you expect us to believe you about anything else?"

The experts are lying to athletes, too, with the same results. In study after study the experts "prove" that drugs don't enhance athletic performance. But athletes know from taking them that drugs do work. It doesn't make any difference what the experts say; the athletes continue to use drugs. Drug use is flagrant in the sports where attempts are made to control it, and epidemic—virtually universal—in sports where it is not controlled, such as professional football.

Because experts lie (or resolutely and dependably fail to find out the truth) about the effects of drugs on performance, then those experts forfeit the right to be believed when they try to warn athletes about the rest of the drug-related phenomena—the long-term effects, the possible damages, the very real dangers that drugs represent. Drugs are the loose cannon on the deck of sports.

That's a moral judgment. The difficulty surrounding drugs arises from our insistence on making moral judgments about chemicals. There is a continuum of substances that begins with the purest and most healthful life-sustaining elements and extends through the deadliest poisons. We ingest substances ranging from air and water through tobacco and heroin, for purposes ranging from the maintenance of life to its outright destruction. The substances are agents of change, and we seem to fear that. Maybe that's why we attempt to cut out a segment of that continuum and label it "drugs," and surround it with all kinds of moral and legal complications. Nobody has ever adequately defined the boundaries of that segment of the continuum which we invest with such frightful powers, so the boundaries remain arbitrary. (There is no reason, for example, under the definitions now in use in sports, that carbohydrate loading might not be considered to be drugging.) When we extend moralistic social judgments about chemicals into the world of sports, we immediately are involved in arbitrary behavior. Arbitrary behavior is extremely difficult to command or control. I will try to excise my own moral judgments from the discussion of athletic drugs to follow. I will probably fail.

*   *   *

An exercise physiologist told me of his own brief personal experience with steroids. As an athlete just out of graduate school, he was still interested in increasing his size, weight, strength, endurance; he was also a Ph.D., with a heavy concentration in biochemistry in his background; that is, he was not some dizzy scatterbrain ingesting anything that anyone told him might work. He did exhaustive research before the fact, planned his dosage and program with meticulous care, and kept exact records of the results. "First, the steroids made me feel terrible for a few days, nauseous and weak as hell," he told me. "But I had a set workout at the time, and after I stopped feeling bad I noticed almost immediately that I was completing my workout in a lot less time. I was doing a certain number of repetitions with each amount of weight in each kind of lift. After a very short time I was doing the workout in less than half the time that it took before the steroids.

"I started gaining weight pretty fast, but before the weight even showed up on the scales, people started remarking about my appearance. I'd run into someone I hadn't seen in a couple of weeks, and he'd say, 'My God you look *big*.' I did bulk up quite a bit. I put on twenty or thirty pounds very quickly. After a couple of months I began to worry about long-term effects and quit taking them. Within a week or two I was back to the original amount of time to get through my workout. It was scary."

The American College of Sports Medicine has issued a position statement that tries to say that steroids don't work, but pulls up short of so unambiguous a declaration. "Based on a comprehensive survey of the world literature and a careful analysis of the claims made for and against the efficacy of anabolic-androgenic steroids in improving human performance, . . ." the ACSM decided that "administration of . . . steroids to healthy humans below age 50 in medically approved therapeutic doses *often* does not of itself bring about any significant improvements in strength, aerobic endurance, lean body mass, or body weight." Since athletes usually choose much larger than medically approved therapeutic doses, "There is no scientific evidence that extremely large doses of . . . steroids *either aid or hinder* athletic performance." (Emphases supplied.) The remainder of the statement is devoted to warnings—liver damage, decreases in testicular size and function, decrease in sperm production—and to a plea for education about these dangers in the athletic community.

In other words, there are scientific studies pointing in both directions. Dr. Allen J. Ryan, editor-in-chief of *The Physician and Sportsmedicine*, was furious with what he called the pussyfooting in that statement. He published it in March of 1978, but with it he published an editorial that claimed the "comprehensive survey" gave too much weight to poorly designed studies, and that a more intelligent analysis would allow a flat statement: the idea that taking steroids will result in increase in strength and improvement in performance is simply a myth. "Athletes are not only wasting money and cruelly deluding themselves, but also endangering their health," said Ryan. My friend with the Ph.D. might agree with the health part, but the rest has to leave him wondering what it was that was deluding those friends—who didn't know he was taking steroids—who came up to him and said, "My God you look *big*."

*   *   *

There are two phases of metabolism: catabolism and anabolism. *Catabolic* processes break down complex substances into simpler materials; *anabolic* processes build up complex substances out of simpler materials, as in the synthesis of new protein from nutrients supplied by the diet. Athletes, particularly in strength-related events, seek anabolism.

"Anabolic-androgenic" steroids are compounds that resemble male hormones, that stimulate the synthesis of cellular protein. Androgens are the natural male sex hormones, such as testosterone, which show a marked increase in the system about puberty. They stimulate development of secondary sex characteristics at that time. Androgenic effects differ from anabolic effects only in location. Both are demonstrated in the growth spurt that occurs at puberty, but androgenic growth occurs in such places as the larynx (deepening the voice), the hair (increasing body and facial hair), the sexual organs (increasing their size and stimulating their function), while anabolic growth is just general increase in physical size, without the "virilizing" effect of androgens. It has been in the attempt to increase the anabolic effect and reduce the androgenic effect that the synthetic anabolic steroids have been developed.

(The reduction of the androgenic effect has not been entirely successful, which led to a famous exchange between the press and the East Germans at Montreal in 1976. The remarkably successful East German women swimmers were so broad-shouldered and slim-hipped, with such deep voices, that they were generally suspected of heavy steroid use, although none was caught in the drug-testing procedures. A reporter asked one of the East German coaches about those deep-voiced women. "Our girls came to swim, not to sing," was the East German reply.)

Medically, therapeutically, steroids are used in cases where stimulation of protein synthesis is desired: for malnutrition, for individuals with low hormone production, after surgery, in skeletal disorders, in any of several "wasting" diseases. They have been found to have a tonic effect on appetite and mental attitude as well as on protein synthesis.

Sauce for the sick is sauce for the healthy: steroids are used by athletes to cheat—at least according to the Olympic definition. The IOC calls it doping: "Doping is the administration of or the use by a competing athlete of any substance foreign to the body or of any physiological substances taken in abnormal quantity or taken by an abnormal route of entry into the body, with the sole intention of increasing in an artificial and unfair manner his performance in competition." By which definition a Brussels sprout diet—taken with the wrong intention—is also doping. Steroids are banned by the rest of the athletic federations as well. But their use is almost universal.

This chapter relies heavily on a remarkably frank book by James E. Wright, Ph.D., entitled *Anabolic Steroids and Sports: A Complete Report on the Controversial Drugs Used to Increase Muscle Size and Strength* (Sports Science Consultants, Natick, Mass., 1978). Wright estimates that over 90 percent of today's athletes in the strength-related sports—weight lifting, football, track and field, wrestling, crew, and others—use steroids on a regular basis. He quotes similar estimates from enough other coaches and officials over the past couple of decades to indicate that if his impressions exaggerate the problem, most others in positions to know have gotten the same distorted view. The stimulus for steroid use, as Wright points out, is almost irresistible:

"This phenomenon is probably the result of the athletic dogma (by now an Article of Faith of the religion of physical culture) which contends that failure to take steroids would leave one with no hope of reaching international or even national status. The feeling among athletes is almost unanimous that these compounds substantially increase muscle strength and, if the diet is appropriate, muscle size and body weight. Although endurance athletes have experimented with steroids, their use has primarily been confined to those sports which rely heavily on strength and/or muscle mass. Other than among the weightlifters and body builders already mentioned, use is substantial in other sports as well. Among track and field athletes, jumpers and especially throwers (hammer, shot, discus, javelin) appear to be the heaviest users. Football players are another group using steroids to build or maintain body weight. One estimate holds that 75 percent of professional players have used the drugs at some time. Noted sports medicine authority Dr. Allen Ryan states in a recent article that not only was it difficult to find a competitive weightlifter or thrower not taking steroids regularly but that, at least at one point in time, football players at all levels (high school, college and professional) were taking the drugs under orders from coaches and even team physicians."

Confusing—or confused—as steroid research has been, some basic principles for their use to enhance athletic performance have emerged, although the source of those principles is more likely to be practical locker-room experience than any carefully designed scientific study. The individual gets maximum results from ingesting steroids when he or she has already trained up to a strength plateau before starting the drugs—when strength gains seem to have stopped, and the athlete needs something more to kick the system onward to additional gain. Similarly, athletes usually find they reach a plateau when using the drugs, which leads to bizarre experiments—changing the type of steroid, doubling up on dosages, ingesting oral steroids on top of injected dosages, and so on. Some top athletes are so sophisticated in steroid use that they vary dosage by the milligram, like gourmet cooks mixing exotic sauces.

When the athlete discontinues using steroids there is some rebound effect—a slight loss of weight and strength, which can be disconcerting (and can also work as a stimulus to continued or increased usage). All traces of orally ingested steroids usually disappear from the system within two weeks, once their use is stopped; injected steroids may take three weeks or more to be completely eliminated. Rumors have it that the Russians and East Germans have techniques for more rapid removal, so that traces of drugs can be flushed out immediately before an event and the athlete can go ahead and compete before the rebound effect saps strength.

That was the suspicion focused on Russian super-heavyweight weight lifter Vasily Alexeyev at Montreal. Track and field expert Neil Amdur described the incident in *Playboy*. Alexeyev didn't show up on the day he was supposed to report for precompetition medical testing; his trainer said he was out of the city that day and thus unavailable. Was he, or, as most rival competitors and some officials suspected, "was he anticipating the drug test and having his system flushed of traces of body-building hormones by a special diuretic?" asked Amdur.

He checked with George Freen, an American hammer thrower who, according to Amdur, "knows the drug culture in sports from amphetamines to Xylocaine and has culled scientific secrets from friends inside the iron curtain." According to Freen, Alexeyev's signs were all positive. " 'Alexeyev's face was so blown out of proportion it looked like it was going to explode out of his skin. That's usually a sign of heavy drugs, especially steroids. And he had these little cholesterol globules that collect under the eyeball from too large a dosage of steroids. You can't tell me that he was missing for three days in Montreal because he was busy competing. I believe nobody could find him because the Russians needed time to clean out his system.' "* Alexeyev was not challenged by the authorities, and won his event.

Steroid research continues to come up with the kind of contradictory results that lead to the "scientific pussyfooting" of the ACSM, and as James Wright explains, that shouldn't be too surprising:

"Problems in human research have centered around the condition of the person taking the drug. How old is he (she)? How highly trained is he? How hard is he training while taking the drug? What kind of training is he doing (general conditioning, running, power lifting, body building, etc.)? What type (oral or injectable), dosage, and how long will the subject be on the drugs? Is he taking protein and/or other food supplements? All these questions have a critical bearing on the outcome of the research. For instance, not only have the drugs, dosages and durations of the studies varied, but some researchers have used untrained people who have never touched a weight in their lives while others have used world class strength athletes who have been training intensively for 8–10 years. Some researchers have given protein supplements, others haven't. Some studies have had the subjects engage in weight training while taking the drugs, others prescribed general physical conditioning, still others did not have the subjects doing any exercise. What the reader must keep in mind is that each investigation is designed to answer one or, at the most, a few specific questions. Every study has limitations and none can answer all aspects of every question."

Furthermore—perhaps most important—there is the placebo effect, which predictably screws up just about every attempt to study

* "Wired to the Teeth," February, 1978.

the effects of ingestion of any substance by conscious human beings. Weight lifters have been given inert pills which they believed were steroids, and have achieved the same level of gains in size and strength as control groups taking real steroids. Placebos, as it turns out, are a larger and more significant aspect of this subject than steroids. We'll get back to them in a moment.

Meanwhile, James Wright is willing to make some cautious generalizations. Conducting his own survey, which may or may not be more thorough and more objective than that done by the ACSM, but which does take that survey into account, Wright says that "the effects of anabolic steroids on gains in weight, size, and strength present a general picture that indicates:

1. That gains in muscle size and, less predictably, strength are facilitated in untrained or inexperienced individuals provided they are ingesting adequate protein and are on an appropriate exercise regimen.
2. That gains in size and usually in strength are almost always enhanced if the subjects are experienced weight trainers engaged in heavy training and on an appropriate diet."

Which is precisely what strength athletes have been telling each other for the past couple of decades.*

*   *   *

As with steroids, so with amphetamines. The sports-medical establishment keeps repeating that "speed"—"uppers," stimulants of various stripes—don't enhance athletic performance, despite studies that have shown that some of them can prolong the time an individual can perform a physical task, and may in some cases even raise the level of performance. It makes absolutely no difference, however, what the establishment says or the studies show about these drugs.

---

* In Chapter 4, I mentioned that strength training has become endemic in sports such as baseball, for which it had not been considered a necessity in the past. A lot of coaches aren't too happy with this development, and try to get their athletes to stop with the weight machines. They run into a lot of resistance from the athletes, who don't want to quit.

If steroids work, they work only when you're engaged in a regular program of heavy exercise. Although Dr. Wright doesn't talk much about it, steroids are generally regarded as mood-enhancers, giving a buoyant, optimistic, aggressive high. Withdrawal from steroids means withdrawal from that high, compounded by a feeling of weakness, weight loss, a general bummer. I suspect that when some athletes resist giving up weight training, they may in fact be resisting giving up steroids.

The athletes already have the experience of taking them and have felt the effects as performance-enhancing. And that means it makes no difference whether there is any physiological basis for their effects or not; in the athletes' terms, the drugs do work. If the placebo effect can cause someone who only thinks he or she is taking steroids to gain weight—by kicking off action in the slow-moving endocrine system—imagine what that effect can accomplish in the lightning-quick and much more subjective nervous system.

Stimulants are less frequently associated with such purist endeavors as track and field than they are with the big-time professional sports—sports that make much less effort to control drug use. Most of the bad press about amphetamines and athletics falls on football, where use of the drug has been traced all the way down to the high school level (just as with steroids). But plenty of other kinds of athletes with long and grueling schedules to fulfill also grow fond of speed. Baseball, basketball, and soccer players have shown a particular predilection for amphetamines' chemical boost. In international bicycle racing there have been amphetamine-related deaths.

Traditionally, amphetamine use starts with something like an innocuous diet pill before game time, just to cut through the fog of jet-lag, to get up for the daily competitive grind. "Well," said Pete Rose in a *Playboy* interview (September, 1979), "I might have taken a greenie last week. I mean, if you want to call it a greenie. I mean, if a doctor gives me a prescription of thirty diet pills, because I want to curb my appetite, so I can lose five pounds before I go to spring training, I mean, is that bad? I mean, a doctor is not going to write a prescription that is going to be harmful to my body. . . . So a greenie can be a diet pill. That's all a greenie is, is a diet pill. Am I right or wrong? I know I am right. An upper is nothing but a diet pill. . . . There might be some day when you played a double-header the night before and you go to the ball park for a Sunday game and you just want to take a diet pill, just to mentally think you are up. You won't be up, but mentally you might think you are up. . . . It won't help your game, but it will help you mentally. When you help yourself mentally, it might help your game. . . . Yeah, I'd do it. I've done it."

Unfortunately, tolerance to amphetamines increases rapidly, and with higher dosages comes the temptation to use sedatives (tolerance for which also increases) to get back down from the amphetamine high—if for no other reason than to fit some rest into the killing schedules of professional sports. It just wouldn't seem that there is enough time in a pro basketball player's 82-game schedule, for example, to get up and back down and back up again for the next game by natural means.

That's one pattern of amphetamine use among athletes. A much more frightening version finds football players who feel they need the "crank," the mood enhancement. With low dosage the athlete feels heightened confidence and what seems like improved concentration; as the dosage is increased, that mood builds to what one team physician has characterized as "pre-psychotic paranoid rage." That was Dr. Arnold Mandell, who served as an unpaid team psychiatrist to the San Diego Chargers, and later had his license temporarily suspended for dispensing drugs to the players. Dr. Mandell is a highly accredited teaching physician and researcher, and his colleagues accept his claim that he was only trying to get the team members off dangerous street drugs and into a program to lessen their dependency on amphetamines. Mandell described the way the pills work for football players to John Underwood of *Sports Illustrated* (August, 1978): "In small doses, they give you the kind of work-drug high you might want to increase efficiency. But in large doses that nervous alert becomes something else, a rage players feel they must have in a game that requires violent aggression at a precise point in time.

"Amphetamines are certainly psychologically, and possibly physically, addictive. The post-use depression is severe. Sexual appetite diminishes. Some suffer temporary impotence. But you can't tell a veteran player that there is another way. He says, 'Doc, I'm not about to go out there one-on-one against a guy who's grunting and drooling and coming at me with big dilated pupils unless I'm in the same condition.' "

Some athletes will say that they thought they were performing exceptionally well on the drugs, but realized afterward—sometimes not until they saw the game films—that their judgment was off, their timing poor, their level of exertion inappropriate for the situations that faced them. This is the amphetamine effect that is most often used to warn athletes off the drug. Penalties for unnecessary roughness and unsportsmanlike conduct are often blamed on speed. The really disconcerting confession, however, is that of the 260-pound offensive lineman who admits he's afraid to face his opposite number without the bottled madness that amphetamines can offer.

There are graver dangers. Amphetamines increase heart rate, blood pressure, and respiration rate; they also mask pain. The health problems that can result from their use are legion, and are not restricted to the immediate effects of the drug. An athlete who is insensitive to pain is likely to overextend himself in several senses, to continue competing long after the body's own good sense should tell him to stop. And willingly to suffer pain himself in order to inflict a little pain on others, as in the paranoid rage that Dr. Mandell describes. Amphetamines and other drugs, particularly street drugs of dubious composition and purity, vastly complicate treatment of injury, since attending doctors can't tell what they're dealing with and can misread drug-altered symptoms. Drugs that are perfectly efficacious by themselves can be fatal in unwitting combinations, particularly in the mysterious biochemical minefield of stimulants and depressants.

Officially, nobody has a good word to say for amphetamines. Yet their use by long-haul truckers, by students at exam time, by harried executives, and by dieting housewives has built up such popular acceptance that their use by athletes seems only a curious offshoot. The revelations of the infamous "Dr. Feelgood" and his coterie of amphetamine abusers in New York society rocked the medical profession a few years back, with horror stories in the daily press about once-productive types driven to destruction by their amphetamine habits. In other words, this particular kind of drug use is not so much an athletic phenomenon as it is a public-health phenomenon, and as such is of less concern here than some other drug-related athletic developments. Nevertheless, amphetamine abuse seems to be the most common and most dangerous kind of athletic drug use, although it probably has less to do with the expansion of the limits of performance than some other less popular forms of drugging. Still, the continuing use of amphetamines by athletes indicates that their practical effect may be greater than scientific evidence would predict.

Meanwhile, the monied upper echelon of athletes seem to have gone on to cocaine. That illegal drug has much the same mood-enhancing qualities as amphetamines, with a heightened sense of awareness and imperviousness to pain. As Neil Amdur described the growing fad in *Playboy:*

"Some baseball players who got their first kicks chewing tobacco believe cocaine helps them 'see through pitches,' sharpens concentration and makes them more perceptive hitters. Those pitchers who occasionally snort coke on game days say it keeps their arms from tightening up and delays pain and soreness. But cocaine is much more expensive than other stimulants, so only the high-priced pros can afford it."

* * *

Blood-doping ("boosting," "packing,")—the reinfusion of the athlete's own blood just before competition—doesn't involve any specific drug use, but it is another kind of controversial laboratory magic that is alleged to improve athletic performance. The name of Lasse Viren, Finland's fabulous distance runner, has become virtually synonymous with blood-doping, on the basis of purest speculation. Viren has a habit of disappearing from the international competition scene for long periods of time, then reappearing in world-beating fettle, without the honing effect of top-level competition to bring him back up to peak. He did it in Munich in 1972 and then again in Montreal in 1976 in the 5000 and 10,000 meter runs, devastating the world's best distance runners.

In between Olympics, Viren doesn't perform up to that standard; and the earliest experiments with blood-doping were Scandinavian. Those two disparate facts seem to be all the track and field cynics need to deduce that Viren must be blood-doping. No such accusation has ever been proved, but then blood-doping is undetectable anyway, so far as exercise science now knows.

Theoretically, this is the way blood-doping works. The athlete gives up some of his or her well-trained blood a few months before a major competition. The blood is stored. Training goes on as before, and the athlete builds back up to normal blood volume by natural processes. Just before the big meet the athlete has his or her own blood reinfused from storage. The "new" blood, which actually is old blood put back into use, theoretically increases the athlete's blood supply, oxygen-bearing capacity, and, therefore, endurance.

One countertheory holds that the blood of a well-trained, non-doping endurance athlete is actually a little thinner than normal—it has to be, it is assumed, to be pumped fast enough to do the job. The addition of transfused extra blood shortly before competition should actually thicken the blood and reduce, rather than increase, oxygen

transport. Furthermore, there seems to be one red-corpuscle substance (2^3DPG) found only in the blood of very well trained people
and essential to their hyperefficient circulation of oxygen, which is
destroyed within a few hours of removal of the blood, according to
Track & Field News. The tone of their report is distinctly sardonic.
Such publications are unavoidably part of the establishment that runs
their sport, and since officialdom doesn't know how to detect blood-
doping and can't predict where its use is likely to lead, the fervent
hope is that blood-doping will just quietly go away.

The problems involved in testing for the effects of blood-doping
are exactly as complex and difficult as they are for steroids, and the
results just as likely to be interpreted to fit the aims and ambitions of
the interpreter. There have been half a dozen reasonably "good"
studies that prove blood-doping can bring real improvement, and
another half dozen that prove just as conclusively that it doesn't work
at all. The studies go on, and the results continue to contradict one
another.

Even its greatest proponents see blood-doping as nothing more
than a superb peaking tool, a means of bringing an athlete up to an
above-normal level of performance for a specific event (although
recent tests seem to indicate the gain may continue, undiminished,
for several weeks). Nobody suggests that it has any other purpose. To
go to all that scientific trouble for nothing more than a short-term
gain used to win a sporting event or set a record would certainly seem
every bit as perverse as using drugs to exceed normal athletic capacity. Unfortunately, at these levels of sports, sportsmanship can be the
first casualty. No one has reported any specific physical dangers associated with the process. The athlete is therefore not likely to be
dissuaded on account of risk. And so long as a single competitor may
have gained an edge, however slight, from blood-doping, then the
athlete is going to remain interested in the process. An anonymous
athlete stated the attitude clearly to James E. Wright:

"Think about how small the differences usually are between first
and second place, between winning and losing (in high level competition). And keep in mind the drive and ambition and the competitive
spirit of somebody competing at that level. Think about the time, the
energy, and the pain invested. . . . I hate to admit it, but an obses-
sive-compulsive personality is practically a requirement (for success
at these levels). . . . It's like everything else in life; when it all gets

down to the nitty-gritty, you grab at anything you can that might give you a winning edge."

*   *   *

The use of marijuana and alcohol is now so nearly universal as to be as much a part of sports as sweat and liniment. As ex-baseball pitcher and recovering alcoholic Ryne Duren is quick to point out, pro athletes are virtually driven to beer drinking after games, just to be a part of the cultural climate that obtains in the locker room, and life on the road seems organized around the availability of booze. Some marathon runners even drink beer during races—it's quick liquid replacement, has plenty of carbohydrates, is a good source of potassium, and (they claim) does not seem to affect performance that much.

Marijuana still puts management and the press into a panic, but its use is so common among athletes now that if it weren't for the occasional Bill Lee, who slyly chooses to make fun of official attitudes toward it, it would hardly be noticed. The most popular use seems as a postgame relaxant, the same as, and often in conjunction with, alcohol. (Some mountain climbers were smoking dope recreationally ten years before it became a national pastime, incidentally. They preferred it, they said, because it was a relaxant that was not a deconditioner.) But it wouldn't surprise me if some athletes were playing stoned. A lot of playground athletes smoke dope before, during, and after playing any of several sports, with no noticeable change in levels of performance (though their drug use may explain why they remain at the playground level). Some ski instructors find that when they teach, being stoned is the only possible defense against degrees of boredom sufficient to bring tears to their eyes. But since General Motors is finding the same thing true of assembly-line workers, perhaps this, too, is not a sports-related issue. I don't think that even the most devoted users of either drug claim that their use enhances athletic performance. Yet.

*   *   *

The gentlemen who control Olympic sport make lists of substances, detection of which in the body of the athlete is grounds for disqualification. From time to time these gentlemen revise the lists. Caffeine, for example, was once on the lists, then was removed and thus declared okay. Now, with the new research discussed in Chapter 9, don't be surprised if it goes back onto the lists. It improves performance; therefore it will probably be banned once again.

It is the arbitrariness of this that causes trouble. We have the habit of questioning arbitrariness on the part of authorities, and we don't quite see why sports should be exempted from this questioning. Those gentlemen are shocked when they are not exempted. They have a point. All games start in purest arbitrariness. The very rules are arbitrary, standards to which we cheerfully agree as a condition for being allowed to play. The rules create the game. We give to the authorities the power to set the rules, just as we give them the power to set the boundaries of the playing field. Unfortunately, we never decided where the rules of the game leave off. The authorities just naturally assume they have the power infinitely to expand their jurisdiction. That's the thing about power.

The issue of amateurism provides a better example of corruption by power than does the drug question. The attempts of the various sports governing bodies to come to terms with IOC definitions of amateurism have led to mannered craziness. There are now intricate, hair-splitting regulations governing the payment of outright salaries to amateur athletes. The authorities assure us that this money is not payment to the athletes for participating in their sport, but is reimbursement for the money the athletes might have made if they had gotten a regular job instead of spending all that time training. Large sums are paid to sports governing bodies by commercial interests for the right to use the names and faces of individual athletes in advertisements—in implied endorsements. Endorsements by amateurs are forbidden of course. If the governing body wants to turn around and give the money to the athlete, however, that's okay: that's broken time payment, to make up for lost income from that regular job. This Alice-in-Wonderland absurdity reached new heights in the case of Dwight Stones, who recently *bought back*—for a sum well into five figures—his amateur standing. As a cash purchase.

Look what happens. We give arbitrary control over the rules of games to a sports governing body, and suddenly that governing body has extended that arbitrary control not only into the details of our personal financial affairs, but also into our diets, into our body chemistry. It is amazing. I haven't a clue to how the problem of drugs in sports will eventually be solved, but attempting to control it through arbitrary rules clearly doesn't work—even when the enforcement of those rules is handed off to the alleged objectivity of the scientific method. It seems to me that drug use is a medical, rather than a legal or social problem, and it may be that in time it will be the nonarbitrary tolerances of the human body that will stake out the limits to their use. But that's a prospect that is every bit as scary as the present situation.

*   *   *

There is one other area of very heavy drug use in sports: pain-killing. It is a drug usage that has more to do with sports medicine than sports science, with keeping the athlete playing (at any level of performance) rather than with improving performance. The nature of sports is such that injuries occur, and the nature of the animal that plays at them is to want to continue playing, injured or not. Enter the chemists, with Xylocaine, codeine, Butazolidin, the opiates, the cortisones, the pain-killers and swelling-reducers—and the trainers, with their ice packs and whirlpool baths, their wraps and straps and braces and bandages. Heroic measures to keep heroic individuals ambulatory, competing, helping their teams.

This, too, is a growing scandal in sports, pointed up in exquisite detail by basketball center Bill Walton's lawsuit for medical malpractice against the management of his former team, the Portland Trailblazers. He claims they injected him with pain-killers and had him "play hurt," which led to more serious injuries. Similar suits had preceded Walton's, but his, coming from the league's most valuable player and growing out of a world championship season, has brought the subject to general public attention. The legal ramifications are still cloudy, but it does appear that team doctors are in direct conflict of interest, ostensibly watching out for the health of the players, but in fact under pressure from their employers to keep those players playing, hurt or not. And, of course, the players conspire with the doctors, against themselves, to keep playing, to advance their short-term careers at the expense of their long-term health. It's a mess.

But it is the armamentarium of those team physicians and trainers that concerns me more. I think Novocain is symbolic of the very force that creates the alchemists in sports. It introduces into the athlete's consciousness the possibility that a chemical substance can completely change the state of the body. What the athlete learns every time he or she gets a shot of Novocain is that drugs do work. It is but a small step from that to the steroid-amphetamine-cocaine consciousness, to the search for the magic potion that will make the athlete *fly*. And it is only a step beyond that to reliance on drugs for the continuance of one's career, to replacement of training and sensible personal habits with chemical assistance. And then onward to the even more bizarre set of fads and gimmicks that infest sports, the bee pollen and megavitamins and super-drinks, the feather in Dumbo's trunk.

There's additional impetus in this direction from the consistent failure of conservative medical treatment to help athletes suffering from so-called overuse injuries, injuries that Dr. George Sheehan calls the "diseases of excellence." These injuries often require a subtle understanding of biomechanics, of lines of force and muscular balance, as well as conventional medical knowledge. A lot of conventional doctors fail miserably in their treatment. Sheehan quotes a South African physiotherapist on the result: "It is a well known fact that a great number of sportsmen lack confidence in the medical profession and turn to quack treatment for a rapid cure." And Sheehan, a practicing cardiologist as well as a marathoner, agrees: "I began running fifteen years ago, before jogging became respectable. And it cost me days and weeks of injuries to learn that I, a physician, knew nothing and my colleagues knew nothing. In my years of running, I have never been helped by anyone with M.D. behind his name. I learned about feet from a podiatrist, muscles from a gymnast coach, the short leg syndrome from a phys. ed. teacher."*

*   *   *

The recent discovery that the brain produces its own opiatelike chemicals promises a complete revision of our understanding of brain function and of much of the rest of the body's chemistry. As Dr. Lewis Thomas puts it, the brain is a different organ than what we thought it was twenty-five years ago: "Far from being an intricate but ultimately simplifiable mass of electronic circuitry governed by wiring diagrams, it now has the aspect of a fundamentally endocrine tissue, in which the essential reactions, the internal traffic of nerve impulses, are determined by biochemical activators and their suppres-

---

* *The Foot Book*, by Harry F. Hlavac, World Publications, Mountain View, Calif., 1977.

sors."* Some of this new understanding is already filtering down to sports.

One small example is a drugless technique for easing pain that is being used with increasing frequency in the treatment of injured athletes. It is *transcutaneous electrical nerve stimulation*, TENS or just TNS. A small electrical device generates current between electrodes which are placed on the skin near the affected area. It works —at least to the extent that medicine understands *how* it works—like acupuncture: stimulation of the appropriate spots on the skin causes the body to generate and release its own natural supply of *endorphins*, the opiatelike endogenous substances that have the capacity to block out pain. So although TNS is drugless in the sense that no foreign substances are introduced into the body, it nevertheless uses natural drugs to ease pain.

TNS treatment doesn't mask pain completely, and therefore reduces the possibility that the athlete will increase the severity of the injury by overusing the affected structure before it heals—which is what Walton claims happened to him. One pro football trainer who uses it regularly claims that TNS treatment can speed healing, because if the pain is eased the athlete can regain his natural motion, and that reduces strain on all affected parts. Favoring one sore part can lead to injuries elsewhere, as in the famous case of Dizzy Dean, whose sore toe caused him to change his pitching motion, which in turn permanently ruined his throwing arm.

(TNS is also claimed to be effective in preventing atrophy of immobilized muscle tissue. Even if the limb is in a cast, TNS causes the motor nerves to fire and therefore gives the muscle fibers the workout they need to keep their size and strength. There's even a theory that increasing the frequency of the electrical signal works out the fast-twitch fibers, and increasing the amplitude of the signal works out the slow-twitch fibers. I'm not sure how much I believe about TNS.)

TNS treatment works to reduce pain the same way the placebo effect does. Placebos work not because of imagination, but because of biochemistry. The brain produces its endorphins when it is stimulated to do so, even if that stimulation is from the imagination. When you ingest a substance that you think is going to bring relief, that belief alone can be sufficient to cause the brain to release the proper

* *The Medusa and the Snail*, Viking, New York, 1979.

chemicals. Those proper chemicals do go to the proper places in the organism, where they ease the pain, stimulate the growth, increase the strength, or do whatever it was you expected the ingested substances to do for you. Since different substances are required to accomplish different physiological tasks, this opens up the startling possibility that the brain is somehow able to select which chemicals will produce which physiological effects. You ask the brain for an effect; it selects the right hormone to cause that effect.

Neither the placebo effect nor TNS is infallible or universally applicable, of course, but when they work they work rather better than medicine does. TNS has been used successfully to treat racehorses, incidentally, which would seem to eliminate the purely psychological element. I don't know of any way of convincing a racehorse that a black box and a couple of wires are going to reduce pain.

Sports stories of miracle recoveries are common; most of us have heard of athletes who have come back after injury in half the time the doctors predicted. Athletes do consistently dumbfound medical science with their recuperative powers, their speed of rehabilitation, their enormous capacity to heal themselves. Now there is speculation that some athletes may be capable of controlling pain by producing endorphins on demand. They may be able to withstand pain not by having more character or stoicism than the rest of us, but by generating, consciously or unconsciously, natural opiates, in response to the pain of the injury itself—by getting rid of the pain, rather than just enduring it. Push that speculation a step farther, and the idea is inescapable that they might also be generating "growth-and-repair" hormones on call, to effect those miracle recoveries.

The next obvious step will be for the rest of us to learn to produce such chemical substances. To do so we might use the biofeedback procedures, for instance, which have already proved effective—occasionally—against migraine headaches, hypertension, peptic ulcer, and other mysterious ailments, particularly those which seem to have an emotional or psychological component. I expect any day now to hear of a training program or device or weekend workshop to teach me—for a couple of hundred bucks—to generate my own natural brain opiates.

In fact, I have already been so proselytized—by the runners. They've been burbling happily about their natural highs for years now. (I've done a little of that burbling myself.) There's a theory that steady, repetitive exercise over an extended period of time may produce some form of these brain chemicals. Ecstatic and visionary states are reportedly achieved by Sufi dancing and other chanting, rhythmic, ritual activities; these states are assumed to result at least in part from the internal production of such natural chemicals.

We are coming to realize more and more clearly that there is a direct link between muscular states and mental and emotional states. (I'm continually amused at how the term "attitude" can be applied with equal appropriateness to a physical or an emotional state. Valium, used mostly to tranquilize the emotions, is actually "only" a muscle relaxant.) In these natural drugs we may have uncovered the chemical basis of that linkage. In any event, the endorphins are so much more than mere pain-killers, so powerful and so little understood that a researcher like Dr. Mandell can speculate that "the equivalent of religion and political systems is in these drugs." *

Getting blissed out is one training effect that the physical education textbooks don't have much to say about, but it might help explain the depth of commitment that some endurance athletes have for their sports.

*   *   *

Much of the foregoing is the airiest of speculation, based on little more than Dr. Thomas' observation that the brain is "fundamentally endocrine tissue." But that notion is so immense that it launches more speculation yet. Some scientists are already predicting a kind of biochemical or hormonal engineering in our future, and it must be assumed that that engineering will be applied to sports. Sports themselves cause hormonal change. Women endurance athletes often find that heavy training can upset them hormonally, interrupting their menses, for example. So far the effect is blamed mostly on the very low percentages of body fat attained by these athletes, the assumption being that with that metabolic reservoir drawn so low, a pregnancy couldn't be carried to term, so the system stops menstruation to stop fertility.

But the larger change works in the other direction: using hormones to change sports. The Eastern Bloc nations are already rumored to be keeping women gymnasts in an unnaturally prepubescent state by

* Boston *Globe*, Feb. 5, 1978.

controlling hormonal levels, to keep down their size and weight. Some European athletes have been disqualified for using steroids, and some American athletes have admitted, more or less formally, to the same offense. Steroids are, of course, hormones. Hormones play a part in all phases of sugar metabolism, which is perhaps the most critical single function in endurance activities.

It is impossible to resist a kind of irresponsible daydreaming about this: there is so much we don't yet know about hormones. Some researchers speculate that the lungs and other organs may secrete their own hormones, signaling changes within themselves and from organ to organ, although as yet we have no means of discovering such a process. One kind of thyroid malfunction slows reflexes, and judicious hormonal balancing is needed to bring that function back to normal. Could additional improvement be possible, to achieve supernormal reflexes? The first artificial production of human growth hormone has recently been announced. Its intended use is in treating afflictions such as dwarfism, but the very idea of using it on normal adolescent athletes raises stupefying possibilities. And dangers. Is hormone-loading in the athletic future?

The point is that this field of research is opening up immense new scientific possibilities. Dr. Thomas (who in addition to being one of the finest living American essayists is also president of Memorial Sloan-Kettering Cancer Center) says without question neurobiology is the most productive place to invest research funds. "The technologies available for quantitative study of individual nerve cells are powerful and precise, and the work is now turning toward the functioning of collections of cells, the centers for visual and auditory perception and the like, because work at this level can now be done," Thomas says. "It is difficult to think of problems that cannot be studied, ever."*

Science and medicine are not athletics, but if the expected new understandings find application in personal health, you can bet your lunch money that their application in the kind of superhealth that athletic performance represents will not be far behind—whether such application is judged to be ethical or not. Athletes have traditionally shown a perfect willingness to undertake experiments with their own bodies and their own health that are of inexpressible riski-

* *The Medusa and the Snail.*

ness. The very power of these methods of hormonal fiddling, and the risk to the individuals undergoing that fiddling, raise horrifying possibilities. The specter of the burned-out husk of an athlete, hormonally crippled or made monstrous, or worse, by the lust for athletic success, is the nightmare that the governance of sport must somehow find a way to avoid. Its performance so far, particularly with regard to steroids and amphetamines, is not one to inspire confidence. In the new science lies modern sports' largest—and most dubious—opportunity. And its most frightening problem.

CHAPTER 14
Tools

Gliders came to our little country airport, turning it into a "soaring center," offering yet another seductive recreation. I couldn't coldly walk away from the chance to acquire another obsession, at least not until I'd learned in some detail how I couldn't afford it. A pilot told me the facts of the soaring life. For example there is one single-seat design, the Schweitzer I-26, that is so popular that competitions are held for it alone, just as in one-design sailboat races. At the time I asked, the basic I-26 cost about $6,000 for the bare airplane, without instrumentation. Or for $7,500 you could get precisely the same airplane, but with flush rivets. That is, for an extra $1,500 the manufacturer would grind off the heads of all the rivets used to attach the skin to the airframe. Since for purposes of drag reduction the quality of finish is of crucial importance to the performance of such a craft, flush rivets are an option worth having.

I managed to avoid buying any kind of glider, but the information about rivets made a deep impression. Fifteen hundred bucks for the removal of something—in order to improve performance—is acutely symbolic of what goes on in the sometimes elegant, sometimes wacky world of sports equipment.

So far we've been looking at the human body as the ultimate piece of athletic equipment, the essential instrument for participating in any given sport. But the other equipment—the wonderful stuff that functions as interface between the athlete and the game—plays an enormous part in the success or failure of that participation. In many sports the development of the equipment has done a great deal more to improve performance than all the physiological and other fiddling that has been so much a part of the modern revolution in sport. It is, of course, a lot easier to modify the tools to improve performance than it is to modify the body (and mind) that uses the tools.

In fact some of this development has been so drastic that it has effectively killed off one sport and replaced it with another, as has almost taken place in the pole vault. That event required a coherent athletic skill with a history traceable through bamboo, steel, and aluminum vaulting poles, with little change other than a gradual increase in the heights being jumped. Then the invention of the fiberglass pole simply turned it into a different event. Pre-fiberglass vaulters relied almost entirely on running speed and arm strength to wrench themselves up to their fifteen-foot heights; today's fiberglass pole vaulters are gymnasts first and track athletes second, working the pole precisely as the diver works the diving board or the trampolinist works the trampoline, pushing now toward nineteen feet. The heights consistently achieved with the fiberglass pole bear little relation to the heights reached before its advent, making a disconcerting hike in the record curve, and begging for some of those asterisks in the record book that the conservative sportswriters so vehemently decry.

(Bob Beamon's epic long jump at Mexico City represents a similar break in the record curve, but one that, never having been duplicated, remains as only a very skinny spike. It was achieved without any external boost other than the thin air of high altitude—and, perhaps, the unusual adrenaline levels that sometimes affect Olympic performers. If modern pole vault records are compared with those of the pre-fiberglass era, the invention of the glass pole has had the effect of moving *all* vaulters into that spooky territory momentarily inhabited by Bob Beamon. No wonder pole vaulters are considered to be a little cuckoo.)

The technological approach to equipment can range from the tiniest personal handicraft—modifying the curve in the blade of the hockey stick, tailoring and shaping the pocket of a baseball glove, even ritually shaving the entire body, as swimmers sometimes do for big meets—to the awesomely complex. The best example of the latter degree of technological input is the very fast "tuned" indoor track at Harvard University, which raises some very hard questions about where the limits lie with sports equipment. Rules are developed to keep constant the conditions under which the sport is practiced; otherwise, painstakingly acquired physical capacities can't be measured against anything but the moment. Many of those rules apply to the equipment used. The track upon which running events are held is a piece of equipment that most particularly must remain constant if records established on it are to have any meaning. But look what's happened at Harvard.

The dimensions of the Harvard track—six lanes, 220 yards per lap—are conventional, and it is built on a supporting substructure made primarily of wood and covered with a polyurethane top surface, which is also in keeping with tradition for indoor tracks. But the substructure and the resulting resiliency of the running surface are designed to fit an analysis of the mechanics of human running. The designers, Thomas A. McMahon and Peter R. Greene, describe the problem:

"One might . . . suppose the hardest track surfaces are the fastest, but that is not the case. A compliant surface acts as a spring, and we found that if the stiffness of the spring is closely tuned to the mechanical properties of the human runner, the runner's speed can be increased. In other words, there is a specific intermediate track compliance at which running speed is optimized. At that optimum compliance the runner stepping down onto the track stores elastic energy in its surface, much as a pole vaulter stores elastic energy in bending a fiberglass pole, which is recovered as the pole propels him upward. A track whose compliance is in the theoretical optimum range can be called a tuned track."*

The analysis done by McMahon and Greene is complex and somewhat controversial, but according to their model, putting the track compliance into the proper range should decrease ground contact time and increase stride length, which in turn should lead to an increase in speed of between 2 and 3 percent. At the end of the first year's use of the new track, records showed an average speed advantage of 2.91 percent. Various other statistical comparisons, including performances of home team versus visiting athletes, bear out its

* "Fast Running Tracks," *Scientific American*, December, 1978.

speed. But the larger gain may be in the forgiving nature of the new surface: ". . . the real advantage of a properly tuned track is probably not its speed enhancement; after all, the opposing teams run faster on it too," say McMahon and Greene. "It is the comfort and safety of a tuned track that give the home team an edge, enabling them to train much harder than they could on an ordinary track. A coach who can train ambitiously without fear of injuring his runners during practice can build a better team. Far fewer runners have been injured on the new track, although the Harvard team trained very hard last year."

The designers also point out that because it is indoors, no world records will be set on the Harvard track. "No outdoor track of optimum mechanical design has yet been built," they say. "If such a track is built, we predict that the world record for the mile could be improved by as much as seven seconds."

At which time another asterisk will go into the record books. Also, track and field rules committees will have to master both biomechanics and landscape architecture, to try to determine just how "tuned" a track can be allowed to be. Otherwise future Olympic Games—which always seem to require that host cities build brand-new facilities—will devolve into track-tuning contests.

* * *

Some sports have become almost purely technological; if that sounds exaggerated, take a good look at the space-age rig (the term "bow" seems completely inappropriate) used by a modern-day competition archer. Often the technological improvement is applied in the most surprising places. In motor racing in the early 1960s a rule change cut the engine size, and thus the horsepower, of Formula One cars by about 40 percent. Yet when the new season started, the much less powerful cars set new lap records on nearly every circuit. The improvement was credited almost entirely to changes in the design and materials used in the tires. Great changes continue to sweep through motor racing—rear-engined cars, turbochargers, wings and aerodynamic downforce—yet those tire improvements keep pace, and in some estimations have by themselves added about one mile per hour per season to established lap records over the past couple of decades.

Another sport that sometimes seems even more technological than motor racing is, strangely enough, skiing. Some credit the invention of stretch pants as the technological breakthrough that made skiing truly popular. Less waggish analysts say it was the invention of metal edges for wooden skis—making secure edge bite and thus much more control available to everyone—that put skiing on the map. But surely as great a contribution to the popularization of the sport was mechanized uphill transportation, beginning with crude rope tows and evolving through chairlifts and bubble gondolas to the massive 120-passenger aerial tramways that now festoon the world's larger ski mountains. Getting people effortlessly up the hill so they could slide down again was clearly the development that turned a hitherto elitist sport into mass recreation.

Ah, but that was just the start. Following steel edges came metal skis (actually aluminum and plywood sandwiches), which made turning so easy they were called "cheaters," but which gave way, in turn, to fiberglass skis. Ski technology expanded rapidly into exotic materials in the early 1960s, and before long ski designers claimed to be able to build in precisely the amount of torque-resistance, damping, camber, stiffness, or anything else you wanted, and put it at any point along the length of the ski. Ski lengths came down, went back up, came down again. (Skiing technique and style, and teaching methods, changed to match the evolving skis.) Finally the ski manufacturers discovered dynamic obsolescence and went to annual model changes, which were mostly cosmetic; a kind of decadence set in. But the modern ski is so far superior to the old woodies that skiing on them is, again, virtually a whole new sport.

As with skis, so with boots: lace boots, double-lace boots, buckle boots, plastic boots, a steady increase in stiffness (and price) coupled with a steady (if belated) reduction in weight. Bindings (the gadgets that hold ski to ski boot) ditto: increasing complexity, increasing sophistication, increasing price. And, the technologists would claim, increasing effectiveness. By the mid-1970s, parents of ski racers saw their kids heading for the slopes with a $500 investment from the ankles down.

Racing has been the impetus for much of the technological development in skiing. Although ski racing is about as far removed from recreational skiing as the Indianapolis 500 is from commuting to work in a station wagon, nevertheless the lessons learned in materials and their application, in making the equipment more controllable and more responsive, have helped shape the consumer product. But in the frantic search for a competitive edge, racing has also shown a tendency to turn absurd. Downhill racers regularly reach speeds—sixty to eighty miles per hour—at which wind resistance becomes significant. They use wind-tunnel testing as a training aid; they ski as much of a downhill course as possible in a tucked-up "egg" position to reduce frontal area. To lower wind resistance further, they put streamlining cones on the baskets on the end of the ski poles, bend those poles elaborately (and nonfunctionally) to allow the racer to tuck the poles more tightly against the body, wrap the turbulence-raising boot buckles in wind-slick spats. Racers have long worn one-piece racing suits in the downhill event to reduce wind resistance. A few years back these suits were switched from conventional stretch fabrics to super-slick windproof plastic, and racers gained another second or two down the mountain.

Unfortunately, the new slick-surfaced suits proved to be rather faster than skis—when the racer was on his or her backside, after a fall. When you fell wearing one of the new suits, you still had the problem of figuring out how to stop. Racers suffered some truly horrendous falls, sliding great distances at hair-raising speeds down steep downhill courses, slamming into barriers. Some serious injuries were blamed on the new suits. In the meantime, recreational skiwear blossomed out in the slick new fabrics, so by the time the International Ski Federation banned the suits from racing, recreational skiers were encountering the same safety problems as the racers. The racers fought the ban, of course, disregarding safety as competitors often do in any sport. One dodge was to wear the slick suit inside out, hoping to show enough nap to the material to pass the officials while maintaining the windproof qualities of the plastic. The controversy goes on; World Cup race results have been protested, and the protests upheld, over the texture of the fabric worn by the racers.

Technological development continues to reshape skiing. The switch from wooden to fiberglass cross-country racing skis forced development of a whole new ski technique. The glass skis are in some senses like wearing McMahon's springy tuned track on the bottom of your feet. In the wooden ski era, cross-country racing was dominated by slim, lightweight, subtly skilled racers built in the marathoner mold; now it has become a power sport, and coaches look for "horses," burly young athletes who can overpower the new skis.

(And, I suspect, steroids have come to cross-country ski racing as a result.) Carbon-shafted ski poles—unbelievably light and strong, and unbelievably expensive—help these young studs power their way to higher rates of speed.

In ski jumping—a sport only vaguely related either to downhill or cross-country skiing—new boots rise well up along the back of the jumper's calf, to help him get the tips of his skis up into proper aerodynamic alignment for his flight, and at Lake Placid in 1980 some jumping skis sprouted ailerons on the rear for additional flight control. (As with pole vaulting, there is no ski jumping competition for women.) I was marveling at this touch of technological fussiness while in the presence of a jumping coach. "Hell, that's nothing," he snorted, and proceeded to tell me of the invention of a catapult device for training, which actually launches ski jumpers into flight—like a giant slingshot, without the necessity of sliding down a hill or jumping off a lip into space—so they can learn to fly better during the aerial portion of their jumps.

I've gone to excessive lengths here to describe technical developments in skiing (while still treating those developments only superficially) just because it is a sport I know fairly well. Precisely the same kind of development is, of course, going on in all other sports as well. There was also a fabric controversy, for example, in women's swimming suits not long ago. American racers refused to wear the new slick suits as too revealing—until the East Germans started winning while wearing the suits, at which point the Americans overcame their concern for modesty. Carbon-shafted golf clubs, bike frames, tennis rackets, and the like have recently been touted as the ultimate—and most expensive—breakthrough in sporting implements. But the carbon filament development is only one of an unbroken chain of technological advancements in sports that continue to raise the levels of performance. It is not always the most positive development, but it is no more likely to cease than are competitors likely to stop keeping score.

*   *   *

A friend of mine is the quintessential southern Californian: surfer, motorcylist, pilot, skier, hang-glider, skateboarder, the works. He told me about a moment of truth in his adolescence. He was equally attracted to skiing and motor racing. He thought it out very carefully. Ski equipment doesn't require much maintenance. If one was a skier, one could ski all day, but what to do at night? He'd be reduced to sitting around with nothing to do. Racing cars require a great deal of maintenance. That meant he could race cars all day and fix cars all night, and never risk a moment's noninvolvement in the sport. He chose motor racing.

My friend's hyperkinetic zeal may be unusual, but I suspect more than one sports enthusiast has made that kind of choice: rather than some recreation like basketball or weight lifting that you just go out and do every day, you choose instead a sport in which the equipment is very hard to get just right. (The equipment nut may have a physiological cousin in the body builder, who spends a similar amount of time maintaining his—or her—flesh. There's also the possibility that some sportspersons invest equal amounts of "maintenance" time in the healing and rehabilitation of injuries. This is a parallel I don't want to think about.) At any rate the fascination of trying to get complex equipment to function just *so*, in support of one's performance in a sport, is enormously gripping.

I think I understand my southern California friend, as I have fallen in love with sports equipment as often as anybody; I have become hypnotized by the fit of fine machinework, the exquisite craftsmanship so often lavished on implements used for play. That fatal weakness led me at one time to work for the Ziff-Davis Publishing Company, a magazine factory that caters to those yearnings. They publish *Car and Driver, Skiing, Boating, Flying, Popular Photography*, a string of so-called special-interest publications, in which the ads for all that delectable hardware are considerably more interesting and more valuable to the reader than is the editorial material used to hold those ads apart. (When you acquire a new sports obsession, you go to the newsstand, right? So you can pick up the magazine about that sport, and study the ads for the equipment used?) By the time I left that company I envisioned the American male as a creature sitting—bored—in a pile of toys: rackets, bats, skis, fishing rods, guns, skateboards, running shoes, outboard motors, motorcycles, scuba gear, cameras, sleeping bags, binoculars, cleats, gloves, masks, sports cars, boats, airplanes. A depressing vision it was, and is. Those magazines are very successful.

Ziff-Davis and I complicate the picture: it doesn't take that much complicated machinery to scratch the itch for good sports equipment. Or maybe the itch just gets more complex with age. As a kid I had a baseball glove that I loved more than I loved my dog. Before I was old enough to warrant such equipment, a wealthy relative gave me a pair of real football shoes—black high-tops of kangaroo leather, with brutal cleats—that were my proudest possession for several years. I wore them—selectively, for special occasions—long past the age when my feet had grown so large I had to double up my toes like a clenched fist to get them on at all.

I also owned, serially, three or four official Lou Gehrig model Louisville Sluggers. Softball, which grown-ups accurately perceived as safer than hardball, was the bane of my childhood years, and I bought my own baseball bat to express my contempt for the playground game. One had only to compare the respective bats to understand the chasm between the two disciplines, the significance of the real McCoy. A softball bat is fat, thick-handled, light in weight, graceless; a baseball bat is a work of the latheman's art, a whippy, almost delicate handle tapering gracefully to an impressively solid and dangerous mass at the business end. (I just realized those proportions always symbolically spoke to me of Babe Ruth, the maximum bat-wielder of all time—the Ruthian ankles corresponding to the slender handle, the Ruthian torso to the barrel.) A softball bat was a kid's toy; a baseball bat was sports equipment.

There were seldom enough kids around to get up a full-fledged game in which to swing my bat in anger, however, so it stood unused for long periods, stimulating the imagination. I acquired a golf ball, and in an inspired moment fungoed it with my Louisville Slugger. It disappeared. I can't tell you how satisfying that moment was, even if it lost me my golf ball. A golf ball solidly hit with a baseball bat takes off with about the same muzzle velocity as a round from a .50-caliber buffalo rifle. I began haunting water hazards, acquired a few more lost golf balls, instantly made them disappear also. In an effort to make them last longer, to make them more retrievable, I tried "golfing" them, swinging underneath and driving them as high as possible. That tactic permanently destroyed my baseball swing but provided me with an engaging if short-lived solitary recreation. I learned to drive a golf ball about twenty stories straight up, so high that if it happened to come down on a solid concrete surface, the first bounce would be higher than I could throw a golf ball unaided.

The reason I owned bats serially was that I would always eventually lose my last golf ball, or drive it into some completely inaccessible location, and then in frustration pick up a rock and smack *that* out of sight. The first time I hit a rock its flight was almost as satisfying as that of a golf ball, and while the rock left a thumbprint-sized dent in the wood of the bat it didn't seem to do that much harm, so what the hell, why not hit another one? Another indentation. After fifteen or twenty such blows, the barrel of that bat was so misshapen that it was no longer good for baseball, so it became my rock-hitting bat. Unfortunately, two or three hypnotic hours of that idiotic pastime proved sufficient to reduce to splintery pulp the last twelve inches of a good Louisville Slugger, making it no longer useful for anything but firewood. I immediately started saving money to buy another bat. Which, inevitably, on one boring afternoon, became my next rock-hitting bat, and so on. A golf ball is a pretty satisfying piece of sports equipment too, isn't it?

* * *

Among the brighter people who go to work for General Motors, the assignment most treasured is to that corporation's Tech Center, a 21st-century technological wonderland where the far-out research and design stuff goes on. Most of what transpires there is secret, so exciting rumors circulate about the Tech Center at all times. One used to hear regularly, for example, that General Motors, which does not officially participate in motor racing, each year builds a car that could win the Indianapolis 500. Purely as a design exercise, the technical mavens examine previous winning performances, assess the state of the art in race car building, and then construct a car that would win the race if it were only let out of the supersecret confines of the Tech Center. I heard that story a dozen times, back in the late 1950s and early 1960s.

I never quite bought that apocryphal tale, but there's another rather more charming story that has the ring of truth to it. In this legend, back in the early 1950s, someone at the GM Tech Center decided that it was time to apply modern technological smarts to bobsled racing, at which the U.S. teams usually did poorly. GM would defend the flag. The Tech Center's wind tunnels and rudimentary early computers were put to work; supersled was created. It was smaller (less frontal area), sleeker (better streamlining), with precision steering gear to replace the crude traditional ropes and pulleys. It had a totally new runner design that was a quantum leap better than the old style, with all new materials, new finishes, new metallurgy throughout. Two supersleds were built—at a rumored $80,000 per—and shipped off with the U.S. team to a big international meet.

But what worked in the wind tunnel didn't work on the bobsled run, of course: the sleds were almost unsteerable, the new runners were unable to withstand the stresses of real-life bobsled racing and collapsed regularly, and on the few occasions when the sleds managed to complete a run they were just depressingly slow. In the story, the disgusted U.S. team shipped the GM wondersleds home as experimental junk, and competed on borrowed sleds. I have no idea whether this story is true, but the other day I heard a strong rumor that a well-known former motor racing driver is going to go bobsled racing. Thirty years after the GM effort, he's planning to use modern technology, computer analysis, and all the rest to build up some worldbeater bobsleds for future competition. Hold your breath.

Whether or not the GM story is true—and some small part of me hopes that it is, as a glimmer of the best sort of human craziness in that corporate megastructure—it points up a recurrent theme in the way man grapples with sports: someone is always fiddling with the equipment.

• Shaving one's body to reduce water friction for important swimming meets may not be enough to stay competitive. An Iowa osteopath, Jon Van Cleave, has invented a spray-on solution that's supposed to "hydrodynamically friction-proof" the swimmer. "Time-Off" is $6.95 for a ten-ounce can, according to *Sports Illustrated*. (The U.S. Navy has studied the water-slick surface of dolphins in search of technological improvement for the exterior finish of submarines—but so far as I've heard, none of that research has yet funneled down to sports.)

• Inventors have recently put gasoline engines on skateboards, roller skates, skis, surfboards, and hang gliders. That wasn't enough for Burt Shulman, who has installed a gasoline engine on a human being. It's a running machine—a one-horsepower engine on an aluminum backpack, driving padded levers which push the thighs forward alternately, leaving the calves to keep up on their own. I don't know how well it works, but the device left *The New York Times* talking wryly about three-minute miles.

• Varying the size of the dimples on the surface of a golf ball can impart a gyroscopic action to the ball in flight that makes it straighten out the slice or hook that the golfer may have unintentionally given it. This development, illegal for tournament play, helps the duffer but not the pro, who often deliberately curves his or her shots.

• Shoe designers have for years devised sports shoes with different tread patterns on the soles for different types of artificial surfaces and different sports. Now they're working on plate-mounted cleats that will swivel away under excessive pressure from the wrong direction, in hopes of reducing or eliminating sports-related knee injuries. Also being tested is an inertia-reel knee brace that bends easily with natural pressure but locks up to prevent motion from sudden blows or in unnatural directions.

• Until recently skaters' boots were evolving in the direction of ski boots, toward a more rigid encasement of the foot to allow instant translation of movement from foot to blade. But medical problems developed from hyper-rigid boots, so now skate manufacturers are working with podiatrists, orthopedists, and biomechanists to correct the problems. Thus skate and ski boots, already reinvented once in the direction of more rigidity, are having to be reinvented once again to solve the problems that rigidity brought.

• Swimming continues to generate more or less wacky technological touches. "Dragin" is a training swimsuit with pockets that fill with water as you swim, creating extra drag and making you work harder to maintain a given pace. "Pasar" is an electronic gadget that straps to the swimmer's head and beeps rhythmically to teach a regular stroke. (Similar gadgets are available for runners.) The coach can also buy a transmitter that allows changes in the Pasar's pace from poolside. "Cybertron" is an electronic mitten that tells the swimmer, by audible tone, how much water pressure is being exerted on the hand, and therefore how hard the swimmer is pulling with each stroke. None of these gadgets is quite so outlandish as an East German scheme attempted a few years back, in which the swimmers' intestines were inflated with compressed air, to increase flotation, get the swimmer higher in the water, and reduce resistance. Too painful for practical application, the tactic was abandoned.

• There have been "tuned" swimming pools longer than there have been tuned tracks. Gutters and lane markers are now designed to damp out water turbulence, which slows racers. A deep pool is a fast pool—the depth keeps down waves—so new pools are being built deeper than the old standards. Electronic starting blocks and touch plates at the pool ends are now in general use, not only to time races to the hundredth of a second, but also to make sure each racer touches each end of the pool and to disqualify relay racers who leave the starting block early.

• Electronic communication between coach and athlete is increasing. Motor racers can talk to their pits, arranging repairs and scheduling stops as they race. Now walkie-talkies are used increasingly by coaching teams out on long courses—in cross-country and downhill ski racing, in marathons, in cycle racing. Racers can be advised of their official positions while the race progresses, can ask for nourishment or equipment changes, can advise team members of changing course conditions, can get tactical advice. So far ski racers don't carry radios themselves, but receive messages relayed from radio-equipped coaches at trackside. Miniaturization should enable racers to send as well as receive during competition before long.

• A few seasons ago Houston Oiler quarterback Dan Pastorini broke three ribs just before a crucial play-off game. Yet in that game he completed fifteen out of twenty passes, painlessly, despite being sacked more than once. He was wearing a five-and-a-half-ounce inflatable "flak vest" to protect his rib cage, designed by Byron Donzis, inventor also of the inertia-reel knee brace. Pastorini continued to wear the vest after his ribs healed; the inflatable concept is now being tested for padding for the rest of the players' bruised and battered bodies, under a half-million-dollar grant from the National Football League to inventor Donzis. It could not only lessen or prevent future injuries, but also improve performance markedly, since the nonrestrictive padding weighs considerably less than current padding. Its use is expected to expand to other sports.*

• Also, in the 1980 Winter Olympics, technology came to luge racing. The Poles were rumored to have a new alloy for sled runners,

---

* Donzis had trouble getting to Pastorini to show him his invention, according to Dave Brady of the *Washington Post*. "He had an unmarked room at Methodist Hospital," Donzis told Brady. "I went there with an associate. He was carrying a baseball bat and I had my flak jacket. The fifth floor nurse stopped us—she probably thought I was going to beat Dan to death. I pleaded with her to open the door . . . I put the jacket on, I put my hands above my head, and my associate . . . hit me as hard as he could with the bat four or five times in the area where Pastorini said his ribs were sorest. I got everybody's attention."

which they shared with the Russians but not with the East Germans. The East Germans had become so dominant in that and most other sports that even their Communist brethren weren't giving away anything else to them. The East Germans won.

A more interesting technical development was the use of plastic mouthpieces by the luge riders. The mouthpieces were intended just to help keep the teeth from chattering during high-speed runs on rough ice, but wearers found that the mouthpieces also helped them brace their cervical spines during the runs, which reduced fatigue. This also reduced headaches—an occupational hazard among luge riders—and radically improved vision.

That reminds me of the Chaparral, a very successful sports racing car in the mid-1960s designed and driven by Jim Hall. Among other innovations, the Chaparral had a fiberglass chassis, in effect glued together. For a more adjustable test-bed, Hall's crew built a duplicate car, but with an all-aluminum chassis held together with conventional rivets and bolts. The aluminum car vibrated so severely that its driver could hardly see to race. The crew named it "E.B.J."—for Eye-Ball Jiggler.

• And so on. Aluminum baseball bats are popular at lower levels of the game, although banned in the big leagues. (Aluminum bats are so lively that players fear someone might be killed if they are allowed in the majors.) Finish lines at most kinds of racing now feature automatic photography to help analyze close results; electronic timing to the hundredth of a second is generally available (but, inconceivably, not considered for records in track and field). Titanium is used in golf club shafts, in racing car parts, in any sporting usage where great strength with light weight is more important than the high cost of fabrication. (It was a similar use of magnesium in the Mercedes-Benz sports car that crashed at Le Mans in the late 1950s which raised the death toll so severely. Car body parts actually caught fire and were spewed into the crowd.) Officiating by instant replay, line calling by electric eye or electronic sensors, scheduling of training programs by computer analysis, all are technically feasible, awaiting only economic justification—and public acceptance—to be put into use. Great breakthroughs still await in many aspects of personal safety, however, and no economic justification should be necessary to push that research forward. The football helmet is still the worst offender in sports, but the breakthrough that will tame that lethal instrument hasn't been made.

* * *

Technological developments often force sports authorities to reach definitions where none existed before. In the tennis boom of the early 1970s, the technologists discovered that tennis rules neglected to define the tennis racket. One result was "spaghetti stringing"— extra, loosely strung filaments that make for softer but trickier and much less predictable returns, with much more spin on the ball. The fate of spaghetti stringing is still up in the air: one body of opinion says it produces unplayable shots and is therefore an unfair advantage; the other view holds that it is only a passing aberration that will have no permanent place in the game. The latter opinion really means that until someone wins a major tournament with the slack strings, they can be ignored.

The other development in tennis is the oversize racket, which top-ranked players disparage but which some lesser players swear by. Big-racket fanciers say it has a larger sweet spot—they're able to make a higher percentage of accurate returns using the racket, since they don't have to hit the ball quite so squarely to make it go where they want it to.

Several years after introduction of the larger racket, a physicist named Howard Brody analyzed what really goes on when a tennis racket hits the ball. Using laser beams, oscilloscopes, and other resources of a Princeton University lab, he dissected rackets big and small. As it turns out, the sweet spot—formally, the center of percussion—is only marginally larger in the oversize racket, but it is closer to the center of the racket's playing surface. In conventional rackets the sweet spot is usually an inch or two closer to the handle than the center of the playing surface. That means that the sweet spot may be easier to hit with the larger racket, not because it is bigger, but because it is closer to where your visual sense of the racket would put it. And strokes hit from that sweet spot may be hit harder than with a conventional racket, since the sweet spot is farther from the hand and thus has more leverage behind it.

Brody took his analysis a great deal farther. He determined that when you miss the sweet spot, the ball stretches the strings asymmetrically, so it rebounds at an angle to where you intended it to go —the farther from the sweet spot the more erratic the return. Also, the farther you miss the sweet spot, the more vibration or torque is transmitted back up to your hand—and your tennis elbow. Tennis balls are not particularly lively, losing about half their kinetic energy upon rebound. The ratio of the ball's speed before impact to its speed after impact is the *coefficient of restitution*. Because of this low return energy, the pace on the shot has to come from the racket head. The speed of the return is a product of *dwell time* (the amount of time the ball stays in contact with the racket's strings) and the *oscillation period*, which is the rebound time of the racket head itself. Optimum power would come from a racket in which the dwell time equaled oscillation time. Most rackets are too slow—the ball comes and goes before the racket has rebounded—and could be stiffened to shorten oscillation time. You could gain further power by matching the racket's oscillation period to the tennis ball's coefficient of restitution, by stringing the racket more loosely than the forty-five to sixty pounds of tension that most good players prefer. How loosely to string the racket depends on the frame design and the liveliness of the balls to be used. Spaghetti stringing goes much too far, of course, but then the spaghetti players aren't interested in power.

Unfortunately, we don't know what kind of tennis balls Dr. Brody used. Arthur Ashe speaks about their variations:

"One of the strangest things in tennis is that for all the fuss always made over the difference among court surfaces, virtually nothing is ever said or written about the differences in balls—and let me tell you that the change in balls is a great deal more difficult to cope with than the change in surfaces. . . . The fastest balls are the Wilson and Spalding. Then comes Slazenger, the Wimbledon choice, then the Dunlop, and finally the Italian Pirelli and the Swedish Tretorn. The last two are really slow balls. Hell, you can stick an ice pick through a Tretorn and it won't make any difference.

"The American balls, in baseball terminology, are much livelier. You hit one right and it goes *bing*. You can wrist them around, flick them, and they get easier to handle the longer you play with one. A Wilson loses its fuzz and gets noticeably smaller. Really. On the other hand, the European balls are heavy and get deader the longer you play with one. You hit a Pirelli or a Tretorn, even a Dunlop, it goes *thump.* You try to wrist one of them, it will just die on your racket. European balls are just not flickable. Not at all.

"Because the Europeans grow up with the slower balls, they tend to build an entirely different game than what we incline to in America."*

Dr. Brody's physics and Arthur Ashe's experiential detail only illustrate the nature and degree of analysis that goes on in all modern sports in the pursuit of performance. Those legends of the bright young GM Tech Center types come from another generation, and also come only from taking too lightly the grasp of detail that championship-level experience with a sport must bring.

*   *   *

Only a few Olympiads ago it was an athletic college boy's lark to make an Olympic team, just to get an expense-paid trip to an exotic locale. You picked some minor sport in which few in the United States had ever competed—canoeing, team handball, the biathlon —and practiced it only enough to beat out the seven or eight other people in the country who were aware of the sport's existence. (The only better dodge was to have the luck to be born in some small nation that couldn't afford to get serious about the Olympics, and get oneself appointed to their squad—in whatever sport.) You got the trip, two or three very unusual weeks in Melbourne or Tokyo or somewhere, and although you would come in 67th in your competition—because no matter how obscure the sport, there would be droves of others who would take it very seriously indeed—nevertheless you would forever thereafter be an "Olympian," a member of the club. More than one business or social career has been built on just that kind of athletic opportunism. But the days when those easy Olympic team slots were available have gone the way of wooden skis, bamboo vaulting poles, and leather football helmets.

*   *   *

The force behind the evolution of sports equipment is expressed idealistically in the horseman's cliché about how racing improves the breed. Competition is the crucible that refines equipment as well as

* *Arthur Ashe: Portrait in Motion*, by Arthur Ashe with Frank Deford, Houghton Mifflin Co., Boston, 1975.

bloodlines. Perhaps. Cynics point out that the only development to make its way from the Indianapolis 500 onto production automobiles is the rear-view mirror. That's unfair; motor racing has generated many more subtle improvements, in metallurgy, lubrication, tire compounds, and the like. But there is some justification for the cynicism. If you use horse track records as the standard, for example, the improvement of thoroughbreds through racing has been desperately slow and inconsistent, for all those compulsively maintained breeding charts and bloodlines.

Perhaps a more intriguing question is just who benefits from these competition-honed improvements in equipment. Leonard Koppett addressed the question in *The New York Times*:

"The golf clubs used by Jack Nicklaus or Tom Watson today are strikingly different in construction from the ones used a generation ago by Ben Hogan or Jimmy Demaret—but the stroke average of the leading players is virtually the same. . . .

"Baseball played on artificial turf requires adjustment in the positioning of fielders, decisions about bunting and newly designed shoes —but neither scores nor statistics are drastically different. . . .

"Football teams use movie film and computer printouts to analyze strategy, evaluate personnel and refine playing techniques—but the actual games produce virtually the same mix (number of plays, points scored, margins of victory) as 30 years ago.

". . . these examples make several points about the nature of technological change in sports. They have a great effect on techniques used by the players without a correspondingly great effect on the results achieved; they make games easier for the ordinary recreational player but don't change the relative strength of professionals competing against each other at the highest level; they make games safer, create better conditions for play and constantly increase the complexity of the paraphernalia, but they do not touch the underlying simplicity of purpose around which each game is built."*

Competition does provide a strong evolutionary force in equipment development, but it is business competition rather than athletic competition. The manufacture and sale of athletic equipment is a huge industry; athletic shoes alone constitute a billion-dollar annual piece of business. Interestingly, the professional athletes, who ob-

* "Can Technology Win the Game?" April 24, 1978.

viously need the best and most meticulously prepared equipment, get all of it free. (Thus you have such extreme cases as basketball player Adrian Dantley, under who knows how large a contract to Adidas, demanding and getting a brand new pair of shoes for every game.) Even when the manufacturer is not paying athletes to use the equipment, it is supplied free for their use, by either the manufacturer or the athlete's employer.

It is the consumer athlete who pays the tab for that competitive development. It is the consumer who, because of lack of practice time or marginal skills or simple delusion about his or her aptitudes, is driven to paroxysms of frustration by the intricacies of the chosen sport. Lured ever upward by performance levels seen on the tube or at the club or playground, operating often as not on distorted or insufficient information about the sport, tantalized by the ads that fill the special-interest publications, the consumer athlete goes to the local pro shop and tries to buy some performance. It is the impulse that fuels the sporting goods business, and it is almost irresistible. Every would-be athlete has experienced it: if I just had that new gizmo—computer-designed putter, high-rise ski boot, aerodynamic racket frame, flush rivets on my glider—I could beat those other guys. I could buy myself an edge. (Although, considering our capacities for self-delusion, it is more likely that what we really think is that the new equipment will allow us finally to play up to our innate potential. And who's to deny that possibility?)

There is some justification for this wistful dream. New equipment very definitely can improve performance. Occasionally, although less often than the industry would have us believe, a new development comes along that makes a real performance difference for the beginning to middle-level participant. Reducing the length of alpine skis, for instance, markedly upgraded the level of skiing technique of most skiers, almost across the board. Fiberglass—making possible small, lightweight, supremely maneuverable surfboards—was practically responsible for the invention of modern surfing. The urethane skate wheel—more compliant and forgiving, not so likely to trip up the user at every pebble and matchstick in the path—put hundreds of thousands of us on wheels, and rescued a near-dead skateboard and roller-skate industry.

But the larger effect of the new equipment may be psychological. It's the feather-in-Dumbo's-trunk effect again: you know you have new equipment, you believe it is going to make you perform better, and—perhaps just because of the confidence that knowledge gives you—you do. The new equipment, by its slightly unfamiliar feel, keeps reminding you of itself, at least until you become inured to the difference. This sensory awareness can keep you conscious of the subtle strengths and weaknesses of your own technique, can help you concentrate better on avoiding habitual errors, can therefore bring about a real improvement in your technique.

I know this is true because the new skis I got season before last did make me fly—and now that I think of it, so did the pair I got the year before that, although, of course, they rather let me down before that season was over. So dependable is this twisted version of the placebo effect that it goes to extreme lengths. When I was professionally employed in ski-biz I was occasionally given a new pair of skis, "just to try out," by one manufacturer or another. Those new skis also helped me ski better, but never did the freebies help as much as the ones I paid for out of my own pocket. (I understand the same technique is useful in medicine, particularly psychoanalysis. The more expensive the therapy, the faster the patient improves.)

I'm sorry if this equipment nonsense makes me sarcastic, but I've been in it for so long—a lustful scrambler after the technological secret that will improve my own game, as well as a reporter on that technology—that I've grown jaundiced. I think it is a very American notion that goes far beyond athletic performance: some gadget is going to make all the difference, in our sports, in our businesses, in our lives. Against that silly hope, as irrepressible in every sense, lies The Legend. In The Legend, the Old Pro is in a situation where the only equipment at hand is hopelessly out of date, broken, ill-fitting, outclassed, in every way unsuitable. The Old Pro picks it up and uses it anyway, and proceeds to whip the socks off the Young Whippersnapper, who, of course, is using the very latest and best in technological gizmos. You've heard a dozen such stories, just as I have.

I'd pay less attention to The Legend if I hadn't once watched a mechanized version of it play itself out. Racing driver Stirling Moss once found himself unaccountably without a car to race at Sebring. This was in the late 1950s, before the accident that forced Moss into retirement, when the twelve-hour endurance race at Sebring was still an important international event. Some kind of contractual foul-up had left Moss temporarily without wheels. At the last moment someone asked him to drive a reasonably well-prepared Austin-Healey roadster, and to the amazement of the world of motor sports, he accepted.

The Healey was only a production sports car, and the field of pure racers against which it would run at Sebring had about three times the horsepower with half the weight. It was roughly equivalent to going up against a sky full of F-116s in a P-40. There was some kind of class award for the little roadster, but a driver of the stature of Stirling Moss just did not drive for a class award, running an itty-bitty car back in the ruck. Moss, however, recognized a situation in which he couldn't lose. He could simply drive the car as fast as it would go until it broke, retire it with honor, pick up his paycheck, and be headed back to England while the serious racers were still droning on.

He did just that—but while the Healey ran, Moss put it well and truly up among the big boys. Nobody ever saw an Austin-Healey go like that before or since. Moss simply turned it, temporarily, into a bona fide racing car, and he did it by the sheer force of his skill and nerve. Since he was giving away thirty—or forty, or fifty—miles per hour on the straightaways, he couldn't afford to slow for the twisty parts, so he didn't. He simply went through, sideways most of the time, at rates of speed that couldn't really be comprehended. The sight of the Austin-Healey passing whole strings of much faster cars is forever etched on my memory—outbraking them on the inside of slow curves, motoring past them on the outside of faster ones, stripping them off in traffic. By the seventh hour of the race Moss had forced the car up to about fifth place overall, ahead of dozens of racing cars with half again the performance of his puny mount. In the process he reduced the poor Healey to a smoking hulk of a burned-out sports car, and, predictably, it finally died. Ah, but while it lasted we got to see a master at his craft. It was clearly a case of an athlete overcoming the equipment he had to work with, an example of The Legend that demonstrates that it is not the gizmo, not the tool, it is the tool-user that makes the real difference. I try to remember that when the urge comes on me to buy a better pair of skis.

I doubt that the Austin-Healey people learned much from the occasion that they could use to improve their breed of sports car. But maybe the experience—especially for pilots of superior machines, who found themselves embarrassed by Moss' demonstration ride—did something to improve the breed of racing drivers.

*   *   *

Although I am continually seduced by the new and the technologically clever, I hope I am sensitive also to the loving craftsmanship lavished on the most traditional of the tools with which we play. Not that the new stuff is necessarily clumsy or gross: various new racket designs, fencing foils, helmets, even an entire racing car, have been displayed at the Museum of Modern Art as exemplary of superior modern design. New or old, there is something in sports equipment that brings out purity of materials and craftsmanship, that hones away the superfluous and merely decorative, that causes the makers to bring an extra degree of care to the making. Some good sports equipment easily lasts an athletic lifetime and is passed on. Other equipment is no stronger than it needs to be (usually in order to save weight), and often is even designed to be expendable, to break and to be replaced. But the expendability doesn't come from shortcuts that violate the integrity of design and material that so distinguishes it in the first place.

The examples that demonstrate this most clearly are the rigorously traditional, frozen in form and duplicated only by the most assiduous attention to detail. In some cases the specifics are preserved as if in amber:

"It weighs just over five ounces and measures between 2.86 and 2.94 inches in diameter. It is made of a composition-cork nucleus encased in two thin layers of rubber, one black and one red, surrounded by 121 yards of tightly wrapped blue-gray wool yarn, 45 yards of white wool yarn, 53 more yards of blue-gray wool yarn, 150 yards of fine cotton yarn, a coat of rubber cement, and a cowhide (formerly horsehide) exterior, which is held together with 216 slightly raised red cotton stitches. Printed certifications, endorsements, and outdoor advertising spherically attest to its authenticity. Like most institutions, it is considered inferior in its present form to its ancient archetypes, and in this case the complaint is probably justified; on occasion in recent years it has actually been known to come apart under the demands of its brief but rigorous active career." *

The subject is the modern baseball, of course, and these are the manufacturing specifications for it. (Surprisingly, the official rules of baseball are far less detailed.) If specifications down to the color of the yarn seem a trifle picky, one has only to consider the continuing disputes over the liveliness of the ball, down through the years. In the face of the occasional spurts and slumps in home-run production that now and then afflict baseball, the authorities are always accused of fiddling with the ball—and always swear they haven't done so. The players themselves often claim they can tell the difference, that the quality of the balls has changed markedly in one direction or the other. (Pitchers claim they're livelier, hitters that they're deader.) And despite Leonard Koppett's assurances that technological changes don't necessarily change the games in which they are made, it is clear that a very small manipulation of the ancient standards of baseball can effect great revisions in the game. During the last great hitting slump in the 1960s, the pitcher's mound was lowered only a few inches, and yet league-wide batting averages immediately took a twenty-point leap upward. (What that says, biomechanically, about the pitching effectiveness of a five-foot eight-inch pitcher versus a six-foot six-inch pitcher is worth considering.)

This kind of structural fragility makes the very primitiveness of the baseball itself reassuring. Science could surely produce a "better" baseball. It might have a petrochemical-based composite core dipped into some kind of plastifiber material, computer-tested to retain the precise liveliness of, for instance, the average baseball in play on July 8, 1972—or 1922, or pick your year. It could be covered with some extruded seamless plastic coating—molded to retain the stitched contour—that would retain the desired characteristics of flight and rebound, yet never wear out, never need be rejected by the pitcher for a duplicate example. A lot of the conservatism of baseball is simply irritating, but that that obvious step has never been taken is somehow admirable.

Instead you have the traditional baseball, just a touch scruffy even as it comes out of the box. In part this is because each individual

---

* *Five Seasons*, by Roger Angell, Simon and Schuster, New York, 1977.

baseball put into play in the major leagues has been previously hand-rubbed with some of the same clay from that same mysterious site somewhere in the mudflats of Chesapeake Bay. In an age of vulcanized computer-wound polywrapped extrusions, to find a piece of equipment made of cork and yarn and the skins of animals, *sewn* together (with bone needles?), is to get a vision of baseball shoved back through time, maybe even out of the reach of the demographers and marketing analysts who have come to control so much of modern sports.

And that the product of those detailed specifications can be so entirely satisfying a physical object—so nearly perfectly round, so warm to the touch, such a satisfactory size and weight to catch and to hit, but most of all to throw—is more reassuring yet. We have to take comfort where we can. What with free-agency and the playing out of options and other terrorist activities against the placid immutability of baseball, those specifications for manufacture begin to take on the flavor of an incantation. One would almost expect them to be handed down orally. I get this image of the assembled major league club owners, hunkered down around a boardroom table, chanting those specifications in unison before their annual meeting. Before sitting down to decide where to shift which franchise for maximum profits, and how to hold up the networks for more cash. Up front.

Well, my imagination gets away from me. Nevertheless, there is something immensely appealing about the official major league baseball. It's only a thing of hide and string and human craftsmanship, but while it is a perfectly suitable and useful implement for the playing of a fascinating game, I'd maintain it's also just the sort of object that an anthropologist might turn up in a mud hut someplace. On an altar, perhaps, along with other curious objects of bone and feathers and beads.

CHAPTER 15
Yokes

"Now we're going to do some O.J.'s," said Denise McCluggage, and began a slight weaving, bobbing motion with her head as she said it. We were in an early morning session of her Centered Skiing Workshop, and McCluggage was taking us through various subtle exercises, in effect warming up our heads for the skiing to come. "You've seen O. J. Simpson do television commercials," she continued, her head waggling gently in an unerring imitation of Simpson's characteristic mannerism: very erect spine, chin tucked in slightly, then jutting out again in a feinting motion. A graceful sway to the entire head, as if he is keeping time with his head to some internal music. Soon she had the whole class doing it; as I began moving my head that way I got the weird feeling I was ready to do an O. J. Simpson impression. It was eerie.

"I call them O.J.'s . . . ," McCluggage said, and proceeded to construct a rationale for this gentle head movement. Movement is necessary for several kinds of sensory input. Put your hand on velvet and you can't tell how soft it is, can't "read" it, until you slide your fingertips over the surface. If you stare too fixedly at a single point your eye develops a momentary blind spot; to maintain visual contact you have to keep your eyes moving, sweeping the target in "searching behavior." (None of our sensory organs operates as simplistically as the biology textbooks say it does, anyway: "What one sees goes well beyond what the eye provides; what one hears is more elaborate and significant than the meagre information provided by the ear," says Jonathan Miller.) Keeping the location of the eyes in constant motion—by this subtle wagging of the head—helps maintain a little better sensory connection with the environment.

More importantly, the neck muscles are among the body's primary controls of movement. "The whole region at the base of the neck, both front and back," says one analyst, "is a veritable maelstrom of muscular coordination." Tension in any part of the body is likely to be reflected in the neck. The righting reflex—the reflex that makes a dropped cat land on its feet—and several other reflexive responses to gravity operate through the neck and the location of the head. So "O.J.'s," by keeping those muscles in gentle use—firing proprioceptors and thus informing the nervous system of where everything is— are as important to skiers as they are to broken-field runners.

Besides, this kind of head movement serves as a neuromuscular reminder to stay loose. Literally. So long as you are loose, with no major muscle groups locked in rigid tension—"blocked"—then balance is improved, reaction time speeded, preparatory movements reduced to a minimum.* Blocking the muscles of the upper body and neck is an effective means of anchoring yourself for powerful movement. "Getting your back into it," as in a tennis serve, means blocking the torso and shoulder muscles so that more than just arm muscles are available to power the stroke. But the blocking is more effective if it occurs just as the movement is launched. Before that time the looser and more adaptable the upper body stays, the more effectively you'll be able to respond. In fact, in the often difficult process of initiating a movement, of finding the proper internal cue that will help you launch a motion, the very act of blocking those muscles can be a superb trigger. You can't pull that trigger, however, if those muscles are already blocked. The loosey-goosey, juking-and-feinting style of movement of many superior athletes is a process, however unconscious, of maintaining this preparatory state: ready to snap the musculature taut to initiate action.

So off we went to the ski slopes, bobbing and weaving and doing

* It's the opposite of staying on your toes. Biomechanical analysis shows that when you're up on your toes, as in preparation to receive a tennis serve, you'll have to rock back onto your heels and then come forward onto your toes again to get into action. Sorry, coach, but that's one athletic cliché that does not hold up.

O. J. Simpson imitations as we went. I can't tell you whether the skiing of the entire class improved; mine did. It is a technique I've subsequently tried to apply elsewhere, whenever I discover that I've become so engrossed in something that I've frozen into stiffness. Of course I forget most of the time, but when I do remember—when I can remind myself to recapture that subtle swaying, that liquid movement of the head—then I feel all kinds of limitations melting away.

There is a wonderful change in athletic thinking behind all this. It isn't terribly new, perhaps, in big-time athletics, but it is slow to filter down to general public acceptance. It is not a movement that is going to revolutionize sports, but it is helping revise levels of performance —upward—in unexpected ways. What I'm referring to is really a kind of yoga, although the yogis of the world will surely be enraged at that simplistic characterization. Maybe the change can best be described this way. Many professional and college athletic teams have completely abandoned "exercise," in the sense of the toe-touches, push-ups, jumping jacks, and other calisthenics that most of us have experienced, with considerable distaste, in organized athletics. In their place has been substituted . . . stretching. Period.

Many teams have hired stretching coaches, personnel whose job it is to teach athletes how (and why) to stretch. These teams have found that static stretching helps to avoid muscle pulls and cramps, that muscle soreness can be diminished by stretching before activity and can be relieved by stretching after activity is over. Stretching is the most important part of any warm-up; it also stimulates increased circulation in the muscle, to remove wastes and to bring in new nutrients to repair and resupply the muscle for future work. It actually reduces the amplitude of the electromyographic signal; that is, it in effect drains off the static electricity, or reduces the background "noise" of such electrical activity in the muscle.

One concrete result of this wholesale adoption of stretching programs has been a sharp downward revision of injury statistics. One national champion junior college football team, for example (Orange Coast College, 1975), never goes through a drill without first spending a full twenty minutes in passive flexibility exercises. In the first three years of this program the team members did not suffer a single muscle pull of hamstring, quadriceps, or groin. That's a record some major league pro teams might look at with wistful longing, after seeing championship seasons slip away in nightmares of rolls of tape and whirlpool baths and other remedies applied after the fact.

Stretching—the relaxed, passive pulling out of each muscle to its maximum resting length—is not the whole story, but it is eloquently symbolic of the sea change in athletic understanding that is taking place. For stretching to take hold in the athletic consciousness— stretching, that is, as a programmatic activity—we've had to undergo a 180-degree switch in our concept of what exercise actually is. Stretching is a kind of antiexercise.

We learn in childhood that exercise is huffing and puffing: the stressing of the physical plant through exertion to the point of fatigue, even to the edge of failure. That's the only way we know how to accumulate the incremental training effect, to achieve hypertrophy. We're taught that exercise is for growing stronger or for growing larger. It extends our reach—linearly.

That kind of exercise is the product of muscular contraction, as all movement is the product of contraction. We do understand quite a bit about muscular contraction (see Chapters 3 and 4), and in some senses all traditional athletic thinking is keyed to that understanding. We comprehend considerably less about the opposite side of muscular function: decontraction, or relaxation. But we are coming to realize that this is a more important aspect of the use of our bodies than we previously dreamed. We are beginning to see that we can extend our reach in other ways, by increasing our flexibility, our suppleness—and that that characteristic is an immensely important part of good physical conditioning.

Muscular function as we currently understand it is curiously one-way. The muscle's reaction to cold, to heat, to fatigue, to pain, to shock, to noise, to touch, to almost any stimulus, is to contract. That's simply what muscle *does*. There are no similar stimuli that cause muscle tissue to decontract.* A muscle that is already contracted can't function fully. If contracted muscle tissue is not pulled back out to length from time to time it begins to accept its contracted state as normal and to remain contracted. It is actually shortened:

---

* When you contract a muscle to move a limb in one direction, the nervous system does send an automatic relaxation signal to the antagonist muscle—the muscle responsible for moving the limb in the opposite direction. But it's a process we still don't know too much about.

the collagen—the network of connective tissue—reorganizes at the shorter length, causing a significant loss of motion. The same state of contracture can result if the muscle is worked beyond fatigue and pain, so that it goes into spasm. To the degree that a muscle stays contracted, whether from spasm or from structural changes over time, it has lost function.

This loss of function has now begun to be recognized as a problem not just of athletic training but of public health. It is a product of a state of residual tension that can lead to an extended list of modern ailments and diseases. Most headaches are caused by "tension"; the tension is of muscle tissue. The muscles involved—of the scalp, face, neck, and back—are supposed to be voluntary, accessible to willful control. But that control is one-way, of contraction only; we seem to have lost the capacity voluntarily to relax those muscles. (O.J's can help.) High blood pressure is epidemic; it is otherwise known as *hypertension*, and conscious muscular relaxation can reduce it. (My bet is that a proper stretching program would significantly lower most hypertension.) Two out of five Americans suffer from lower back pain; most lower back pain is caused not by disk degeneration but by muscle spasm—uncontrolled contraction of muscles that we've lost the capacity to relax. The skeleton is festooned with voluntary muscles that we can contract but can't relax. Muscles we can't relax can still be passively stretched to relieve tension.

We misinterpret most of this tension. "Emotional tension" is located not in the mind, where our dualistic Western understanding puts it, but in the body. "We generally think of an attitude as a mental set," says one writer. "An attitude is a bodily set. Our attitudes are the framework of our form." The flight-or-fight syndrome expresses itself in our musculature more clearly (and more accessibly) than in our glandular secretions. We are poised for flight, our muscle systems cocked for emergencies—and release—that never come. We get tired of being poised, but we can't willfully let go. Fatigue itself is a snowballing mechanism: tired muscles contract themselves involuntarily and thus use still more energy, generating more fatigue in the uncontrolled effort. We reach for the Valium.

In recent years there has been a great wave of self-help disciplines aimed at enhancing, balancing, harmonizing bodily function—an altogether worthy goal, but one that is usually lost in a welter of physioideological gibberish. These disciplines are not necessarily at war with each other, nor are they mutually contradictory, although they are usually presented that way. Many of them use some form of stretching as a starting point. (Other pop disciplines have come along which take an exclusively "mental" approach, promising some kind of steady-state of reduced tension through purely mental relaxation. As if the mind could be relaxed while the musculature is still tensed; as if muscle tissue could be relaxed merely by thinking about it, without first being stretched out to length.)

All of these disciplines may produce perfectly terrific results, for whatever reasons, by whatever means. I don't mean to discount or disparage any particular scheme; there are, after all, world-class athletes who find their performances improved by the ingestion of bee pollen, and I'm not about to knock whatever works. But the stretching disciplines are so much more directly related to the athletic use of the body that they are of direct concern here.

The original stretching discipline, yoga, is thousands of years old; it does take into account these complex interactions of stress and tension, muscle contraction, loss of control of voluntary muscle groups, and the chimerical nature of relaxation. That discipline's name comes from the Sanskrit word for "yoke," referring to the goal of linking the physical and mental, the muscular and the emotional. Yoga is an attempt clearly to reestablish the link implied by the Valium conundrum. *Hatha yoga* ("body" yoga) uses stretching and breathing exercises almost exclusively to cool out the physical self and, by damping out its jittery, noise-filled response to the distractions of the external world, prepare it for effective action. That would seem to make yoga precisely the technique that a modern athlete might best be able to put to use.

(The emphasis on breathing and breath control is striking, since maximum oxygen uptake is still the sports physiologist's best single measure of overall athletic capacity. Yoga's concern with the breath is keyed to breathing's curious position astride the dividing line between conscious and unconscious bodily functions. We can leave breathing entirely to automatic systems, but it is also a function that we can bring under conscious control. The yoga masters regard it therefore as a gateway leading from the conscious to the unconscious processes, one that can lead us to ways of controlling functions not ordinarily amenable to conscious control.)

But yoga is so wrapped in foreignness, retains such an odor of mysticism, and is usually presented in such plodding fashion that it is virtually unavailable to most of us. (The yogis will cry foul at this observation too.) Yoga is just too much trouble, at least for most of us, to use as a workaday tool for feeling better. This shouldn't be surprising: we know perfectly well how to feel better than we ordinarily do, but to do so takes a little forethought, a little bother—as in watching one's diet, getting exercise, avoiding overindulgence—and that, too, is too much trouble. Feeling good is too much trouble.

For athletes, however, whose primary resource consists of the state of their bodies, the complexities and time-consuming minutiae of a discipline such as yoga are not too much trouble. Nothing is too much trouble. The trainers for pro sports teams, the sports physicians, the coaches and dance teachers and especially the physical therapists—the bona fide members of the practical world of applied physical discipline—have always recognized the efficacy of stretching, although that recognition has usually been in bits and pieces, for limited specific applications, never quite pulled together into a codified form such as yoga.

You can see the importance given to stretching when you watch the pregame activities of a major sports team. Most of the attention will be to a gradual, leisurely stretching out of the major muscle groups; only after the stretching is done will the athletes begin to run, to throw, to perform the increasingly vigorous acts that will bring the body up to athletic operating temperature. Watch the kickoff return man in football as he awaits the start of play. He'll touch his toes, do splits, stretch out his hamstring and groin muscles and tendons in preparation for the sprint (and the collision) to come. Even on the eighteenth hole on a blistering hot day, a tournament golfer will not tee off without three or four practice swings to stretch out the long muscles of the back, shoulders, and arms. To do otherwise is simply to invite injury.

But for illustrating the significance of stretching, the dance is better than the game. Consider the dancer's sacrificial altar, the *barre*—the simple grab-rail where so much of the dancer's time is spent working out, warming up, *limbering* up. The barre is only a stretching aid, a prop upon which the dancer balances while pushing and pulling the body to its elastic limits. Most of the barre time is pure stretching exercise; dancers speak of it as working on body line, but the best body lines are the property of the most supple dancers, and the work at the barre is aimed at increasing that flexibility. "Extension" is the dancer's goal; amplifying the stretch.

Several years ago in *Sports Illustrated* dancer Edward Villella made a clear (if subjective) case that dancers are among the best-trained and hardest-working athletes alive. More recently the Institute of Sports Medicine and Trauma at Lenox Hospital affirmed Villella's assessment. In a study of the physical demands of the major sports, ballet was ranked first, ahead of basketball, soccer, football, and baseball. I asked Robby Barnett, a dancer with the extremely athletic dance troupe called Pilobolus, how many times a year he performed. After some calculation, he came up with the figure of eighty-two. I pointed out that this was equivalent to the regular NBA season. (He was appalled.) That is, the scheduling, the work load, of a topflight dancer is as exhausting as that of a starting forward in professional basketball. As with other athletes, dancers frequently perform despite injuries, in the artistic equivalent of "playing hurt." They suffer so many overuse injuries that sports medicine, running up against similar problems, comes to the dance physicians and therapists for advice. Yet dancers often continue their careers well past the age at which conventional athletes find their sports too demanding physically to continue. (Gordie Howe excepted.) It is the continual daily stretching (I claim) that keeps the dancers dancing. The barre is their fountain of youth.

Yoga is often touted, informally, as an antidote for aging. Gerontologists use loss of flexibility—in joints, muscles, tendons, even skin —as an index of aging. Stretching maintains flexibility.

*   *   *

If "stretching" seems too simple an idea to carry the weight I give it here—and I admit that the term sits there a trifle baldly, even to my own enthusiastic eye—then perhaps it should be considered only a fancy way of warming up. There are several dozen references to warm-ups in the preceding pages, a development I find ruefully amusing. I've been nagged at about warming up properly at least since Boy Scout camp (thirty-five years ago). Yet I've stumbled, half-frozen, off the chairlift after a twenty-minute ride in ten-degree weather, and skied down—hard and fast—without doing anything more in the way of a warm-up than to bend over and fasten my boot buckles. I suppose I was undertaking sizable risks, but I just never seemed to find the time for warming up. But then I've never been a very serious athlete.

Age, however, will do the job that all those coaches and camp counselors and instructors never could. Aging has taught me that a warm-up is a better investment of time than almost any other. (Maybe you know you're getting old when the warm-up becomes more pleasurable than the activity you're warming up for.)

I think I finally got the message about warm-ups from the kitchen. As I researched this book I necessarily became interested in muscle structure. I found I could no longer slice a steak without pondering fascia, aponeurosis, cartilage, and tendon. Looking at a stiffened, lard-laden leg of lamb as it came out of the refrigerator, I began to make certain unavoidable connections with my own physiology. And once my imagination was directed down into the muscle cells, down there in among the actin and myosin filaments and tissue-thin membranes, in the wash of fluids and the squeezing out of wastes, my empathy for bodily processes began to grow. I began to envision, with something akin to horror, the destruction that could result from action unprepared for, in the cold.

Now when I want to enjoy any large physical motion or expend heavy muscular effort, my imagination goes first to the cramped, cold, dry muscle cell, maintained by its various support systems at a metaphorical idle, at a pilot-light level of metabolism. (Lately I find I stiffen up so quickly when I sit still—my muscles taking a set like the hair on your head when you sleep on it wrong—that it takes little translation to apply to muscle cells what my whole body is feeling.) I see stretching as a gentle force to pull the cells toward new shapes, to begin to soften their stiffness as a child pummels Plasticine into workable warmth. The fats and oils and other liquids of the cell must be melted into motion; as the faint heat starts to build they finally begin to run a bit, to trickle down to lubricate the congealed internals of the cell. Gradually the temperature rises, at first from sheer friction, then from the wash of hot blood as circulation picks up. The cell begins to warm up into its natural rubbery resilience.

I keep remembering a childhood birthday party, for which I was supposed to blow up the party balloons. I couldn't do it, defeated by the cold stiffness of the balloons, until a grown-up showed me how to stretch the rubber first by hand, warming it, making the membrane pliable enough for my lungs to overcome its resistance. Lungs, too, must need warming up, their elasticity gradually brought up to work-ability, the energy required to expand them therefore reduced. Not to mention the heart. . . .

The warmer I get, the smoother the motions I can make. The friction is less, the entire physiology more workable. Now, as I actually stretch and feel my muscular resilience begin to improve, I can follow this process—or I can imagine it, which is just as satisfying. Synovial fluid pumps into the joints, providing the lubrication that allows the cartilaginous bone ends to slip over each other without those distressing creaks and cracks of unpreparedness. Tendons and ligaments that were dry rope now become slickly greased cables, with their own snappy elasticity. Even the nerve endings must get warmed up, the messages finding their way more easily once there are hot receptors waiting on the far side of the synapses, the circuits awakened and ready for business. Marvelous. Cold, I am foil-wrapped roast beef in the fridge, awaiting slicing for tomorrow's sandwiches; warm, I am a slippery, rubbery animal, and can't be hurt. I can begin to use myself without fear of pain. Or at least that's the way it feels. At any rate, as long as I can remember to picture it this way, I can convince myself to take the time to get a proper warm-up.

Of course, all this verbiage is only a tedious and complicated way of reiterating Satchel Paige's recipe for agelessness, which avoids warm-ups entirely: "Keep the juices flowing by jangling around gently as you move."

* * *

The abandonment of structured calisthenics, the wholesale adoption of stretching programs, the intensive concentration on thorough warm-ups—and yoga, and "jangling around gently as you move"—are all symbolic of a curious turning away from force in modern athletics. The trend is toward sports as a kind of jujitsu—literally, the "yielding art"—in which one uses the opponent's weight and strength instead of one's own, in which gravity and balance and timing, rather than sheer muscle, are used to do the job. Denise McCluggage talks about it in *The Centered Skier:*

"There is a way of using the body that is perfectly suited to the task at hand. A *basal effort* that is just enough to get the job done with the least wear and tear. It might be called the Baby Bear Effort. Not too soft, not too hard. In the words of Goldilocks, 'just right.' Whatever the job—toting barges, lifting bales, or quietly sitting in a chair and sipping tea—there is an optimal expenditure of energy, a particular marshaling of musculature that is totally relevant to the task. Ideally there is in the action nothing superfluous, nothing redundant, nothing contradictory.

"Bodies used so aptly are aesthetically stirring to watch whether they belong to dancers, athletes, or construction workers. Such bodies are also rare. Our culture appears to be overpopulated with Papa Bears, splattering the landscape with the excesses of the old college try—straining, overdoing, grimacing at jar lids. . . ."*

Julius Erving and O. J. Simpson are examples of this appropriateness of effort, "catlike in their economy of movement." Pete Rose is a Papa Bear, "a singularly successful ballplayer, although economy is not his forte. He is master of excess. He kills snakes at third [now at first] and explodes in bustling efforts around the bases. We call it 'hustle' and cheer it lovingly. Little League coaches urge their young players to emulate him. Try! Try! Try! . . . Everyone can try, if they try. True, trying hard has enough apparent success to be much favored and honored. Its negative sides are unknown or unnoticed. We live by the Philosophy of Overwhelm."

But it isn't necessary: "Actually the gift of fluid movement and appropriate effort is one granted all but a few; but it is a gift generally compromised, squandered, and misplaced over the years. As we grow day by day, we make our deals with gravity and collect our share of frustrations—dangling in awkward steps from the fingers of encouraging adults, falling off garage roofs, hunching over homework, cringing from real or imagined physical and psychic blows; in short, by our habitual responses and attitudes, we give ourselves our shapes. And our shapes, in turn, shape our further responses and attitudes. This is the high gloss of our sensory abilities grimed over and dulled with disuse. Instead of stripping our gifts back to their shining basics, we slap on another thick coat of effort."

My comparison of this trend in sports with jujitsu is deliberate, although the name of that ancient Oriental discipline sounds as out of date, in these days of aikido and kung fu and T'ai Chi, as six-day

* Vermont Crossroads Press, Waitsfield, Vt., 1977.

bicycle races. There is a strong Oriental influence throughout sports these days, stemming principally from the martial arts. Those arts are still generally misunderstood: despite the porno-violent promotion they have popularly received, their emphasis is not on violence at all but on balance, centering, economy of motion, harmonious use of the body, and various other unusual states of mind and body that are hardly the kind of thing that the traditional American football coach can be expected to teach.* The martial arts have more to do with dance than with violence, but the film and TV entrepreneurs have successfully concealed that fact.

There are forces working to reject the Philosophy of Overwhelm. In the face of steroids and weight training, of 280-pound football linemen and 7'3" basketball centers, it is clear that this rejection has not swept all before it, but it nevertheless is a growing influence in sports. Its origin is often traced to a wave of overdue political activity in sports in the late 1960s—Harry Edwards' efforts to organize a black boycott of the 1968 Olympics and the gloved fists of sprinters Tommie Smith and John Carlos at those games, attacks on the football establishment by Dave Meggesy and Gary Shaw, and other efforts to jar sports loose from their conservative, middle-class, largely white and largely militaristic ideology and control. But I suspect other forces at work in the late 1960s—not excluding revolutionary changes in attitudes toward drugs, music, and sex—had more to do with this softening and gentling of our approach to sports.

It is tempting to lay it all at the feet of Esalen, that countercultural vortex that spewed out the human potential movement. Esalen also produced, or gathered, or somehow otherwise legitimized some dozens of more or less mystical entrepreneurs who thrived, for a while, on introducing us to the flip side of all our established institutions. Michael Murphy, Esalen's cofounder, whose family estate became headquarters for the movement, is passionately interested in sports. He has written a mystical novel about golf (*Golf in the Kingdom*, Dell, New York, 1972) and coauthored a roundup of mystical experiences of athletes (*The Psychic Side of Sports*, with Rhea A. White, Addison-Wesley, Reading, Mass., 1978). Others have described the

* The traditional American football coach may be missing a bet. I was told by a reasonably good source—who kept a perfectly straight face as he told me—that every member of the defensive line of the Dallas Cowboys' 1979 Super Bowl team had achieved black-belt-level proficiency in karate.

change, most notably George Leonard in *The Ultimate Athlete* (Viking, New York, 1974). Still others have attempted to refurbish the timeworn how-to approach, beginning with Timothy Gallwey's *The Inner Game of Tennis* (Random House, New York, 1974), a best-seller which spawned dozens of variations. *The Centered Skier* is one of the more clearly realized evolutionary developments out of Gallwey's approach to sports.*

There are dozens more of these titles, most of which are accompanied by workshops, clinics, visiting lectures, expensive lessons, and elaborate rationales. What all of these approaches have in common is an inward turning, a focus on the athlete's own internal state as a function of performance. It is an emphasis on the athlete as conscious participant, rather than as only a single element functioning within the overarching and dominating structure of the game. The new approaches to sports put heavy emphasis on feeling —in the sensory rather than the emotional sense. The emphasis is on the athlete's own capacity to feel what it is one is doing with one's body to participate in the sport, and also on how those sensations play against any preconceived notions of what should be happening.

In the older style of presentation of athletic tasks, the athlete is told how to do the act in order to achieve the result—a kind of engineering approach, tab A in slot B. In the newer style the athlete is encouraged to become conscious of the sensations that surround the performance of the task, and to become aware of how the task fits into the larger context of the game, and then is left alone to hone those feelings, to turn them into a skill. This opens up the argument that the new style is only one more manifestation of Christopher Lasch's New Narcissism: it requires that the athlete focus on internal states to a degree that more conventional athletic thinking regards as downright self-indulgent.

In fact this contrast illuminates one facet of a continuing ideological battle going on between the two approaches to sports, not only between the self-indulgent (or merely self-absorbed) New Athlete and the old-style, self-effacing Team Player, but also between the mystical and nonmystical. The older consciousness in sports has always seen itself as proudly no-nonsense: cut out the bullshit, get the job

* Actually the precise point of origin of this entire movement in sports—and certainly all of these books—is probably *Zen in the Art of Archery*, Eugen Herrigel's slim little classic published by Pantheon clear back in 1953, and still in many senses the best of the bunch.

done, knock off the scary stuff about nonordinary states of consciousness. Execute the fundamentals—harder, faster, maybe even meaner
than the other guy—and let statistics (otherwise known as the odds,
or the breaks) take care of the rest. Let us not confuse ourselves with
any of this psycho-what's-its-name and other faddish manifestations
of an unstable society.

The New Athlete is much more accepting, more curious about new
possibilities. And stretching, with the tiny modifications to athletic
thinking that it implies, is the kind of phenomenon that opens the
door for all the rest. Consider calisthenics, the traditional form of
preparation for action. A leader stands in front of the group and takes
them through the exercises. The pace, the length of time spent on
each exercise, the level of effort, are governed by a single individual
operating only on a personal sense of what is appropriate for all those
unthinking followers. Nobody has much chance to pay attention to
the results of the exercise, to the accommodating state of the body,
to what is actually transpiring. Nobody has time to notice whether
the calisthenics are enough or too much or simply beside the point.
Indeed, the factor governing the number of repetitions is often pure
competitiveness, the drill masters attempting to embarrass their
charges into overexertion. Or some other such macho trip.

Compare the gentle self-absorption of a stretching drill. You start
with the long muscles of the hamstring or back, and work gradually
to the shorter muscles. You select a particular muscle and bend your
frame as needed to pull it out to length, preferably by locking the
appropriate joints at maximum extension. (If the joints can be
locked, more relaxation of the muscles is possible.) You take the
muscle to the point at which it feels taut, but stop short of pain
(because pain causes contraction, wiping out the benefits of stretching). You hold the position—the longer the better—and try to relax.
Usually after a few seconds at maximum length you find there is
additional slack, which you then take up.

Almost unavoidably your conscious attention is focused within the
muscle. You locate the amount of tension at which pain starts, in
order to stay short of it, and feel the gradual relaxation of the underlying tension. (The yogis recommend that you release the tension as
you release each breath.) All kinds of more or less pleasurable sensations are kicked loose. You find you can focus your attention at either
end of the muscle, where it ties to bone, and by subtle variation of

the stretching tension you can bring specific stimulus to those two points. You can bring your attention slowly down the length of the muscle, and while you're doing it you'll find that the stretch, the point of maximum tension, seems to travel down the muscle as your attention does, giving a kind of sliding massage down its length. After about a minute, usually, the muscle stops sending out signals of change, indicating a steady state of accommodation to the stretch. When it does, you let up on that muscle, choose another, and continue. Once you've started stretching a given muscle you'll usually be surprised at its length. Simply tracing out that length—using stretching to provide the sensory indexing that tells you where the muscle really goes—is marvelously therapeutic, relaxing, restorative.

(When the batter swings the weighted bat or the golfer swings the club as a warm-up preparatory to hitting, that's *ballistic* stretching. Proponents of static or passive stretching say that ballistic stretching is counterproductive. When you try to touch your toes by bobbing down at them, for example, you generate pain in the muscles being stretched, making them yank tight in another contraction. But for increasing the amount of flexibility or range of motion, studies have shown that ballistic stretching can be slightly more effective than passive stretching. Nevertheless, everyone seems to agree that for unkinking muscles before and after action, the slow, gentle, passive techniques are best.)

*　　*　　*

In recent years "uptight" has become the pop vernacular for maximum psychic distress. When a muscle is pulled up tight in contraction, it needs stretching out to relieve it. This is stretching as Valium.

*　　*　　*

The athlete who stretches is required by the very act to enter a cocoon of self-absorption, in order to pay enough attention to what is going on with the muscle to get any benefit from the process. It is a solitary, introspective, withdrawing kind of "exercise," one which requires that the athlete deliberately step away from the cheerful group activity that we traditionally—and healthfully—associate with sports. That's a significant loss: the gregarious sociability of sports is one of its great benefits. But there's a certain balance to be sought here, too. Unexamined participation can be as distorting as total withdrawal. The distracted athlete may be attracted to a discipline such as stretching for that very reason—its peace and quiet. Stretching does coerce self-absorption, but it is a reassuringly meditative occupation.

Yoga, for all its Sanskrit terminology and metaphorical reference, is simply the stretching discipline taken to its logical end. In practicing yoga one stretches organs as well as muscles, tendons, ligaments; one gradually works over the entire physical plant, making sure that no element—gland, connective tissue, bodily function—is allowed to escape the gentle stimulation that prevents atrophy from disuse. In fact, despite the distorted popular view of yoga as some kind of vague posturing and religiosity, it is actually a concrete expression of the absolutely practical philosophy of use-it-or-lose-it. It's a system of organization that prevents neglect of those physiological areas that otherwise might be overlooked in the scattered confusions of modern life. As such its first appeal is to the harried and hypercerebral, the otherwise sedentary individual in search of physical release that seems elsewhere unobtainable.

Seen this way, yoga is not so much a nutball fad as it is merely a loosener, a toner, an antidote to tension. It's all very Western and logical. And it is in this sense that yoga has also begun to have a considerable influence in modern sports: as a counterdiscipline to the harder-stronger-faster-tougher methodology—and ideology—of traditional athletic training.

Ah, but practical or not, yoga (or stretching) does open a quiet little door in the consciousness. To get any real benefit you must pay attention as you do it. It is not like calisthenics, during which you often deliberately turn your mind elsewhere in order to ignore fatigue and pain. Because yoga demands intense attention to the moment, some athletes feel it can serve as a training method for the kind of concentration required in sports. Many athletes who practice the focusing necessary to follow the changing state of a specific muscle feel that they are also sharpening their powers of concentration for more active tasks. I know of no studies that measure any such improvement; the would-be scientist in me says that to try to improve concentration on athletic tasks in this fashion may be roughly akin to the quaint Victorian notion that studying Latin or playing chess improves "logical" thinking. The athletes who realize benefits, however subjective, from such practices couldn't be less concerned with scientific verification.

As I say, much of this influence in athletics springs full-blown from the martial arts. Practitioners of those arts perform feats of remarkable athletic effectiveness, such as the breaking of bricks with bare hands. The athlete witnesses these almost sideshow demonstrations and hears them credited directly to superior concentration. Inevitably the athlete starts thinking about connections between the mental and the physical, about physical capacities coupled—yoked, if you will—with extraordinary mental states. About putting back together the physical and mental capabilities that the rest of Western society —the nonathletic part of society—seems to have let slip apart. A degree of mysticism is the almost unavoidable result. The athlete sees that there is tremendous power there, somewhere, if one can just figure out how to grasp it. Time after time the athlete bumps up against his or her absolute physical limits; eventually there is no place else to turn—for improvement, for change—but to the mind.

When I wasn't catching any fish, my father always used to tell me I wasn't holding my mouth right. The parallel isn't exact, but it may be closer than it appears. Athletes who suddenly begin espousing strange metaphysical (*meta* = "beyond") theories are not what you would call rare in sports. First thing you know they're proposing some bizarre miracle cure-all to solve all your problems. Such as stretching.

Nonsense, says the grizzled old veteran, who knows perfectly well that all that mumbo-jumbo about what the muscles are actually doing won't help you get the job done. He knows that nothing is going to affect the outcome of the game except preparation, execution, hustle, and the Philosophy of Overwhelm. Just so the coach doesn't forget to wear his lucky socks and nobody steps on the third baseline and no green racing cars (or women) are allowed in the pits. And nobody mentions the no-hitter the pitcher has going for him. If you want to meet a modern-day mystic, don't go to a Buddhist monastery, just find some baseball player who has a hitting streak—or slump— going for him.

Cynics might say that the Fellowship of Christian Athletes is an organization that owes its existence to streaks, slumps, and other irrational occurrences in the athletic career. A superior athlete always feels "blessed," the recipient of an inexplicable gift—and likely as not just a bit guilty about whether he or she deserves such a blessing. A slump is a temporary withdrawal of the gift, for whatever reason, and one can easily imagine the complex rationales the athlete must come up with to endure the withdrawal. A streak—a period of particularly outstanding performance, when the athlete gets "grooved," "hot," "in the zone"—is even more mysterious; what already gifted athlete would have the moral arrogance to feel that he or she truly deserves this kind of bonus? It is all inexplicable, mysterious, mystical.

(Thus sports' fascination with statistics. The attempt to demystify chance by reducing it to statistical probability is nothing more than odds-making, the stuff of gambling, .perhaps the most mystical of man's nonreligious activities—and an activity intimately and historically attached to sports. Our very language is littered with profane attempts to deal with the inexplicability of athletic performance. But I guess that's just the way the old ball bounces.)

I am not cynical about these matters. It is not the degree or the amount but only the nature of the mysticism in sports that is changing. Athletes have always been mystified by their own skills, and therefore driven to elaborate belief structures to maintain their sanity. Nowadays they are apt to learn so much more about what is involved in those athletic skills and capabilities that the unknown occupies a narrower range, along an edge of human performance where much finer subtleties operate. Which only makes the final result that much more mysterious, teasing us with the possibility that there is some final knowable secret that will explain all. If your free-throw percentage is off, you can haul out the high-speed cameras and perform a computer-based biomechanical analysis of where that hitch in your motion comes from, or you can pay a gypsy to remove the curse. One method may be as efficacious as the other; it all depends on what the athlete's belief system requires.

*　　*　　*

"Attention" literally means a "stretching out" of the mind. . . .

As I sit here and write this, tension begins to build in my shoulders, in the back of my neck. I have to remind myself every now and then to let go of that knot of tension, to relax those muscles. (O.J.'s help.) Of course, if my back really knots up, if I have one of those kernels of minor pain from sitting stiffly in one position for too long, then I stretch it out, working the cramped muscle loose. Everyone does that, even people who aren't nutball mystics on the subject of stretching. How could stretching not be an effective treatment for tension when it is what we always, unthinkingly, use for relief when we really need it? Just as naturally as we rub a hurt spot?

There's another clue. Bang an elbow and you'll rub it, maybe a little sheepishly, the rubbing an almost superstitious response to pain. What could rubbing the skin over a bruised place possibly accomplish? Well, quite a bit, actually. It stimulates extra circulation, to bring healing nutrients to and take damaged cells and other wastes away from the injury site. It slows or reduces swelling by that stimulation. It fires other nerve receptors in the area, spreading additional sensation—more pleasant sensation—on top of the sharp pain that distressed you in the first place. It diffuses the pain. Besides, it gives you something to do in reaction to pain besides cursing and gritting your teeth—other natural responses, but not quite so productive as self-massage.

Or there is massage itself, which is making a big comeback as part and parcel of this change in sports. "Swedish massage" and similar nonmedical therapies were all the rage around the turn of the century, but more dramatic forms of intervention—drugs such as antibiotics, and more and more sophisticated surgical techniques, for instance—superseded these gentle therapies. We became convinced that the "scientific" way to deal with trauma was to cut, to fix, to pour in chemicals. It is the engineering mentality; one often sees it in orthopedists. And dentists. (The folks who are concerned about the state of sports medicine sometimes say that skeletally we're doing okay, but we're still in the dark ages when it comes to *soft tissue medicine.*)

Now, much of the public is finding the dramatic interventions, the heroic measures and technological overparticipation of many aspects of medicine, to be increasingly offensive. At the same time the subtleties and gradual accretions of the body's own capacity to respond have recaptured our attention. As in the training effect. We're looking at the gentler therapies with renewed interest. Formal AMA-type medicine still has little use for the kind of tender loving care, the slow and patient application, that is required for such subtle disciplines to have any effect. But the public and the athletic world are becoming more sensitive to the possibilities in these nondramatic, noninterventionist therapies.

I confess to a certain obsessiveness with this whole business. I can't help it. I am in my late forties, still in possession of most of my faculties but beginning to be subject to small physical surprises in that regard. Sometimes it seems as if my entire adult life has been spent in an ongoing war against stiffness. (It escalates every year, of course.) Aging specifically attacks the flexibility of the body, causing the basic connective tissue to lose its elasticity. Age drapes me in cobwebs of disuse; stretching helps clear those cobwebs.

As a matter of fact, age exaggerates the mind-body split in one's self-concept. (I hate this kind of talk, but it is true.) Consciousness is a relative continuum: I don't notice any aging of my consciousness. I don't feel that the person I am, here inside, is changing at all. But I keep running across things that my body doesn't want to do—athletic things, yes, but other, daily-life things as well. So here I sit in my head, watching my body begin to sag into an entirely different, older, form. I have to believe that it is some separate thing, distinct from my unchanging self, that is deteriorating. Aging pulls me out of my body, into my head. Stretching puts me back into my body.

But that's not entirely it. Oh hell, I might as well confess the rest: stretching just feels good. Stretching makes me smile. (And, of course, smiling stretches the mouth. Laughing, on the other hand, stretches great sheaths of muscle reaching all the way down to the groin, discharging their tensions. So does crying; thus the tonic effect of an emotional workout, he said stoically.) When as a result of anything from too little activity to too much my physical self begins to quiver in physiological indecision, hung at some undiscoverable, unreachable point between dead slack and wire-tight tension—threatening to go numb, to sink into the abyss of nonfeeling—then stretching is the gentle restorative that pulls me back into comfortable contact with myself, that tells me what my body is up to. Stretching is just purely wonderful. I recommend it.

CHAPTER 16
Free Lunch

The trouble with working on a project such as this is that after a couple of years of digging into the subject, after researching all the details and gaining some degree of understanding of the mass of complexities involved in the athletic process, I now cry at track meets.

At World Cup II, the track and field finale of the 1979 season held in Montreal, Canadian Debbie Brill won the women's high jump. Before the meet she had revealed that she was in the process of changing her jumping technique. She had become very consistent with the motion that would carry her to 6'2" or so, which would win a lot of North American meets but which wasn't quite competitive in world ranks. If she were to progress she had decided that she had to "get very technical"—athletic slang for experimenting with her jumping technique.

Dwight Stones, who for all his flakiness probably does know as much about the high jump as any athlete, was a TV commentator. Early in the competition he pointed out that Brill was "bottoming out" at foot plant. Grossly oversimplifying high jump technique, there are power jumpers (the Russians favor this style and do very well with it, currently holding the men's world record) and speed jumpers (the style of former record-holder Stones). Brill is a speed jumper, approaching the bar at high speed, then converting horizontal motion abruptly into vertical motion. But in the early going at Montreal she seemed to be using power alone, with a labored last foot plant that left her taking off almost from a squat. "When a jumper spends that much time on the plant," Stones pointed out, "it's awfully hard to get much height from it."

Then Brill pulled her technique together. She began approaching the bar with brilliant speed, with a kind of electric excitement that seemed to carry over into the very springiness of her musculature. She started clearing heights easily, and won the event with a jump three inches better than her previous personal best. The Canadian crowd naturally became swept up in this minor drama, and it turned into an emotional occasion. But the emotional content was significantly heightened, for me, anyway, by the enrichment of the technical detail, by understanding something of the process with which she was experimenting. Habit and power were being superseded by experiment and technical innovation, and with that switch came sufficient momentum to lift Brill another three inches upward.

Contrast that telling small moment with the performance of Edwin Moses in the same meet. Moses runs the 400-meter hurdles so much faster than anyone else in the world that he really hasn't been pushed since 1976. He's a physicist with an analytical mind, as well as being a whopping stud of a world-class athlete, and at World Cup II he missed breaking his own world record only by a few hundredths of a second. His concentration failed, he said, in the last thirty meters or so. He was disappointed, but it fit into a larger plan. "I've been running very technical races all season," he said. (Translation: I've been working on the fine details of my hurdling technique, honing it so I know precisely what I am doing at every point.) "Now all I have to do for the Olympics next year is *power back up*." (Work on strength, amplify the physical plant, fine-tune it to match the polished technique of the previous season.)

Both Moses and Brill are experienced, intelligent athletes; both are juggling strength vs. speed, power vs. finesse, to continue to advance to the highest possible levels in their respective events. At Montreal they happened to be on schedules that had them working almost in opposite directions. One, Brill, had a ten-year base of strength and speed training, and therefore could begin toying with sweet spots, could start experimenting successfully with time. The other had invested a year in exploring the rhythms and timing of his specialty, and now was ready to begin reaching down (again) into the related intricacies of muscular and cardiovascular preparation, to begin unleashing new physical power to fit the new rhythms. One was exulting in a breakthrough, the other proceeding along a performance curve that looks as if it will extend inexorably upward.

Moses and Brill were, for me, symbolic bookends at World Cup II, between which were packed plenty of other small dramas, now frozen in my memory. (And I wasn't even in Montreal—I watched World Cup II on television.) I can still recapture images of the second-best long jump in history by Larry Myricks; of the flicker of emotion, almost of panic, in the otherwise cool, impassive face of Evelyn Ashford as she realized she had finally emerged as the best woman sprinter in the world; of the miraculous finish of Renaldo Nehemiah in the 110-meter hurdles. I tend to think of strength and skill as almost contradictory traits—a traditional bad habit of dualistic Western thinking, I guess—but time after time that track meet demonstrated how complexly they can be interlocked. A sprinter, for example, must get stronger to get smoother, which seems contradictory. (Physical strength is needed to control the wild flailing that characterizes so much raw sprinting talent. I understood that speed is supposed to be innate, but now I began to understand what coaching must attempt to accomplish with sprinters.)

Track and field also demonstrates convincingly and in precise detail how fatigue destroys technique, how the first sign of failure in an overextended athlete is always the disintegration of form. You can pick it up in the tiniest of subtleties—a two-inch chop in the stride of a hitherto fluid runner, a slight bob of the head that was steady up until now. (The head and neck are remarkably acute indicators of muscular state: see O.J.'s, Chapter 15.) Fatigue puts a gauzy film of restraint over the flowing freedom of movement that we associate with the practicing athlete. Style—completed movement—is the first casualty.

(With animals as well as with human athletes. I've been amazed to see this whole business demonstrated in TV broadcasts of horse races. The two favorites round the last turn dead even, but in the stretch run, one better conditioned horse begins to forge ahead. The other, in a desperate bid to keep up, begins bobbing its head frantically, trying to squeeze a tiny bit more speed out of its tiring muscles. Trying to recruit more muscle fibers—and, in the effort, recruiting other, nonapplicable motor units. I'd never have recognized the desperation of the motion if it hadn't reminded me so clearly of footraces I lost as a kid, and the way my own head would start to bob, seemingly of its own accord, as I tried to keep up with faster runners. At the moment you can pick up excess motion in the horse's head, its race is to all intents and purposes lost.)

I keep thinking of the amazing set of neurological messages that must have gone through Renaldo Nehemiah's system in the last thirty meters of his stunning race (the same one discussed in Chapter 1). He was exhausted from an extended European campaign and from the pressures of a year-long winning streak. He started badly and kept himself in the race only through grunting effort, instead of the fluid grace that usually characterizes his performances. He crashed through, rather than over, the next-to-last hurdle, and was yanked off-stride, almost out of control, by the impact—and the lead had already slipped away when that happened. Yet he somehow managed to win the race. I suspect that if we had any clear picture of what kind of signals passed between which centers of thought and action to enable him to bring his body back under control, accelerate it, drive it forward to break the tape, we would have an enormous leg up on understanding how the brain and nervous system actually function. Until we do we must be content with recognizing that that, too, Dr. Costill, was a major-league job of recruitment of muscle fibers.

What is really intriguing to me about a good track meet (or any other more or less high-quality sports event) is my sure knowledge that I know so little. The minor dramas I could grasp from World Cup II were only those that my limited background exposed, or that television chose to elucidate for me. I am simply too ignorant of what was really happening to understand the full drama. Imagine the intensity of the experience if you could really know the whole picture of any sports event, of each of those individual athletes—every one of whom is also juggling the eternal athletic questions of strength vs. speed, power vs. finesse, and all the rest. The athlete knows a thousand times more about what is going on than I can know, knows details of every step of the training process, can apply a gut knowledge of what is happening with fatigue levels and the cardiovascular system and neurological patterning. The athlete can relate these things to precise feeling states, pains, pleasures, emotions. Imagine how deeply and personally that athlete can experience a major sports event, even if only as a spectator.

I can't attain that depth of experience, I suppose, but working on this book has so expanded my appreciation that almost any athletic performance is immeasurably richer for me. Forget about "world-class" and other such vague categories: if seen from this physiological point of view, a mile that's run in 4:05 can be as interesting, and under the right circumstances as moving, as a 3:50 mile. This view of sports—of the human body as athletic instrument, of sports as expressions of the finite limits of the body and as means of exploring the mechanisms at work to set those limits—positively illuminates great athletic performances, at least for me. I can only hope that some of that illumination, that great joy, becomes available to the reader. I guess what I'm trying to do is make sure that you, too, cry at track meets.

*   *   *

Sportscasters and coaches are always talking about the good athlete, as in "We're going to draft the best athlete available, regardless of position." Nobody ever says what it is that elevates a given individual to that particular category. I've done the same thing throughout these pages, and the question has nagged at me as I've done so. The quality that elevates a good athlete is positively glaring—but what *is* it? Almost any good athlete has competitiveness, canny tactical sense, strength, stamina, self-possession under fire, balance, quick reactions, and, yes, coordination, no matter what the motor-learning people say—the ability to coordinate all these qualities into superior performance, anyway. But none of these traits snaps your head around in sudden attention when it is demonstrated. Something else does that. I think what we are looking for is a quality of movement.

The show-biz personality who hasn't danced regularly in ten years attempts a big production number. He or she obviously *can* dance— knows the moves, has the fundamentals, can learn the routine—but the fine edge is gone. The dancer stands in front of the troupe and is . . . exposed. The gypsies of the chorus line are highly skilled performers who dance every day, who are in rigorous training, who believe that by polishing these very skills they may achieve stardom. The contrast—the fluidity, the precision, the amplitude of movement of the members of the chorus line vs. the rickety imitation of those same qualities by the star—is shocking. The difference is in the tiniest of degrees and fractions, but it is appalling. We get a quick object lesson in what dancing is all about. The analogy is not exact, but it is close. Put a truly great dancer in front of that chorus line, and his or her skills will be as glaringly superior as those of the chorus line over the has-been.

James Cagney, floating through a tap number with those curiously steady, squared-off shoulders. Fred Astaire, whom Mikhail Baryshnikov has called the greatest dancer who ever lived, yet with skills so coolly understated that you can't imagine him *not* dancing. Buster Keaton and Charlie Chaplin, choreographing linked series of pratfalls. (Does any contemporary performing artist move as well as these ancients?) Or Muhammed Ali, Walt Frazier, Lynn Swann, Jean-Claude Killy, Russ Francis. There is a connection here, teasingly beneath the surface.

Choreographer Twyla Tharp was asked whether for her style of dance she preferred candidates with classical or modern dance training. Classical, she said: "People with ballet training are more centered. I don't mean that in any mystical sense—they just know where their center is. They know how to get their weight between their feet and keep it there, how to arrange their limbs around a central body core. They have a reference point. When you work with them you have some place to start from." Fancy talk for a sense of balance, one might say, but I think there is more to it than that. When I think about the names in the preceding paragraph—dancers, comedians, athletes—the images I get are strikingly similar for their quietness of movement. All of them, by trade, make very large body movements; all do so in a similarly damped-down, smooth, almost minimalist style. All remain remarkably still in their upper bodies; there is no excess, no flapping, flopping, disjointed-looking motion above the waist. (The same is true of good racehorses: little motion above the legs; the jockey gets a quiet ride. Remember Silky Sullivan.)

Watch Tony Dorsett run: no head bob. When the upper body is still, so is the head; when the head is still, so are the eyes. The major organs of balance are the inner ear and the eyes.* A superior sense

* O.J.'s again, but the other side of the coin. As discussed in Chapter 15, it is athletically helpful to keep the head in (subtle) motion to keep the sensory equipment stimulated. But the larger goal is to make of the neck a gimbal device—as in the mounting that keeps the compass level on a sailboat—so gross body movements don't unnecessarily displace the head, the inner ears, the eyes. O.J.'s keep the neck gimbal freed up, lubricated, ready for action.

of balance keeps the body arranged around its center so that movement in any direction is possible with a minimum windup, miminum response time, minimum wasted motion. Each new motion, each new direction is initiated as efficiently as possible, usually taking some small measure of momentum from the motion before. Here comes the Sweet Spot Theory again: each separate movement (to the extent that movements can be separated) has its own clear, clean trajectory. We do see this when we watch a good athlete at work, although it is so buried in the swirl of activity that it may be impossible visually to distinguish these subtleties.

(That's okay, we'll pick it up on the replay, in slow motion. Slo-mo has been wonderful in helping us understand athletic motion, but it has lulled us into forgetting how very quickly the athlete actually must put his or her motion together. We almost don't bother to watch the real-time version, knowing the replay will be along in a moment. Most of us, television-spoiled, suffer a certain disorienting frustration when we go to a live event, waiting for replays that never come. The installation of giant overhead replay screens in the newer indoor sports venues tells us more about what TV has done to our attention spans than has all the nagging from all the educators in the world.)

There are as many styles of athletic movement as there are athletes, even if there is some organizing principle such as a quiet upper body or superior sense of balance that characterizes them all. Lynn Swann's electroglide smoothness, Alberto Juantorena's pounding strength, the eerie floating of Julius Erving, the rigid, small-motion tightness of John Havlicek (and many other aging athletes), the loosey-goosey flexibility of Charlie Scott, the rebounding rubber-ball quickness of Walter Payton. (Football would convince us that athletes move in peculiar ways, mostly because of the restrictive padding. That may change with the application of Byron Donzis' technology.)

These are the visual riches of sports, and much of our enjoyment comes from marveling at and learning to identify these characteristics, on whatever subliminal levels. What is most surprising to me is to realize that the truly great practitioners of any sport are so *un*distinctive about it. It turns out that the correct performance is the best performance, and it is one to which the better athletes naturally evolve. Good athletes seem to be able to come up with the "correct" performance in absolutely impossible circumstances, to go ahead and execute the move in textbook fashion despite utter lack of time or space, or the threat of personal disaster.

But it is the signature of individuality laid on top of the textbook-correct performance—the fillip of personal genius—that makes sports so lovely. That's the tragedy when the great ones leave the field. Quantitatively there may be no great loss when an O. J. Simpson's knees go bad and he is forced to retire. There are better running backs to come. With the sheer numbers that funnel through football in this country, more O. J. Simpsons will emerge, will break all those O. J. Simpson records, will surpass all his achievements. The tragedy is only that we will never again see the precise beauty of that individual performance. That characteristic grace of movement may be equaled or surpassed but it will never be duplicated. That's the irreplaceable loss. That's why I so treasure the curious little piece of cerebral film that's stored in my head, the one that lets me replay Babe Ruth's bat-swing on the back of my eyelids. All the records will eventually go, but nobody, ever, will swing a baseball bat just like that again. And that's why the contemporary, real-time performance of a great athlete is to be savored so. That in itself is reason enough to punch off the TV and go out to the ball park.

*　　*　　*

I've also been talking a lot about "the athletic task" without ever attempting to define what that vague phrase might mean. For my purposes, the athletic task is to make preliminary judgments about the amount of effort, motion, and speed that will be required to accomplish most effectively a given physical end, and then to carry out those judgments in the most efficient manner possible. (I suppose such a definition should say something about sports, but I'm not sure it's necessary. I've seen people mow lawns athletically, paint cupboards athletically, shuck corn and slice tomatoes athletically.) The person who does this is an athlete, in my view—and that means racing drivers, billiard players, jugglers are athletes (but chess players are not). The best athlete is the individual who is able to make and carry out the best judgments, of course.

I was musing about this to long-suffering Chris, speaking of finer judgments resulting from the happenstances of better sensory equipment, better proprioceptive equipment, better neurological equipment to connect all these varied faculties. It is a vision of athleticism

that strikes me as dangerously neo-Nietzschean, but to a degree physiologically inescapable. "You mean the athlete has better register,"
Chris pointed out. She was using the term *register* in the printer's
sense—as in the precise alignment of the overlying color plates that
allows fine reproduction of color photography. It is an appropriate
metaphor for a physiology that would provide athletic superiority, a
handy way of thinking about how those superstars can do so much
more than you or I can with our poor bodies. An alibi, if you will:
they have every connection, every molecule and fiber laid down with
better alignment, closer to perfection.

It is an Apollonian, left-brain vision of athletic prowess; it ignores
the Dionysian, humanistic vision of our possible skills, which is much
more satisfying. In the latter view it is the little guy, the underdog,
the nonblessed, who manages by dint of cleverness and dogged effort to succeed athletically where the genetically overendowed
superstars often fail. I think this is the stark comparison that makes
life so tough for Reggie Jackson: he is so very gifted, and so consistently disappointing. His gifts promise us more than any mortal could
possibly deliver, and we end up hating him for his small imperfec-
tions. We save our love for the Yogi Berras of the athletic world.

There goes another simplistic dualism. Sports have never been
grounded in a terribly sophisticated philosophy, but it is still surprising how often we sucker for such dualisms, how often we use these
oversimplifications to organize our understanding of sports. Red vs.
white muscle fiber, sprint vs. endurance training, strength vs. skill,
brains vs. brawn, fundamentals vs. fireworks. Offense vs. defense.
Coaching—in the sense of team management during a game, as
opposed to the teaching of athletic skills in preparation for the contest—often devolves into choosing the proper personnel and the
proper moments for switching back and forth between the bold offensive stroke and the careful defensive posture, between conservative fundamental play and all-out risk-taking. Coaches—and athletes
—seem to end up thinking that way about sports in general.

Understanding sports by these either-or dualisms alone is missing
the point: balance is the key, the essential metaphor that extends far
beyond the level eyes and quiet upper body that help the performing
athlete keep his or her feet. One must also maintain a certain level-
headedness (an interesting coinage) about the diversely complex demands of the total athletic equation. Single-minded training of an

isolated muscle, for example, will lead to muscular imbalance so severe it can actually be crippling. That, too, is an accurate metaphor. The goal must always be balance, harmony, the broad increase, the view that keeps open the maximum possibility. I suspect that the people in sports too often lose sight of this reality: that sport itself is a kind of yoga, a linking device for teaching us, both literally and figuratively, to be balanced.

*   *   *

This book grows out of a pile of news clippings about the revolution in athletic performance that is right around the corner. Breakthroughs are imminent, says the press, because of all this research in nutrition, exercise physiology, biomechanics, high-tech training gadgets and sports equipment, miracle drugs, magic potions, and who knows what else. (And always, overshadowing all else in the imagination of the popular press, there are the infinitely greater improvements to come if we can only find out what's being done by the East Germans, those godless Communist superscientist/athletes.) As I've researched beyond the headlines, however, one after another of these bubbles has seemed to burst. Scientists, coaches, trainers, all keep telling me that the press has blown everything out of proportion, including the alleged advances of the East Germans. Nobody should expect any big breakthroughs.

In nutrition they've known for ten years about carbohydrate-loading, which does aid performance in some kinds of endurance tasks but which has lately proved difficult to manage and less effective than expected in general use. More recently caffeine has been shown to provide a further boost, but its use is extremely controversial. Beyond that, well, athletes should eat a lot to restore what they burn off in exercise, and the increase should be well balanced among the basic food groups. Any variations on these 1930s truths about nutrition begins to smack of drugging—as with caffeine—from which sports scientists shy away in near panic.

In exercise physiology some very basic questions about training phenomena, about the production of energy and other aspects of the biochemistry of exercise are now coming clearer, but none is going to make us start producing 3:40 milers, sub-two-hour marathoners, or nine-flat sprinters. Science hasn't begun to get a handle on skills—how they're acquired, how they can be increased beyond the perfectly amazing (and nonscientific) levels at which they are now practiced. Biomechanics probably provides the best method yet for digging out that information, but its application so far, with a few notable exceptions, is much too rudimentary to be of practical or immediate service to athletes.

The high-tech approach does make some measurable differences, here and there (measurable mostly because something other than soft, lumpy, hard-to-pin-down human beings can be measured), but it gives a lot of athletes the creeps. Improving the tool rather than the athlete somehow seems to be working counter to the purposes of sports. Besides, improving the implement improves the level of performance for all athletes equally—as with the fiberglass vaulting pole —so that the end result is more like changing the rules than improving performance.

Drugs have proven effective and dangerous in just about equal measure, and their use *really* gives people the creeps. No respectable scientists look to drugs for additional performance, at least not publicly. And the magical potions—and the mystical disciplines, the psychocybernetics and hypnotism and martial arts and yoga and meditation—are so subjective and, well, flaky, that nobody dares admit dependence on them. Individual athletes may find their methods useful for self-psyching, for attaining mental states and levels of consciousness that they feel improve performance, but that kind of private use is a long way from underwriting any sea change in performance levels.

So where is the athletic revolution that started all this talk? It is right there, above, in the cracks and crevices of this list of failures I've just recounted. It is all there, and if we can't see it that's only because the scale is wrong. We look for too much.

Most world records are broken by the smallest of measurable increments. Sebastian Coe's spate of record-breaking during the summer of 1979 was a monster breakthrough, perhaps the greatest one-season group of performances by a single individual in track history. In a forty-three-day period he lowered the marks for three of the most difficult and most tightly contested distances in running. Coe broke the records for the 800-meter run by 1.1 seconds, for the mile by 0.4 second, for the 1500 meters by 0.1 second. That totals 1.6 seconds over a little more than nine minutes of racing: three new world records squeezed out of a total improvement of less than three tenths of one percentage point. The 1500-meter record was an improvement of the old mark by less than five one-hundredths of a percentage point.

We expect our sports heroes to be off-scale in some recognizable attribute—just one attribute will do, but we really do want there to be some absolutely shining area in which our hero has total dominance of his or her peers. We want to be able to explain our hero's greatness; it just isn't enough to be able to say only that he or she is "better." Much of sports' obsession with statistics must spring from the frustrating search for these explanations.

But most of the clearly superior athletes have only the tiniest of edges, and their superiority is an amalgam of advantages so small as to be indiscernible if taken each by each. As Coe is superior (in the record books) for being five one-hundredths of a percentage point faster (on one day) than Filbert Bayi, the previous record holder (on another day years before), so are the superheroes possessed only of similarly minute percentage points of advantage over their competitors. It is the total package—and the career-long demonstration of those minute advantages—that establishes their superiority. Or more acutely to the argument here, it is the balance—of skills, strengths, capabilities—that enables the great ones consistently to outperform the rest.

It is not unusual in a World Cup slalom ski race for the first ten finishers to be separated by less than a second; many races are won by one or two hundredths. Over the long World Cup season, those same ten may often swap positions from time to time, but still finish in the same general grouping. And yet it is also not unusual for one skier to win eight out of ten of those races. That is, the World Cup slalom winner may only be a few hundredths of a second better than the field, but he or she is very likely to be those few hundredths better in race after race, able in some inconceivable way to hang onto those hundredths despite anything the competition can figure out to do. It's uncanny.

The popular press does tend to overrate the possibilities of sports science. But the sensationalized overinterpretations grow out of real research that is slowly, patiently winnowing the solid and useful out of the sensational. Nutrition, for example, may seem to be a somewhat backward science; we know all that old stuff, don't we? Yet as Dave Costill observed, there are professional football training camps still serving protein-heavy, carbohydrate-light meals—exactly wrong for the circumstances—to athletes who should know better than to eat them. (Or there were until recently; if the revolution is indeed taking place, perhaps the message has begun to sink in by now. But there are still coaches who allow no drinking water during hot-weather football practices, which in the scientists' eyes is tantamount to manslaughter.) There are junk-food junkies at the highest levels of professional athletics; get them to follow modern nutritional principles and their performance levels should improve—to say nothing about their professional longevity. There are great strides still to be made in applying the details of all these disciplines. It is in the details that the strides—the accretion of percentage points that adds up to a breakthrough—will be made.* "A pawn, now," says the chess master, "*that*'s worth a little something."

The American scientists who seem to be discounting East German efforts are misinterpreted by the press. Of course the East Germans are realizing gains in performance, as the press says they are; just look at the recent records, at the medal shares in international events. And of course those gains are not from any huge break-throughs in the principles of athletic training, just as the scientists maintain. The gains are from attention to detail, the accumulation of tiny percentage points of advantage. The East Germans are not doing anything in the training of athletes that we don't know how to do. It is just that they *are* doing it, and we're not—or we're doing it in dibs and dabs, bits and pieces, outside of any rigid organizing structure. The athletic miracle of the recent years may not be the accomplishments of the East Germans after all; it may simply be that we've managed to keep them in sight. But the reasons why this is miraculous are much too subtle to fit into a headline, and the press chooses not to try to explain subtleties, particularly in sports.

*   *   *

* In one sense nutrition is demonstrably a backward field. It has always looked not to increase but only to maintain some nebulous state of normality, of "health." The carbohydrate-loading techniques—which, incidentally, developed out of exercise physiology, not out of nutritional science—showed improvements of as much as 15 percent in the amount of work done before exhaustion in endurance activities. The caffeine studies showed similar increases. Any method of understanding human performance which is still discovering changes of that magnitude must be considered to be in a primitive stage of development. Imagine the results if nutritionists (or anyone) turned up similar improvements for the work loads involved in all-out three-and-a-half-minute tasks—such as the 1500-meter run!

After all this talk of things to watch for, to look at, I don't want to obscure the possibilities for participation in this approach to sports. I come to sports late—or perhaps I should say I come back to sports, after a twenty-year period when I paid rather less attention to sports than the average fan. My interest was rekindled by aging itself, by the early stages of sagging and stiffening that my body began to evince. As I began to work that body back into something resembling fitness—and began to learn a bit about what was happening as I did so—my first reaction was one of astonishment at how very much there is *to* all this, how much to learn, how interesting it all is when it is happening to your own physiology. I came into the subject wide-eyed and somewhat innocent, I suppose, at the whole new world of intriguing possibility that opens up when you approach sports from this direction. Maybe all modern athletes do so, but I don't think so. I think it is a vision of sports that is just now emerging into the general athletic consciousness.

I quickly became irritated with most programs intended for public consumption, which take perfectly wonderful exercises and reduce them to charts and numbers—so many repetitions of this and that, repeated every so many days, without ever an explanation of what can happen, what it can mean, if you follow those meaningless numbers. The Royal Canadian Air Force approach: calisthenics again. That immortal line from James Jones' *From Here to Eternity* keeps echoing in my head: "Hips on shoulders, *place!*"

Another thing began to bother me early on: the soft, uncritical mysticism that is beginning to be troweled onto sports, particularly as represented by the Michael Murphys and Mike Spinos and other human potential movement types, who seem to want to come at sports through the metaphysical, even through the occult. They put me off with talk of body auras and force fields and energy centers. I think they leap too early to nonordinary explanations for the seeming dislocations of time and space, the exalted states of consciousness and other remarkable occurrences that can be produced by the peculiar conditions of sports. I think I'm sensitive to that impulse; God knows I've had experiences as a result of athletic effort that have left me bemused, unable to explain my own reactions. But mysticism must be rigorous. Besides, it isn't necessary.

There's metaphysics enough in this material, marvels to satisfy the deepest cravings for wonder without going an inch beyond a freshman physiology textbook. As I ponder these matters I find myself metaphorically scuba-diving through the cell structure, down there among the actin and myosin fibrils, the axons and dendrites, feeling the exhilarating wash of hormones, the jittery shocks of electrochemical signals sizzling along their way to fire off muscles and start the action going. I can almost feel fatigued muscle cells sponging up extra nutrients, to build themselves up bigger, stronger, for the next effort. I experience the aerobic buzz; I search my own frame for muscle fibers to recruit when all energy is drained from the habitual sources; I watch the melting heat of early, tentative action let lubricants trickle into the joints. I take a magical mystery tour of my own anatomy, witnessing the athletic process, the miracle of use. Who needs force fields when we have synapses, muscle spindles, rods and cones?

* * *

Picture a fine natural athlete who makes his way to the top in baseball, and has a solid career for five or six years, honing his skills, learning the small intricacies of the game, getting better and better at it, and who *then* undertakes a well-planned, scientifically designed weight program to increase his strength. As Fred Lynn, Jim Palmer, and several other major league ballplayers have done in recent years. A yogalike, unforced acquisition of the skills first, and then the application of extra power. It's almost frightening to contemplate.

Consider how much more effective a warm-up might be if instead of just moving around loosely until one breaks a sweat, the athlete paid conscious attention to the levels of heat in the body of the muscles, to prestretching specifically to enhance contractility (and reduce injury), to stimulating the actual neuromuscular pathways that will be called upon in the task to come—as Dwight Stones in fact does to prepare for the high jump, to name just one world-record breaker.

Envision the physiological consequences of "choking"—of going into an athletic panic—as the precisely wrong response to competitive pressure. One's normal skills and abilities seem to evaporate, the feet feel leaden, you may even be nauseous or dizzy. What's happening? Overthinking and indecision interfere with the smooth, sure motor patterning that ordinarily guides your responses—the ones you've invested so much time and energy in acquiring. Respiration goes shallow, reducing oxygen supplies, forcing you to go anaerobic, reducing endurance, increasing anxiety. Tensed muscles—overprepared for action from lack of confidence—knot the body, making movements jerky, hindering balance, slowing reaction times. Hurry, that athletic poison, overtakes you. Take deep breaths, says the coach; move around a bit. Relax your shoulders. It's appropriate advice. Imagine how much more helpful it might be if the athlete understands the physiological mechanisms that underly the tensions, and how that advice deals with those mechanisms.

Picture the way sports could be if every aspect and every participant—coach, trainer, athlete, even observer—were informed by this kind of broad understanding of the workings of the physical plant and its operation in the real-world time frame of the athletic task. If the natural athlete (which most of us are, at least until socialization robs us of trust in our bodies) had a complete and intrinsic understanding of how that natural athleticism might be enhanced, augmented, amplified, then envision what could happen to sports. Well, it *is* happening, and as a result sports—all sports—have been irrevocably changed. We are beginning to look at and take part in sports with what might be termed physiological eyes. It radically alters and enriches the experience.

This radical alteration is most visible, most accessible, in individual sports—track and field, gymnastics, diving—in which the athlete usually performs alone, and in which the athletic body is extended, however briefly, to its absolute maximum. But grasp this vision securely in the isolation of individual sports—with the technical assistance of replays and slow motion, if you will—and it quickly translates to the swirling confusion of the faster-paced team sports. Then when you see groups of athletes letting their astonishing individual skills play off each other, sharing the immense range of possibilities that open up when a team begins to click, it is doubly moving. (Quadruply so, I'm sure, to take part at such a time.) I can't yet quite hold with my friend Nick Howe, who maintains that good hockey provides a metaphor for the organization of the cosmos. But when I see a group of good athletes arrive at that curious state in which they are truly in phase with each other—when I see a bunch of "stars" pull up their socks and start working together in that snowballing symbiotic relationship that is known as teamwork—then I do begin to see a little hope for the species. Even if that state of cooperation only holds for ten or fifteen crisp, wonderful minutes at a time, then falls apart in fatigue and discord, as it always does.

Athletes often talk of the advantage of running in second place, of having a leader to chase. Mere psychology, I always thought: other than a slight reduction in wind resistance, what possible real physical effect could arise from being in second place? But performances like Nehemiah's hurdle victory at Montreal, and some other last-second overtakings I've witnessed since, put a different light on the situation. Having the backside of a competitor before you, on which to focus, must concentrate the mind wonderfully, damping out distractions, permitting a more intense cortical input to help you search among the neuromuscular possibilities. In such a fix a runner can throw into the fight everything that works, discard everything that hampers. A level of concentration should be made possible that generates extra energy, better selectivity of motor units, abandonment of every microerg of effort that is not devoted to pulling the runner forward, contributing to speed and acceleration. The effect must be like a towrope in the imagination, pulling the runner onward.

(That imaginary effect, the towrope in the mind, is very likely one source of ideas such as energy centers and force fields and the like. I can't prove that my notion of neuromuscular focusing actually happens, but physiologically it has to be a more likely explanation than a force field of *ki* energy that extends from the second-place runner's navel and latches onto the track shorts of the runner ahead.)

It is a mistake to assume that obscure sports haven't yet had much science laid on them—that the limited numbers of practitioners of the sport are just going out and trying hard to do the particular thing, without much analysis of the task. As the Lake Placid games demonstrated—to my surprise—even speed skaters are now an extremely sophisticated bunch, applying the most advanced training and conditioning principles assiduously to their (numerically) minor sport. My surprise is naive, of course; no sport that offers an Olympic medal is any longer obscure.

But one major sport that has not had a hell of a lot of modern science applied to it is the sweet science itself, boxing. The old pugs, the old-style trainers, are firmly in control of that brutal art, and aren't about to let modernists confuse the issue with facts.

An interesting violation of that custom occurred in 1979, when heavyweight Duane Bobick attempted a major comeback against

John Tate. With a great flurry of publicity, Bobick announced that he was applying scientific principles in his training. He dropped a considerable amount of flab, training himself down to an attractive leanness; he ran forty miles a week, much more than the usual amount of roadwork, to give himself a cardiovascular base. He used Nautilus weight machines to build specific strength in carefully analyzed parts of the body, and so on. It seemed that boxing finally had a thoughtful, analytic practitioner.

Unfortunately, Tate dropped him like a bad habit at 1:22 in the first round. So much for science. Actually, all the fight really proved was that Bobick was still a sucker for a right lead, of course; science couldn't do anything about that, and the rest of the fancy principles never had a chance to be tested. But I'm sure the boxing community has now pushed science out of its collective mind for another couple of decades. It's too bad. Eventually a boxer will combine a modern training approach with enough talent to give science a proper test, and boxing, too, might be revolutionized. Meanwhile, of course, the ultraconservative but tried-and-true training methods in general use do prepare a boxer well for his sport—so long as he's only going up against other pugs who use the same methods.

I have to confess to something of a love/hate relationship with boxing. It was once characterized to me as the only sport the object of which is to inflict brain damage on one's opponent (and then hope it is temporary), and in those terms clearly there is no excuse for boxing's continued existence in modern society. We don't have room for that kind of athletic stupidity; there are too many other fascinating sports which don't violate our medicohumanitarian principles. Ah, but good boxing is indeed such a starkly elemental and direct test of athletic capacities, and when it is done well it is so stirring to watch. I watch it, and hate watching it; it is like a secret vice.

As with boxing, so with football. There is much to meditate upon in that very American game. The dramatic flamboyance of the college game versus the almost bored precision of the professional version. (Once you know how to play it, the hardened pro seems to be saying, drama is bush.) The unspectacular, codified efficiency of good interior line play. (If you notice the performance of an offensive lineman, he's doing a bad job.) The scrambling quarterback, and the inevitability of his interception. (He creates opportunities by breaking the habitual patterns; the opportunities for the defense expand to match, and there are more interceptions.) The frenetic abandon with which certain players approach their duties (kickoff and kick-return teams, free safeties) versus the cool minimization of effort that the good running back eventually learns. The knee: we envision it failing the swiveling, whirling running back, but it is the 270-pound lineman who really subjects that poor joint to unbearable stress, who suffers the most damage when it lets go. His rehabilitation is also much more difficult, of course, for the same reasons of size and weight.

It was in between football seasons when I first began to think hard about what goes on with the body athletically. Much of that time I had spent snorkeling through the muscle fibers—in my imagination —was in the off-season; that was also when I began to understand the ramifications of drug use in large, highly skilled athletes, and the virtual panic of sports medicine at its inability to protect and restore broken football players sufficiently. With my head freshly filled with that viewpoint, when the new season started I could hardly bear to watch anymore. When you have the largest people the species can produce (who are also good athletes, i.e., effective with their bodies), who build themselves up into monstrosity with steroids, then crank themselves into psychosis with amphetamines in order to play their game, it gets simply frightening. When men that big and strong go at each other that hard, it stops being fun to watch. At least it was for me, with my imagination still raw with newly understood pain receptors, with a new sense of the fragility of flesh. A few weeks of the usual network overdosage of football, however, and I was benumbed back to normal. I never said I could resist it. I love to watch football, but it makes me very uneasy. I only hope that the application of modern medical science can soon reduce the unacceptable casualty rates of both football and boxing.

Meanwhile, it's interesting to me that the one thing the gentlemen who govern football fear most of all is not free agency, or players' unions, or even congressional meddling with the boundaries of their plantations. It is soccer. It is the existence of an alternative game that has proved elsewhere to have the capacity to seize the public imagination, but which is so much less destructive to athletic health that parents are now routinely forbidding their children participation in American football, and offering them soccer in its place. What will football do without a captive farm system, and the captive audience to go with it?

I also think it is revealing that football and basketball are in at least moderate trouble with the fans, their market shares beginning to decline, while baseball resurges dramatically and soccer begins to climb. I think the public is beginning to grow uneasy with any sport that gives an advantage to the giant player or to the freak, the goon. I think the great wave of athletic participation now sweeping through the country is causing a rekindling of interest in those sports in which the ordinary-sized individual has an equal chance.

In fact I think that the point of view I'm proposing here represents a couple of problems for big-time sports as they exist in this country. In the first place, if you really get interested in what the athletes are *doing*, you tend to lose interest in all that distracting stuff about scores, leagues, standings, results. The action, the flow, the exuberant joy of the moment is enough. The other stuff—numbers, mostly —becomes only a kind of vague organizing fabric against which the athletes show their skills, play their games, light up our lives with possibility. Furthermore, if one has much moral sensibility, and pays any attention to the scandalous shenanigans that surround modern big-time sports, then this becomes the only view of sports that is bearable. The moral issues still exist, in sports as elsewhere. But you can escape them for a while in the graceful movement, the courageous finish, the exhilarating *try* of the athletic human being. And that escape is a large part of what sports—or re-creation—is supposed to be for.

*   *   *

It should be possible to trace through these pages the progression of athletic seasons, as I've drawn examples from the sports that were in season as I worked on each section of the book. As I was finishing up, the 1979 World Series was taking place. And there was a moment, there was a moment . . .

If you watched or were there, you will remember. In the seventh game, with a 2–1 lead and one out in the bottom of the eighth inning, Pittsburgh Pirate relief pitcher Grant Jackson walked Oriole pinch-hitter Lee May and center fielder Al Bumbry. Runners on first and second. Jackson was yanked for Kent Tekulve, and in the delay for the change of pitchers, the crowd began to go jittery with the possibilities. Pinch-hitter Terry Crowley grounded out, but the runners advanced. Tying run at third, go-ahead run at second, two outs, powerful Ken Singleton at the plate. He was given an intentional walk. That brought up Eddie Murray, a good hitter having a terrible series. Murray was overdue for a hit.

It was perhaps not the most dramatic moment in the history of baseball, but it would do. The camera panned around the infield, catching at least eight different styles of nervous mannerism, as the individual players worked to keep their composure. Waiting.

I began thinking about adrenaline, that chemical supercharger that was pumping through those players. It also had to be flowing pretty freely on the respective benches, I realized. And in the umpires, the announcers, the sportswriters, and, my God, the fifty thousand or so spectators, the uncounted millions of television viewers. It had to be rushing through the TV technical people, the cameramen, who in some senses were faced with their own sharply challenging athletic task, to capture adequately the action to come. And me, my heart pounding, my hands beginning to shake. All that adrenaline, all those hormones pumping, a nationwide *river* of adrenaline, preparing all those millions of physiologies, appropriately or not, for action.

"There's a lot of electricity in that backfield," I once heard Frank Gifford say, describing the collection of talent operating in an all-star game. He was speaking of metaphorical electricity, of the sheer excitement of watching all that talent in operation, but I kept thinking of the real electricity in those talented nervous systems and muscles, of the electrochemical signaling going on to make all those superb athletes operate as effectively as they do. Of the surges of electrons as the pace picked up, as the action got more exciting. Well, you could've run the stadium lights off the electricity being generated in those players and that crowd as Eddie Murray came up to bat.

Tekulve is a tall, skinny individual with a buggy-whip arm in the Ewell Blackwell tradition, a long and complicated sidearm throwing motion that looks impossible in real time, a succession of seemingly disconnected swoops and swirls that couldn't conceivably result in a pitch across the plate. (Commentator Don Drysdale kept insisting that it is, in fact, the most natural throwing motion of all.) Slow-motion replays—as Tekulve dueled with Murray—provided a bio-mechanical comic cartoon of the Sweet Spot Theory. Linked arcs of motion start with the rotation of the upper body from the waist, then absolutely *ripple* on through the shoulders, upper arm, flying elbow, whipping forearm, like a shock wave running down through the throwing arm, cocking everything at impossible angles. Tekulve seems to have two or three extra elbows scattered down the length of his arm as he throws. As he comes past his hip in his low-down sidearm motion, everything in his shoulder and throwing arm gets so far ahead of his hand—and the ball—that it looks impossible to bring the ball through in time. But that appearance doesn't take into account the incredible speed built up in the long series of accelerating arcs; in the last few possible inches the hand and ball snap through, the pitch is made. Steee-rike!

Murray's bat waggles as he awaits the next pitch. My wife points out that the movement is very like the wriggle in the hindquarters of a cat as it prepares to pounce. That makes me realize that Murray is doing something similar with his feet, in fact with his whole body— moving it slightly, rocking, firing proprioceptors like crazy to keep himself informed, instant by instant, of exactly where everything (bat, hands, arms, feet, weight, power) *is*. The pitch tails away low and outside for a ball. Murray steps out of the box to regroup.

As a man the infielders take a deep breath and blow it out forcibly, raise their shoulders and then drop them, set them low, attempting to discharge the unused tension. They slam fists into gloves; they wait.

Tekulve worked Murray—in shuddering tension—to two balls and two strikes; then Murray "hit the heck out of the ball," as Oriole manager Earl Weaver said later. (Eyes picking up the ball as it flicks out of the pitcher's hand, decision made to swing, hands started, hips turning ahead of the arms to bring full power through, searching for a sweet spot as he swings. . . .) It *was* a well-hit ball: "If it goes down the line or in the gap, they'd be talking about him all winter," said Weaver.

Now, there is a sweet spot in time in the trajectory of Murray's swing, at which, if he had met the ball there, it would have gone down the line. He started an instant, a microsecond or two too late for that. There was another instant in the trajectory of that swing which would have punched the ball into the gap, but Murray was too early for that one. He hit it instead at a spot that was sweet for Tekulve, for right fielder Dave Parker, for the Pirates, rather than for Eddie Murray and the Orioles. A microsecond too early, and a microsecond too late, for the championship of the world. The enemy has his sweet spots even in your trajectories, as it turns out.

The drama wasn't quite over. Parker started for the ball. "The first step I slipped," he was to say later (jarring visual perception, causing balance mechanisms to override the message to chase the ball, making Parker reflexively seek equilibrium rather than the third out). "The second step I slipped. It was amazing I was still on my feet." ("I was wondering," said Tekulve, "when he was going to stop stumbling and catch the ball.") Parker did, however, keep his feet, make the catch, retire the side.

I exaggerate. The tension really wasn't in the physiological minutiae I've described, of course, it was in the hard-thinking duel between Tekulve and Murray, the confrontation of skills. That was the story. But the physiology did provide the rich background upon which such a story can be spun out. It always does in sports. Six outs later, with little more drama, the Pirates had won it 4–1, and a lot of other electricity was released, adrenaline resorbed, emotions drained. All over with. I was drained too. It was my first physiological World Series. It won't be my last.

*   *   *

And listen, there's more. In addition to all that you also get free lunch.

I hope the solid optimism of this presentation is clear. The message of the cells, of the organism, is simply that improvement—increase, expansion, growth—is possible. It is there for the taking, if only the effort will be invested. The attempt to bring the physical organism to its best possible state, which is the goal of training, can result in fatigue, in wear and tear, even in a kind of violent destruction. But that is not the tendency, not the direction. The body's impulse is to heal, if we will only provide the conditions that make that possible. The direction is toward increase. That's the training effect: more capability. Maybe that, too, is neo-Nietzschean, but if it is, so be it. I'm too cheered up to care.

I've tried to survey here the major areas where science—more or less "hard" science, more or less scientific in its methodology and approach—is looking to find room for improvement in human performance. That search covers a considerable array of points of entry into the problem, places where clever attention to the processes at work may produce improvement. A bit of biochemistry here, a superior piece of mechanical engineering there, a new training method,

332 / John Jerome

a technical analysis that simplifies what was previously complex: each bit contains the possibility of gain, however small. (Each bit also contains the possibility of loss; that's what record keeping is for.) Multiply the points of entry by the increasing numbers of people who understand where these wedges of investigation might best be driven, by the increasing numbers of people who are involved in human performance, by the accrual of information, the gathering of experience, the deepening of comprehension, and the stage is set for a massive revision upward in the limits of performance, in the capacity of the organism.

But there's another result of all this investigation which is much more important for athletics—and for the species—than any wholesale revision of the record books. This great swelling body of understanding is spreading far beyond the limited world of athletics, into the general public consciousness. It is doing so at the same time that the public is learning, by direct physical experience, of the optimism of the cell.

The ecologists keep telling us that there is no free lunch. In a finite universe infinite growth is impossible. There are these basic laws of nature, of the physical governance of the universe, which say you don't get something for nothing. We must accept limits; we must begin to think small, reduce our appetites, cut back. For decades we've devoted great portions of our massive resources to nothing more ennobling than the reduction of physical effort in our lives. One result has been the construction of a society around the laws of entropy, around the eventual running down of the universe. A kind of paralysis of despair is the perfectly reasonable response. After all, there is the entropy of aging, too, a running down of the organism that is irreversible.

No thanks, says the cell. Only test it—just require of it a little more than its existing, steady-state capacity—and it responds by thumbing its metaphorical nose at the laws of entropy. In fact the more you require of it, the more it gains in response.

We give a great deal of romantic lip service to the indomitable human spirit. That's chauvinistic anthropomorphism. What is truly indomitable about us is this characteristic of all living tissue, this capacity of the cell to flout the laws of entropy: to steal energy out of stress, and with it to construct new health. Free lunch. The only free lunch there is.

Paradoxes abound. When a cell divides it multiplies. Taking time to finish a move makes more time for the next move. Most shocking of all, the expenditure of energy creates more energy. At the same time that the laws of physics seem determined to grind us down, the paradoxes of the cell—the laws of life—point toward new possibility. They point upward.

END

Index

Acetylcholine, 114
Actin, 46–48, 68
  energy and, 79
Actomyosin, 47, 79
Adaptation syndrome, general, 204
Adenosine triphosphate, 79–82, 84, 85, 88
  fatigue and, 212
Adidas, 283
Adolescence, 145
Adrenaline, 329
Aerobic pathway, 81–82, 84, 89
  fatigue and, 211
  lactic acid and, 89–90
Aging
  flexibility and, 296, 297, 308
  motor skills and, 145–46
Alarm reaction, 204
Albritton, Terry, 189
Alchemics, 242–64
Alcoholism, 256
Alexeyev, Vasily, 248–49
Alveoli, 97–99
Amateurism, 257
Amdur, Neil, 248–49, 253
American Athletic Union, 222–24
American College of Sports Medicine, 245
Amino acids, 165
Amphetamines, 250–53
Anabolic steroids, 228, 242, 246. *See also* Steroids

Anabolism, 246
Anaerobic pathway, 81–84, 88
  threshold of, 89–90, 224–25
  training and, 225
Anderson, Paul, 44
Androgens, 246
Anemia, sports, 167
Anesthesia, 119
Angell, Roger, 287n.
Ankling in cycling, 183
Anxiety, 148
Arc, sweet spot of, 14, 15–16
Archery, 268, 301n.
Archibald, Nate, 139
archy the cockroach, 218
Ariel, Gideon, 189–90
Arousal, 148
Arrector pili, 121n.
Ashe, Arthur, 280–81
Ashford, Evelyn, 311
Astaire, Fred, 314
Åstrand, Per-Olof, 120
Atherosclerosis, 164
Athletic capacity, 89
Athletic IQ, 30, 32
Athletic task, 316
ATP (adenosine triphosphate), 79–82, 84, 85, 88
  fatigue and, 212
Attention, 132, 306
  yoga and, 304
Attitude, 56, 262, 293

335

About the Author

John Jerome was born in 1932, grew up in Texas, attended school and later taught there. He moved to New York and worked for *Car and Driver* magazine, was the editor of *Skiing*, and did a brief stint in advertising in Detroit before becoming a freelance writer. He reported on motor racing and ski racing for about ten years each, for various publications. He lived in the mountains of northern New Hampshire for twelve years before recently moving to western Massachusetts. He is married and has three grown children.